Field Guide
to the
TREES
of Britain & Europe

LAROUSSE

Field Guide
to the
TREES
of Britain & Europe

Written by
DAVID SUTTON

LAROUSSE

LAROUSSE plc
New Penderel House
283-288 High Holborn
London WC1V 7HZ

First published in 1990 by Kingfisher Books
This edition published 1998

10 9 8 7 6 5 4 3 2 1

Text copyright © David Sutton and
Larousse 1990
Illustrations copyright © Larousse plc 1990

A CIP CATALOGUE RECORD FOR THIS BOOK IS
AVAILABLE FROM THE BRITISH LIBRARY

ISBN 0-7523-0053-9

Editor: Stuart Cooper
Editorial Assistant: Sophie Figgis
Map (p. 6): King & King
Cover design: Mike Smith

Phototypset by Southern Positives and
Negatives (SPAN), Lingfield, Surrey
Colour separations by Newsele Litho SpA,
Milan
Printed in Portugal

CONTENTS

INTRODUCTION
Page 6

SCOPE OF THIS BOOK
Page 7

THE HISTORY OF TREES
Page 8

THE IMPORTANCE OF TREES
Page 9

HOW TO IDENTIFY TREES
Page 10

HOW TO USE THIS BOOK
Page 13

KEY TO SPECIES
Page 14

TREE NAMES
Page 16

THE TREES
Page 18

INDEX
Page 186

BIBLIOGRAPHY
Page 192

INTRODUCTION

There is something special about trees. They are plants on a grand scale and have long inspired philosophers. An imposing feature of most landscapes, they define the character of an area, telling you where you are – billowing crowns of elms and sturdy oaks at middle latitudes, or slender spires of cypresses and umbrella-shaped pines in the Mediterranean region. Trees also hold many of nature's records: the tallest, most massive and oldest living things are all trees. They can be objects of great beauty and many are grown for this reason. We plant cherries from the Orient and Indian Flame-tree for flowers, and maples and Black-gum for their brilliant autumn colour. Many trees are grown for their imposing form, such as Cedar-of-Lebanon, with its massive flat plates of foliage; Lombardy Poplar, which forms narrow columns; and Golden Weeping-willow, with its hanging curtains of foliage.

Some of the choicest fruits of the earth come from trees. Orchards of apple, plum and pear are planted in the cooler areas, whilst oranges, peaches and nectarines are grown in the warmer south. Even in death, trees contribute to the quality of human life. Softwoods, from conifers, and hardwoods, from broad-leaved trees, provide everything from basic materials for construction to the highly decorative, beautifully figured wood of the walnuts. Timber, converted into paper, holds the world's literature.

Using descriptions, facts panels and illustrations, this book provides the means to identify 430 of the native and most widely planted trees of Britain and Europe.

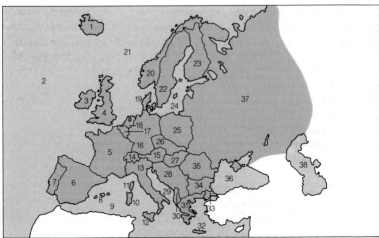

1 Iceland **2** Atlantic Ocean **3** Ireland **4** Britain **5** France **6** Spain **7** Portugal **8** Balearic Is **9** Mediterranean Sea **10** Sardinia **11** Corsica **12** Sicily **13** Italy **14** Switzerland **15** Austria **16** Germany **17** Belgium **18** Holland **19** Denmark **20** Norway **21** Norwegian Sea **22** Sweden **23** Finland **24** Baltic Sea **25** Poland **26** Czechoslovakia **27** Hungary **28** Yugoslavia **29** Adriatic Sea **30** Albania **31** Greece **32** Crete **33** Turkey **34** Bulgaria **35** Romania **36** Black Sea **37** Russia **38** Caspian Sea

Introduction

SCOPE OF THIS BOOK

The area covered by this guide extends from the tree limit in Scandinavia and northern Russia to the islands of the Mediterranean; from the Atlantic coast in the west to the Ural Mountains, Black Sea, Caspian Sea, and Aegean Islands in the east. Emphasis has been placed on those species that are most abundant and visible to the majority of people. Most native species are covered, with the exception of the more restricted and obscure trees. A few of the uncommon species have been included where space permits. The book describes most of the commonly planted trees that have been introduced, including timber trees, fruit trees and amenity trees. The last-named category embraces those grown for shelter, shade or ornament in public places, and

Chilean Wine Palm is commonly planted along streets in the Mediterranean region.

street trees, many of which are planted along thousands of miles of roads. The reason for such a broad coverage is that it is often impossible to know whether a tree is native or not without specialist knowledge. Some of the introduced species regularly produce seed and spread, behaving like native trees. Ornamental trees which are also native may be planted far beyond their natural limits of distribution.

What is a tree?

A general working definition of a tree is a plant with a single, woody stem, which grows to 6 metres or more tall. However, many of the trees that are planted for urban use, in streets, parks and gardens, are typically much shorter, for example Dwarf Cherry. Furthermore, the size of a tree can vary according to the habitat in which it is growing. A native species may be tall at low altitudes but just a few metres high in the mountains. A broader definition has been adopted in this book as there is no precise botanical distinction between trees and shrubs, the latter being typically smaller woody plants with multiple stems. Some large trees, which unquestionably belong here, regularly produce multiple trunks by growing sucker shoots, for example English Elm. Trees that grow in hedgerows, and that at some time have been cut to height, will also sprout extra stems. A few shrubs have been included in the book where they reach tree size, particularly when a common, large shrub represents a group which includes some less common trees.

Although it usually occurs as a shrub, Hazel can sometimes attain tree size.

Introduction

THE HISTORY OF TREES

Forests and woodland may appear to have been there forever but they are all in a continual, gradual state of change. In the last Ice Age, much of northern Europe was covered by a continuous sheet of ice. As the climate warmed around 10,000 years ago, the ice began to retreat and the bare ground left behind became available for colonization. Light, wind-borne seeds of trees surviving south of the ice soon arrived, with birches, willows, then pines acting as pioneers, and woodlands were gradually established in the north. Trees with heavier seeds arrived much later but as they grew they overshadowed and eventually replaced the pioneer species.

During the Ice Age and when the ice began its retreat, colossal volumes of sea water were frozen solid and the sea-level was about thirty metres lower than it is today. France, Britain and Ireland were connected by land and early colonizing trees easily spread through the area. As the ice melted the sea rose, and some of the forested area disappeared beneath the sea. It also prevented some of the trees with larger seeds, which were spreading from the south, from colonizing many of the islands of northern Europe. Eventually a pattern of fairly continuous tree cover developed, with the northern forests of Europe dominated by conifers, and middle latitudes by broad-leaved oaks, elms and beeches. In the drier south, species with tough leaves resistant to drought formed extensive forests.

The recent history of trees is dominated by humankind. The most profound effects have been in the south, where the longer history of human habitation has resulted in most of the forests being destroyed. Further north, prehistoric people, using stone implements, found it easier to clear for crops upland areas with more open woodland than the rich valleys with their dense forests. With advances in materials and agricultural tools, more and more of the forest fell. Even if land was subsequently no longer farmed, domesticated grazing animals often prevented the trees from becoming re-established. Timber for construction has long been a highly prized commodity and has accelerated land clearance around the more densely populated areas. Though there has been much planting for timber on a forestry scale in recent years, it has often been done with imported species from other temperate regions of the world.

THE IMPORTANCE OF TREES

The economic importance of trees to humankind is immense. Yet it is nothing compared to the role they play in regulating the world's climate and ecosystems – a role which, because of the scale on which we exploit and destroy trees, is increasingly under threat.

A tree takes up water and mineral salts from the soil, moving them up from the roots to the leaves, where energy-rich sugars are produced using sunlight and carbon dioxide. These simple sugars are the building blocks for materials which are incorporated into the tree as it grows during a life-span of hundreds or perhaps even thousands of years. In an act that takes but a few minutes, it is difficult to see the long-term consequences of cutting down a single tree, but deforestation on the scale that has happened in the past and continues to happen around the globe is another matter.

A single tree can take up 1000–2000 litres of water from the ground a year, releasing most from the leaves as water vapour. Carried by the wind, this water vapour will later fall somewhere else as rain. On a forest scale, this capacity to move massive amounts of water has a profound effect on the local water-table and regional climate. Forested ground acts as a gigantic sponge, holding rainfall and releasing it gradually. Without trees, most of the water immediately runs off the land after rain and results in flooding alternating with drought. If the slope is steep or the rainfall heavy, the soil is eroded away to where it silts up rivers, reservoirs and estuaries. Without returning water to the atmosphere, the winds are drier and less rainfall is received somewhere else.

As well as affecting the local habitat, uncontrolled deforestation could have grave consequences for the world as a whole. As trees are destroyed and much material is burned or left to decompose, the carbon dioxide combined for centuries in the tree is released. This is one of the gases that at excess levels causes the Greenhouse Effect that threatens to change the world climate in a profound manner, raise sea-levels, and possibly cause species extinction on a vast scale.

It is important to conserve remaining natural forest, or manage it very carefully as a renewable resource, and re-establish tree cover in many places where it has been lost. Increased planting of native hardwoods in Europe would take longer to yield financial rewards than exotic softwoods, but would take the pressure off the tropics where massive deforestation must rank as one of the greatest crimes against the environment ever committed by humanity.

Introduction

HOW TO IDENTIFY TREES

When first learning to identify trees, it is important to resolve the general look of a tree into individual characteristics, which can then be checked against the illustrations, key and descriptions. The most useful features for identification are summarized in the following section, with an explanation of the terms used in the book.

Type of tree
A basic distinction to make is between cone-bearing trees (conifers) and flowering trees, which bear typical flowers or specialized flowers, such as catkins. Each type of tree may keep its leaves throughout the year (evergreen), or may lose all its leaves for part of the year (deciduous), either during a cold or a dry season.

Trunk
Unlike most wild flowers, a tree's stem keeps growing from one year to the next. Stiffening materials are laid down and it becomes a woody trunk, almost invariably increasing in size around its periphery each year. By definition, a tree has a single trunk, but some, such as Coast Redwood, can produce multiple trunks from shoots called suckers that grow around the base of the original trunk. The heavy lower branches of Western Red-cedar become bowed down to the ground, rooting and forming extra trunks in many old trees. Trunks of some species have broad flanges (buttresses) near the base, offering additional support to the tree.

buttresses 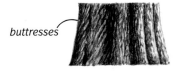   plates

Bark
The outer protective layer of the trunk is the bark, which accommodates increases in girth of the trunk in various ways. Older layers of bark commonly split, with new bark laid down internally, resulting in the vertical fissures of Sweet Chestnut or the small, square plates of Evergreen Oak. Cork Oak has a bark which proliferates rapidly to form a thick, soft layer; the fibrous bark of Wellingtonia is also thick and soft. Smooth barks, such as that of London Plane, often peel off in layers.

Crown and branching
The branches, twigs and foliage together, termed the crown, may have a distinctive shape which helps identify a tree. The shape is largely formed by the major branches, which may be spreading, angled upwards or weeping. A very regular pattern with rings of radiating, successively older branches in many young conifers results in a conical shape. Another distinctive shape is the very narrow crown of Lombardy Poplar, with almost vertical branching. Usually the shape is characteristic for an individual species but some trees can have very narrow or weeping cultivated forms as well as the typical form with widely spreading branches.

Introduction

Twigs and buds

Twigs offer a number of useful characteristics and are particularly important in deciduous trees, as they provide most of the characters for identifying the tree when it is leafless. On bare twigs, there is often a distinctive pattern of scars left where the leaves have fallen. Some trees have stout and rigid twigs, such as Fig and walnuts; others have slender and pendulous twigs, such as Silver Birch. Spines or thorns narrow identification down to a few species scattered through the book.

leaf
scar

sticky
bud

At the tip of a twig, and usually at the base of each leaf-stalk or leaf-scar, are buds. Most of these buds, with the exception of flower-buds, are juvenile shoots, with the young leaves covered by scales and the growth more or less arrested. The bud at the tip of the twig is generally largest and very noticeable in most deciduous trees. Horse-chestnut has a broad, sticky bud, while that of beeches is slender and smoothly tapered above and below the middle. That of ashes is smooth and blackish while White Willow has buds covered with pale grey hairs. The position of the side buds reflects the arrangement of the leaves and can be a useful feature.

Leaves

Trees are leafy for most of the year, but flowering and fruiting may be restricted to a few months. It can take many years before flowering commences and some mature trees may not develop any mature flowers or fruit in certain years. Consequently, leaves provide the most useful features for general identification. Note the position and whether the leaves are paired or otherwise arranged on the stem. The basic outline of the blade (expanded part) is important. See if the edge is unbroken, toothed or lobed. If the leaf is divided into leaflets, then they may be paired or radiating. Leaves of deciduous trees are commonly thinner than those of evergreen trees and often change colour dramatically in autumn. Leaf surfaces vary from smooth and glossy through varying degrees of hairiness, particularly on the underside. Needle-like leaves occur in many conifers, whilst others have small, scale-like leaves. Junipers can have both sorts on the same plant. A pair of stipules occurs at the base of the leaf-stalk of many flowering trees; they can be large, or small and falling quickly.

Lobed
leaf

Needle-like
leaves

Leaflets

Introduction

Flowers

Petals are usually the showiest part of a flower in most insect-pollinated trees. Look to see if they are equal or unequal and separate or joined together towards the base. Sepals are positioned beneath the petals and are usually green. If the petals and sepals are not readily distinguishable, then the term perianth applies to both. The male (♂) parts of a flower are the stamens, which produce pollen in anthers; the female (♀) parts are the stigma, usually supported by a stalk-like part (style), attaching it to the ovary. Most flowers have both male and female parts and are called hermaphrodite (☿). There may be separate male and female flowers, either on the same tree or different trees. The flowers of some trees are tiny and massed in elongated heads called catkins; such flowers are usually wind-pollinated. Conifers bear the male and female parts on the scales of male and female cones respectively.

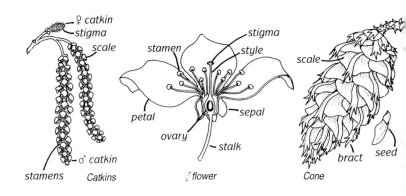

Fruits and seeds

Important things to note about fruits are shape, colour, whether they are fleshy or dry and, in the latter case, if they open to release the seeds. A berry is a fleshy fruit. Berry-like fruits, such as that of Wild Cherry, often have a hard stone inside enclosing the seed. Many fruits have outer layers which become dry as the fruit ripens. Pods are elongated dry fruits that split open to release the seeds when ripe, and are found in species of the Pea family such as Honey Locust. Dry fruits that do not open are commonly nut-like, as in the hazels, and usually contain a single seed. Dry fruits of ashes and maples have a long wing which aids dispersal; the wing of elms and Caucasian Wing-nut encircles the part containing the seed. Conifers mostly have woody cones with seeds carried beneath scales. Individual seeds often have membranous wings. There are sterile bract scales in conifer cones, which may project beyond the seed-bearing scales, as in Douglas-fir, and provide an important identification feature. Cones of pines and spruces usually hang downwards, but those of firs, cedars and larches are upright. Pine cones fall intact, in some species after many years on the tree. Cones of firs and Monkey-puzzle break up on the tree. Yews and junipers are unusual conifers in which the cone scales become fleshy and berry-like as they mature.

HOW TO USE THIS BOOK

If you want to identify a tree and have no idea of what it is, refer to the key starting on page 14 – which should limit your search to a specific group of pages. If, on the other hand, you have a rough idea of the identity, then turn to the relevant section of the book (using the colour code explained on page 16) and you will find similar species grouped on adjacent pages. Match the species against the illustrations, but always check carefully through the descriptions for confirmation. The description of the tree is mostly summarized in a facts panel, which contains comparable elements for every species. This layout differs from the practice in most other field guides and floras, where the descriptions are often very brief and inconsistent.

Each page of the guide features a main species and up to three similar trees. These may be cultivars, subspecies, or similar species, and may sometimes be as common as the main species. The elements illustrated for the main species include the general habit and details such as leaves, flowers and fruit. For the similar trees, only one or two distinguishing details are shown.

This colour shows which group of plants each species belongs to. Use it to help you find the different groups as you flick through the book. The colour code is explained on p. 16.

A text summarizes the general look of the tree or how it looks when part of a forest; it draws attention to important distinguishing features and adds points of interest regarding biology or significance to man.

A fact panel provides a detailed summary of the main features of the main tree; where it grows and when it flowers and fruits; with details on the crown, trunk, leaves, flowers, fruit and seeds.

Accurate illustrations of the whole tree, plus details of the flowers, fruits or other parts of the plant important for identification.

Labels pick out the best clues to identification.

Up to three similar trees are illustrated on the same page, with details of how they differ from the main tree.

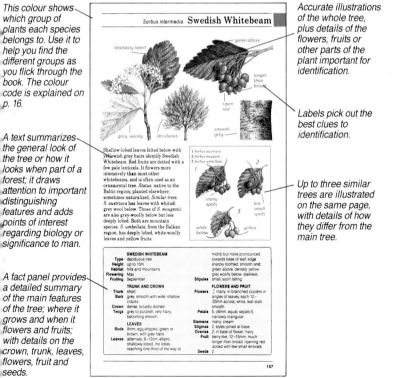

Sorbus intermedia **Swedish Whitebeam**

green above
shallowly lobed
longer than broad
ripen red
grey, woolly deciduous smooth, grey

Shallow-lobed leaves felted below with yellowish grey hairs identify Swedish Whitebeam. Red fruits are dotted with a few pale lenticels. It flowers more intensively than most other whitebeams, and is often used as an ornamental tree. *Status:* native to the Baltic region; planted elsewhere; sometimes naturalized. *Similar trees: S. austriaca* has leaves with whitish grey wool below. Those of *S. mougeotii* are also grey-woolly below but less deeply lobed. Both are mountain species. *S. umbellata*, from the Balkan region, has deeply lobed, white-woolly leaves and yellow fruits.

1 *Sorbus austriaca*
2 *Sorbus mougeotii*
3 *Sorbus umbellata*

many spots
few small spots
white below
yellow

SWEDISH WHITEBEAM		midrib but more pronounced
Type	deciduous tree	towards base of leaf, edge
Height	up to 15m	sharply toothed, smooth and
Habitat	hills and mountains	green above, densely yellow-
Flowering	May	grey woolly below, stalkless
Fruiting	September	**Stipules** small, soon falling
	TRUNK AND CROWN	**FLOWERS AND FRUIT**
Trunk	short	**Flowers** ♀, many, in branched clusters in
Bark	grey, smooth with wide, shallow	angles of leaves, each 12–
	cracks	20mm across, white, leaf stalk
Crown	dense, broadly domed	smooth
Twigs	grey to purplish, very hairy,	**Petals** 5, c6mm, equal, sepals 5,
	becoming smooth	narrowly triangular
	LEAVES	**Stamens** many, cream
Buds	8mm, egg-shaped, green or	**Stigmas** 2, styles joined at base
	brown, with grey hairs	**Ovaries** 2, in base of flower, hairy
Leaves	alternate, 8–12cm, elliptic,	**Fruit** berry-like, 12–15mm, much
	shallowly lobed, the lobes	longer than broad, ripening red,
	reaching one-third of the way to	dotted with few small lenticels
		Seeds 2

107

Introduction

KEY TO SPECIES

This key provides an illustrated guide to the groups of species and their page numbers. At each stage, read the first numbered statement and see if it describes your tree. If not, then the second statement with the same number includes all other plants at this stage of the key. Move on to the next statement below and repeat the process until you key out to the correct group.

1 leaves crowded at top of trunk or tips of thick branches
Agaves 180–181; Palms 182–185.

1 leaves spread along branches and twigs
2 leaves all or mostly scale-like, pressed against stem
Monkey-puzzles 19; Redwoods 38–39; Cypresses 42–45, 47–49; She-oaks 89; Tamarisks 154–155.

2 leaves not all scale-like
3 leaves all or mostly needle-like, spreading
4 needles all spirally arranged or forming 2 parallel rows
Pines 20–29; Redwoods 39–40; Yews 41.

4 needles mostly borne in clusters, tufts or whorls of 2 or more
Pines 30–37; Cypresses 46.

3 leaves not needle-like
5 leaves divided into separate leaflets
6 leaflets in 2 rows
Walnuts 90–92; Roses 104; Peas 124–125, 127–129, 131; Quassias 134; Mahoganies 135; Cashews 136–138; Soapberries 139; Maples 144; Olives 170–171; Honeysuckles 178.

6 leaflets radiating from leaf stalk
Peas 130; Citruses 133; Horse-chestnuts 140–141.

5 leaves not divided into separate leaflets
7 leaves in opposite pairs on stem
Maples 142–143, 145–147; Spindles 149; Boxes 150; Buckthorns 153; Dogwoods 161; Pomegranates 167; Olives 172–173; Bignonias 176–177; Honeysuckles 178.

7 **leaves alternating or scattered around stem**
8 **flowers (at least males) in slender catkins**
9 **leaves lobed, spiny or fan-shaped**
   Maidenhair-tree 18; Willows 58;
   Beeches 70–75.

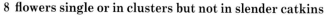

9 **leaves sometimes toothed but neither lobed nor spiny**
   Willows 50–57, 59–61; Birches 62–64;
   Hazels 65–67; Beeches 76; Bog-myrtles 77.

8 **flowers single or in clusters but not in slender catkins**
10 **leaves lobed or spiny**
11 **flowers white**
   Roses 105, 107, 112–115; Hollies 148.

11 **flowers red, yellow or green**
   Mulberries 85; Witch-hazels 86;
   Planes 88; Magnolias 95.

10 **leaves sometimes toothed but neither lobed nor spiny**
12 **evergreen**
13 **crushed leaves strong and pleasant-smelling**
   Laurels 96; Myrtles 162–166.

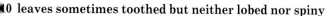

13 **crushed leaves not strong-smelling**
   Pittosporums 93; Magnolias 94;
   Roses 108, 121; Citruses 132;
   Heathers 174; Myoporums 175.

12 **deciduous**
14 **leaves heart-shaped**
   Mulberries 83; Peas 126; Limes
   156–158; Davidia 159.

14 **leaves not heart-shaped**
15 **petals white or pink**
   Roses 98–103, 106, 109–111, 116–
   120, 122–123; Storaxes 169.

15 **petals yellow, greenish, dull red or absent**
16 **leaves with edge toothed**
   Beeches 69; Elms 78–82;
   Mulberries 84; Witch-hazels 87;
   Buckthorns 152–153.

16 **leaves with edge not toothed**
   Beeches 68; Mulberries 84;
   Oleasters 151; Buckthorns 153;
   Black-gums 160; Ebonies 168.

Introduction

TREE NAMES

English language names for native trees have been standardised to the list published by the Botanical Society of the British Isles (Dony, Jury and Perring, 1986). Some plants will have no common name if they only grow in other countries of the area.

Botanical names are more stable and international in usage. Most are those given in the standard European flora (Tutin *et al.* (Editors), 1964–1980) but some are updated according to the British Excursion Flora (Clapham, Tutin & Warburg, 1985). Each Latin name is made up of a genus name (starting with a capital letter) and a species name (starting with a small letter). A third, subspecies (abbreviated as subsp.), name is used to distinguish geographical variation within a species. A multiplication symbol between the first and second names indicates that the plant is a hybrid between two species; if the sign is before the first name then it indicates a hybrid between species of two different genera. Particular selections of cultivated trees are often given horticultural names, indicated in single quotation marks.

Order of trees

The trees in this book are arranged more or less in systematic order. Those that have a similar construction of flowers and fruit are placed together in families. Each group of families is given a colour reference marker. Use this coloured square at the corner of the pages to help you find the different groups of plants as you flick through the book.

Maidenhair-tree and Monkey-puzzles		Roses
Pines		Peas
Redwoods and Yews		Citruses, Quassias and Mahoganies
Cypresses		Cashews, Soapberries, Horse-chestnuts and Maples
Willows		Hollies, Spindles, Boxes and Oleasters
Birches and Hazels		Buckthorns, Tamarisks and Limes
Beeches and Bog-myrtles		Davidia, Black-gums and Dogwoods
Elms and Mulberries		Myrtles, Loosestrifes and Pomegranates
Witch-hazels, Planes and She-oaks		Ebonies, Storaxes, Olives and Heathers
Walnuts and Pittosporums		Myoporums, Foxgloves, Bignonias and Honeysuckles
Magnolias, Laurels and Phytolaccas		Agaves and Palms

THE
TREES
OF·BRITAIN·AND·EUROPE

Maidenhair-tree   *Ginkgo biloba*

An unmistakable tree, with unique fan-shaped leaves, distinctive irregular crown, and marble-sized, fleshy fruits. This odd species belongs to a group of trees that was important when dinosaurs roamed the earth, but now all but this one species is extinct. Fruits give off a nauseous odour when over-ripe, making the female tree unsuitable for planting in towns of warmer countries. The tree was cultivated for centuries in gardens of Chinese temples and palaces. It is virtually unknown in the wild state. *Status:* introduced from China; planted fairly commonly for ornament, often as a street tree. *Similar trees:* none.

♂ catkins

irregular outline

deciduous

rough

paired ♀ flowers

fan-shaped leaf

stalked fruit

leaves clustered

some paired

	MAIDENHAIR-TREE		
Type	conifer, deciduous tree		short shoots, 3–12cm, fan-shaped, notched or deeply cleft, irregularly toothed, base wedge-shaped, many veins diverging from base, yellowish green, turning bright yellow in autumn; stalk up to 4.5cm
Height	25–30m		
Habitat	street tree, parks		
Flowering	March–April		
Fruiting	September–October		
		Stipules	absent
	TRUNK AND CROWN		
Trunk	slender, straight or forked		**FLOWERS AND FRUIT**
Bark	deeply fissured and ridged, brownish grey	**Flowers**	♂ and ♀ flowers on different plants
Crown	irregularly cylindrical or sometimes broad, branches few, short, irregular	♂	cluster of 3–6 yellow catkins, each 60–80mm
Twigs	of two types: long and straight, with short, stubby side-shoots	♀	1 or 2 on stalk up to 40mm long, pale yellow
		Fruit	1–2 on long stalk, 25–30mm, globular or slightly elongated, fleshy, yellowish
	LEAVES		
Buds	conical, reddish brown	**Seeds**	1 per fruit, large, nut-like
Leaves	spirally arranged, widely spaced on long shoots, clustered on		

Araucaria araucana Monkey-puzzle

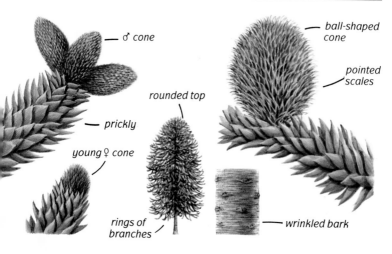

♂ cone

ball-shaped cone

pointed scales

rounded top

prickly

young ♀ cone

rings of branches

wrinkled bark

A most unusual conifer with broad, pine-tipped leaves, thickly set all round the stems. It is the source of a commercially important timber, but rarely produces wood of sufficient quality in Europe. In its native South America, the seeds are eaten as a delicacy but they often fail to set in Europe. *Status:* introduced from Chile and western Argentina; commonly planted in western Europe for ornament. *Similar trees:* Norfolk Island Pine is another ornamental species, but only survives to tree size in the warmer south and west. It has finer foliage, in broad plates, and regular branching.

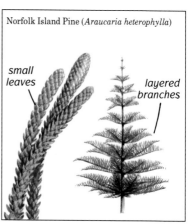

Norfolk Island Pine (*Araucaria heterophylla*)

small leaves

layered branches

MONKEY-PUZZLE	
Type	conifer, evergreen tree
Height	25–30m
Habitat	parks, gardens
Flowering	June–July
Fruiting	August–September

TRUNK AND CROWN

Trunk	straight, stout, not forked, sometimes with suckers from roots
Bark	with horizontal ridges, later becoming vertically ridged, blackish grey
Crown	conical, becoming broadly domed; branches in rings at same level, angled upwards or gradually drooping
Twigs	concealed by overlapping leaf-bases

LEAVES

Buds	conical, hidden by leaves
Leaves	spirally arranged, 3–4cm, triangular or broadly oval, thick, tip spine-tipped, edge unbroken, base broad, dark, glossy green; stalkless
Stipules	absent

FLOWERS AND FRUIT

Flowers	♂ and ♀ flowers on different plants
♂	cone, *c*10cm, egg-shaped, brown, clustered at shoot-tip
♀	cone, globular, spiny, on upper side of shoot
Fruit	globular, upright cone, up to 15cm, green with yellowish spines, breaks up on tree when ripe in second or third year
Seeds	up to 4cm, brown, often sterile

Common Silver-fir *Abies alba*

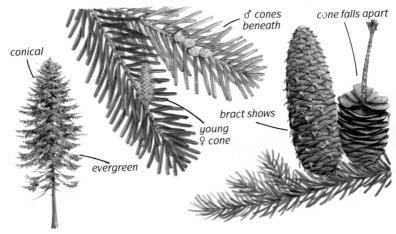

conical

♂ cones beneath

cone falls apart

bract shows

young ♀ cone

evergreen

Once commonly planted in north-western Europe, this species is intolerant of exposure or pollution, and is badly damaged by aphids, so other species are now preferred. Older trees have only a cluster of branches left at the top. *Status:* native to mountains of central and southern Europe; widely planted for timber and ornament in northern Europe. *Similar trees:* Caucasian Fir has a denser and broader crown, crowded leaves, and thicker cones with longer bracts. Heavily branched, with a stout trunk, Grecian Fir differs from the latter in the stiff, spiny leaves, and resinous buds.

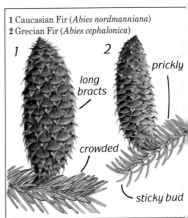

1 Caucasian Fir (*Abies nordmanniana*)
2 Grecian Fir (*Abies cephalonica*)

long bracts

prickly

crowded

sticky bud

	COMMON SILVER-FIR		
Type	conifer, evergreen tree		
Height	40–55m		
Habitat	forests, plantations, parks		
Flowering	April		
Fruiting	September		

TRUNK AND CROWN

Trunk stout, more or less straight, not forked below

Bark dark grey, smooth with resin-blisters, gradually becoming cracked into squarish plates

Crown narrowly conical; branches in groups at same level

Twigs greyish brown, shortly hairy, with circular leaf-scars

LEAVES

Buds egg-shaped, reddish brown, not or scarcely resinous

Leaves arising spirally, twisted to either side, parted above twig, 15–25mm, rarely 35mm, needle-like, flattened but thick, tip shallowly notched, dark green with 2 whitish bands below; stalkless

Stipules absent

FLOWERS AND FRUIT

Flowers ♂ and ♀ on same tree
♂ globular, yellow cone, on underside of shoots,
♀ egg-shaped, greenish cone, on upper side of top branches
Fruit cylindrical, upright cone, 10–20cm, brown, with woody cone-scales and slender-tipped, downward-pointing, projecting bracts, disintegrating on tree leaving slender spike
Seeds 2 per scale, winged

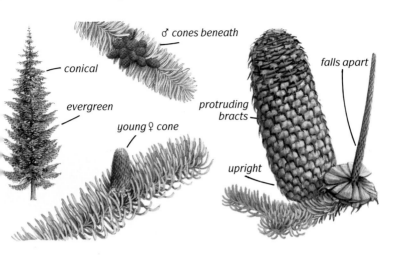

conical

evergreen

♂ cones beneath

young ♀ cone

protruding bracts

falls apart

upright

A striking tree, with huge, upright cones that have distinctive, downward-pointing bracts. It is commonly planted for its close-grained timber, and plantations thrive even under harsh conditions. *Status:* introduced from western North America; widely planted in northern and western Europe for timber or ornament. *Similar trees:* two species have very resinous buds and smaller cones, which are bluish until maturity. Native to north-eastern Russia, Siberian Fir has cones with short, hidden bracts. Introduced from Japan, Veitch's Silver-fir has cones with the bracts just projecting.

1 Siberian Fir (*Abies sibirica*)
2 Veitch's Silver-fir (*Abies veitchii*)

1 bracts hidden

2 bracts just show

bluish young cones

	NOBLE FIR	
Type	conifer, evergreen tree	
Height	40–50m (taller in America)	
Habitat	cultivated mainly in plantations	
Flowering	May	
Fruiting	October	

TRUNK AND CROWN

Trunk stout, straight, not forked
Bark pale grey, smooth with resin-blisters, becoming fissured
Crown narrowly conical or columnar, becoming flat-topped; branches level, forming irregular rings
Twigs reddish brown, finely hairy, with circular leaf-scars

LEAVES

Buds resinous only at the tips
Leaves arising spirally but curved up at sides, parted below, crowded above, 1–3.5cm, needle-like, 4-angled, blunt, greyish green, 2 pale grey bands beneath; stalkless
Stipules absent

FLOWERS AND FRUIT

Flowers ♂ and ♀ flowers on same plant
♂ globular, crimson cone, c6mm, clustered beneath shoots, becoming yellow with pollen
♀ cylindrical greenish cone, 40–50mm, scales orange-tipped
Fruit barrel-shaped, blunt-tipped, upright cone, 15–25cm, with green, downward-pointing bracts protruding beyond purplish brown cone-scales, disintegrating on tree leaving slender spike
Seeds 2 per scale, winged

Grand Fir *Abies grandis*

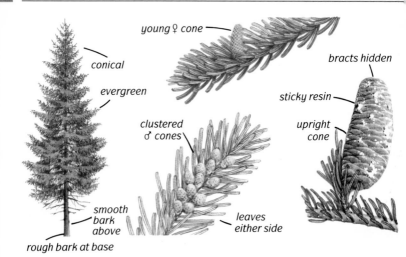

young ♀ cone

conical

evergreen

bracts hidden

sticky resin

upright cone

clustered ♂ cones

smooth bark above

leaves either side

rough bark at base

This large tree is readily distinguished by feather-like shoots with leaves spreading horizontally to either side, and upright, cylindrical cones with hidden bracts. The foliage has a distinct orange-like scent. Remarkably fast growth and tolerance of most soil conditions contribute to the value of this species as a forestry tree. *Status:* introduced from western North America; widely planted in northern and central Europe, mainly for timber. *Similar trees:* Colorado White-fir differs in the dark, rougher bark, longer, upward curving, often bluish leaves, and a larger cone.

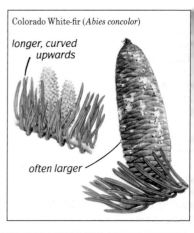

Colorado White-fir (*Abies concolor*)

longer, curved upwards

often larger

	GRAND FIR		Leaves	arising spirally but turning to either side leaving parting above and below shoot, 2–6cm, needle-like, notched, glossy green above with 2 whitish bands below; stalkless
Type	conifer, evergreen tree			
Height	40–60m (over 90m in America)			
Habitat	plantations, especially in wetter areas			
Flowering	April		**Stipules**	absent
Fruiting	October			
				FLOWERS AND FRUIT
	TRUNK AND CROWN		**Flowers**	♂ and ♀ flowers on same plant
Trunk	straight, not forked, fairly stout		♂	purplish, cone, *c*2mm, in cluster below shoot, becomes yellow with pollen
Bark	brownish grey, smooth with resin-blisters, eventually cracked into squarish plates			
			♀	solitary cone, above shoot
Crown	narrowly conical or columnar; branches in rings at same level		**Fruit**	woody, upright cone, 5–10cm, cylindrical, reddish brown exuding whitish resin; bracts hidden by cone-scales; cone disintegrates on tree leaving thin spike
Twigs	with sparse, short hairs and circular leaf-scars			
	LEAVES			
Buds	*c*2mm, conical, purplish, becoming covered with resin		**Seeds**	2 per scale, winged

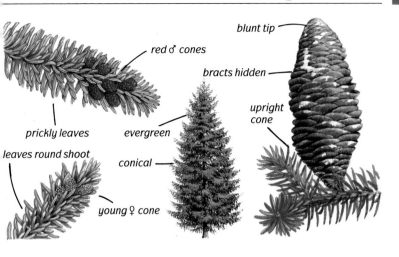

red ♂ cones

blunt tip

bracts hidden

upright cone

prickly leaves

evergreen

leaves round shoot

conical

young ♀ cone

Also known as 'Hedgehog Fir', this species is easily distinguished by stiff, prickly leaves set all around the shoots. Though naturally limited to a few sites in Spain, near Ronda, it is cultivated elsewhere. *Status:* native to mountains of southern Spain; frequently planted for ornament or sometimes timber. *Similar trees:* Algerian Fir has longer, broader, more flexible leaves with whitish bands below, and cones with a raised centre to the otherwise squarish tip. Nikko Fir has very pale, grooved shoots with leaves pointing slightly forwards, and violet-blue young cones.

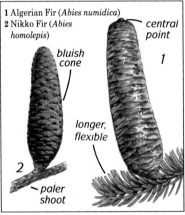

1 Algerian Fir (*Abies numidica*)
2 Nikko Fir (*Abies homolepis*)

central point

bluish cone

1

longer, flexible

2

paler shoot

	SPANISH FIR		
Type	conifer, evergreen tree		
Height	20–30m		
Habitat	north-facing slopes on limestone mountains; also planted elsewhere		
Flowering	May		
Fruiting	October		
	TRUNK AND CROWN		
Trunk	stout, straight, not forked		
Bark	smooth, becoming cracked into squarish plates, dark grey or blackish		
Crown	conical, becoming irregular; branches in rings at same level		
Twigs	orange-brown, smooth except for circular leaf-scars		
	LEAVES		
Buds	3–5mm, egg-shaped, purplish, sticky with resin		
Leaves	spreading outwards all round shoot, 10–18mm, needle-like, stiff, spine-tipped, greyish green with 2 greyish bands above and below; stalkless		
Stipules	absent		
	FLOWERS AND FRUIT		
Flowers	♂ and ♀ flowers on same plant		
♂	cluster of cones below shoot, each c5mm, globular, red, becoming yellow with pollen		
♀	solitary cone above shoot		
Fruit	upright, cylindrical cone, 10–16cm, tip squarish with small point, ripening brown; bracts hidden by cone-scales		
Seeds	2 per cone-scale, winged		

Douglas-fir *Pseudotsuga menziesii*

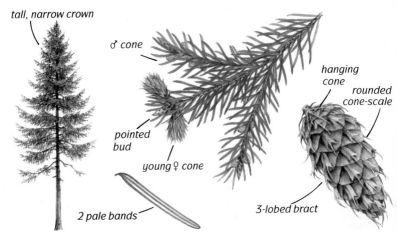

tall, narrow crown

♂ *cone*

pointed bud

young ♀ cone

2 pale bands

hanging cone

rounded cone-scale

3-lobed bract

A magnificent conifer, outgrowing most other trees in Europe and rivalling Coast Redwood and Sierra Redwood in height where these three conifers are native in western North America. A most distinctive characteristic of Douglas-fir is the hanging cone, with protruding, three-pointed bracts. *Status:* introduced from Pacific coast of North America; widely planted in Europe for timber, shelter and ornament. *Similar trees:* Large-coned Douglas-fir has stiff, spiny foliage. Rarely produced in cultivation, the larger cones have bracts which scarcely project beyond the thick cone-scales.

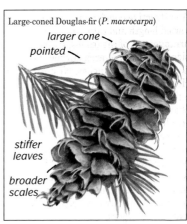

Large-coned Douglas-fir (*P. macrocarpa*)

larger cone

pointed

stiffer leaves

broader scales

	DOUGLAS-FIR		
Type	conifer, evergreen tree	**Leaves**	arising spirally but turning to either side of shoot, 2–3.5cm, needle-like, dark green, 2 white bands below; stalkless
Height	55m (100m in America)		
Habitat	cultivated in plantations, parks, gardens	**Stipules**	absent
Flowering	May–July		**FLOWERS AND FRUIT**
Fruiting	October	**Flowers**	♂ and ♀ cones on same tree
	TRUNK AND CROWN	♂	at leaf-bases of previous year's shoot, yellow
Trunk	straight, not forked		
Bark	smooth except for resin-blisters, greyish green, becoming deeply fissured, corky, reddish brown	♀	near tip of previous year's shoot, 5–10mm, red or green
		Fruit	hanging, oblong, tapered cone, 5–10cm, ripening in first year; cone-scales rounded; 3-toothed bracts project
Crown	narrowly conical, becoming flat-topped; branches in groups at same level		
Twigs	with raised, elliptical leaf-scars, softly hairy	**Seeds**	winged, 2 per cone-scale
	LEAVES		
Buds	tapered both ends, pointed		

Western Hemlock-spruce

Tsuga heterophylla

dark green

young ♀ cone

small ♂ cones

pale bands below

conical crown

small cone

bracts hidden

An attractive conifer, recognized by the varied length and rather random arrangement of the leaves, set either side of shoots that arch downwards from spreading branches. Western Hemlock-spruce is highly productive as a timber tree. The foliage has a characteristic odour resembling Hemlock. *Status:* introduced from western North America; widely cultivated in Europe. *Similar trees:* Eastern Hemlock-spruce is smaller, with shorter, tapered leaves, and smaller cones. Mountain Hemlock-spruce has spirally arranged, bluish leaves and larger cones.

1 Eastern Hemlock-spruce (*T. canadensis*)
2 Mountain Hemlock-spruce (*T. mertensiana*)

2

1

upper row turned

shorter, tapered

spirally arranged

larger cone

	WESTERN HEMLOCK-SPRUCE		
Type	conifer, evergreen tree		
Height	45m (up to 70m in America)		
Habitat	cultivated in plantations, parks, gardens		
Flowering	April		
Fruiting	October		

TRUNK AND BRANCHES

Trunk straight, unforked

Bark reddish brown, rough, becoming cracked and fluted

Crown narrowly conical or cylindrical; branches in groups at same level

Twigs slender, tip droops, greyish brown, hairy

LEAVES

Buds globular, greyish

Leaves arising spirally, turning to either side of twig, 0.5–2cm, of different lengths, needle-like, flattened, blunt, dark green, 2 white bands below; peg-like base remains after leaf falls

Stipules absent

FLOWERS AND FRUIT

Flowers ♂ and ♀ cones on same plant

♂ clustered at leaf-bases near shoot tip, small, red, turning yellow

♀ solitary at shoot tip, *c*6mm, purplish pink

Fruit single egg-shaped cone, 2–2.5cm, hanging, brown, ripening in first year; scales rounded, persisting

Seeds winged, 2 per cone-scale

Norway Spruce *Picea abies*

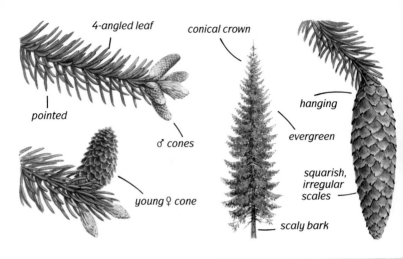

4-angled leaf

conical crown

pointed

♂ cones

hanging

evergreen

squarish, irregular scales

young ♀ cone

scaly bark

An important timber tree, though perhaps more familiar as a Christmas tree. Spruces are distinctive in the long, hanging cones with thin scales, and needles borne on short, peg-like projections. *Status:* native mainly to northern Europe; planted elsewhere for timber, shelter and ornament. *Similar trees:* forming intermediates where they grow together, Siberian Spruce is sometimes regarded as part of the same species as Norway Spruce. It is smaller with a shorter, more pointed cone and short, dense hairs on the twigs. Oriental Spruce is easily distinguished by its very short leaves.

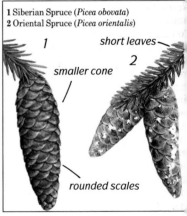

1 Siberian Spruce (*Picea obovata*)
2 Oriental Spruce (*Picea orientalis*)

short leaves

smaller cone

rounded scales

	NORWAY SPRUCE		
Type	conifer, evergreen tree		side of shoot and leaving gap below, 10–25mm, needle-like, 4-angled, pointed, dark green with greyish band on each side; peg-like base
Height	30–40m (rarely to 60m)		
Habitat	forests, plantations, parks		
Flowering	May		
Fruiting	September	**Stipules**	absent
	TRUNK AND CROWN		**FLOWERS AND FRUIT**
Trunk	straight, not forked	**Flowers**	♂ and ♀ flowers on same plant
Bark	reddish brown, rough, scaly, darkens, cracks into plates	♂	globular cones, *c*1cm, near shoot tips, crimson, turning yellow with pollen
Crown	conical or columnar; branches in rings at same level		
Twigs	orange brown, grooved, rough with peg-like leaf-bases, usually hairless	♀	solitary cone, dark red, upright, on upper branches
		Fruit	cylindrical cone with rounded tip, 12–20cm, hanging, woody, brown; scales thin, diamond-shaped or oval with squarish, irregular tip
	LEAVES		
Buds	4–7mm, egg-shaped, glossy dark brown		
Leaves	arising spirally, turning to either	**Seeds**	2 per cone-scale, winged

young ♀ cone

flattened

conical

♂ cones

pointed

hanging

scales thin

evergreen

irregular tips

Native to the Pacific coast of North America, this tall, graceful conifer is now an important timber tree in Europe. It has shallow roots and is often blown over in high winds. *Status:* introduced from North America; commonly grown in northern and central Europe for timber or ornament. *Similar trees:* two species differ in the short, blunt leaves and smaller cones. Hondo Spruce, from Japan, has a blunt cone with toothed scales. Serbian Spruce, from Yugoslavia, has hairy twigs and pointed cones with rounded scales. Also with rounded scales, Tiger-tail Spruce has sharp, four-angled leaves.

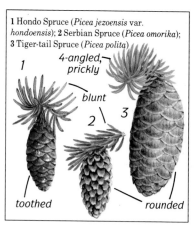

1 Hondo Spruce (*Picea jezoensis* var. *hondoensis*); 2 Serbian Spruce (*Picea omorika*); 3 Tiger-tail Spruce (*Picea polita*)

4-angled, prickly

blunt

1

2

3

toothed

rounded

	SITKA SPRUCE	
Type	conifer, evergreen tree	
Height	40–55m (up to 80m in America)	
Habitat	plantations, parks; often in areas of high rainfall	
Flowering	May	
Fruiting	October	

TRUNK AND CROWN

Trunk	usually straight, not forked
Bark	dark or purplish grey, cracking into irregular, lifting plates
Crown	narrowly conical; lower branches arch downwards
Twigs	pale brown, grooved, rough

LEAVES

Buds	egg-shaped, pale brown, purplish with resin
Leaves	spirally arranged, mostly turning to either side of shoot, the upper close to shoot, 2–3cm, needle-like, flattened, tip sharply pointed, bright green above with 2 narrow, pale bands, 2 bluish white bands below; stalkless
Stipules	absent

FLOWERS AND FRUIT

Flowers	♂ and ♀ flowers on same plant
♂	blunt, egg-shaped cones, 25–35mm, yellow or purplish
♀	pale red or green cone, 25–50mm, mostly near top of tree
Fruit	solitary, cylindrical, hanging cone, 5–10cm, ripening pale brown; scales thin, papery, crinkled, irregularly toothed
Seeds	2 per scale, winged

Colorado Spruce *Picea pungens*

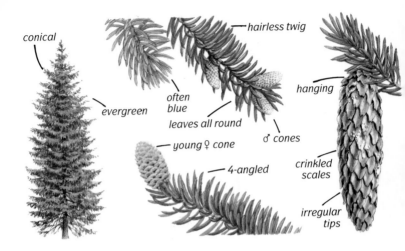

conical

evergreen

often blue

leaves all round

young ♀ cone

— hairless twig

hanging

♂ cones

4-angled

crinkled scales

irregular tips

A variable tree with stiff, prickly leaves and hanging cones with thin, crinkled scales. Where native in western North America, forms with both grey-green and bluish leaves are found. Ornamental trees in Europe are almost always blue-leaved. *Status:* introduced from western North America; grown for ornament and timber in northern and central Europe. *Similar trees:* two species have unpleasantly scented foliage, leaves parted beneath the shoots and smaller cones. Engelmann Spruce has dense, short hairs on the twigs; White Spruce has shorter leaves, and cones with rounded scales.

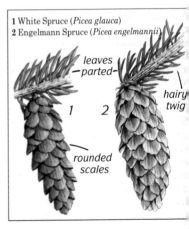

1 White Spruce (*Picea glauca*)
2 Engelmann Spruce (*Picea engelmannii*)

leaves parted

hairy twig

rounded scales

	COLORADO SPRUCE		
Type	conifer, evergreen tree	**Leaves**	spirally arranged all round shoot, 2–3cm, needle-like, stiff, 4-angled, spine-tipped, grey green or bluish with paler band on each side and waxy layer; stalkless
Height	to 30m (rarely 45m in America)		
Habitat	plantations, parks		
Flowering	May		
Fruiting	October		
		Stipules	absent
	TRUNK AND CROWN		
Trunk	straight, not forked		**FLOWERS AND FRUIT**
Bark	purplish grey or brown, cracking into flakes or plates	**Flowers**	♂ and ♀ cones on same tree
		♂	egg-shaped or shortly cylindrical cone, *c*2cm, yellowish
Crown	narrowly conical, dense; branches level or lowest arched downwards		
		♀	upright cone, *c*4cm, near shoot tip
Twigs	whitish or yellowish brown, rough, grooved, hairless	**Fruit**	cylindrical, hanging cone, 7–12cm, near top of tree, pale brown; scales diamond-shaped, thin, crinkled with squarish, irregularly toothed tip
	LEAVES		
Buds	egg-shaped or conical, pointed, scales curved back		
		Seeds	2 per scale, winged

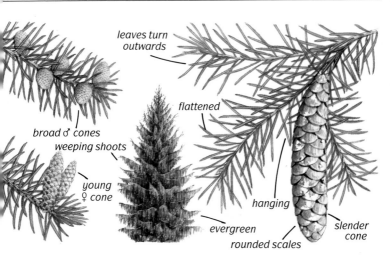

leaves turn outwards

flattened

broad ♂ cones
weeping shoots

young ♀ cone

hanging

evergreen

rounded scales

slender cone

A beautiful tree with curtain-like, weeping foliage from upswept branches. An uncommon North American tree of the Siskyou Mountains in California and Oregon, it is not closely related to any other spruce. *Status:* introduced from western North America; frequently planted for ornament. *Similar trees:* Morinda Spruce has a less dramatic weeping habit and hairless shoots. The buds are smaller and rounded, and the leaves, square in cross-section, are very long and green all round. Relatively broader, the cone has rounded scales which become irregular at the tip as they ripen.

Morinda Spruce (*Picea smithiana*)

hairless twig
broader cone

4-angled

	BREWER'S WEEPING-SPRUCE
Type	conifer, evergreen tree
Height	10–20m (to 35m in America)
Habitat	mainly grown in parks, gardens
Flowering	May
Fruiting	October

TRUNK AND CROWN

Trunk	straight, not forked
Bark	purplish grey, smooth, eventually with roughly circular flakes
Crown	irregularly conical or columnar; branches level or upswept, lower bent downwards
Twigs	long, slender, weeping, rough, pinkish brown, finely hairy

LEAVES

Buds	egg-shaped or conical, blunt, with reddish brown hairs
Leaves	arising spirally, curving out all round shoot or sometimes parted below, 2–3.5cm, needle-like, flattened, blunt, dark bluish green with 2 whitish bands below; stalkless
Stipules	absent

FLOWERS AND FRUIT

Flowers	♂ and ♀ flowers on same tree
♂	egg-shaped cones, 15–30mm, clustered near shoot tip
♀	cylindrical, upright cones, 25–35mm, red or pinkish green, clustered on upper branches
Fruit	narrow, hanging cone, 10–14cm, cylindrical, blunt, purplish, turning brown marked with whitish resin; scales rounded
Seeds	2 per scale, winged

European Larch *Larix decidua*

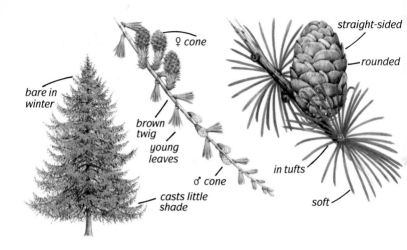

- bare in winter
- ♀ cone
- brown twig
- young leaves
- ♂ cone
- casts little shade
- straight-sided
- rounded
- in tufts
- soft

Leaves of this deciduous conifer turn yellow before falling to reveal knobbly twigs. Soft tufts of emerald-green young leaves in spring accompany pink young female cones and golden male cones. *Status:* native to mountains of central Europe; planted elsewhere for timber and ornament. *Similar trees:* Japanese Larch differs in the orange twigs, bluish leaves with white bands beneath, yellowish young female cones, and ripe cones with scales curved outwards. Its vigorous hybrid with the former species has intermediate cones. Dahurian Larch has cones with fewer, scarcely curved, hairless, broad scales.

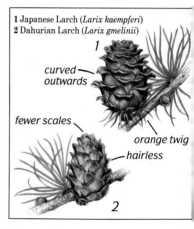

1 Japanese Larch (*Larix kaempferi*)
2 Dahurian Larch (*Larix gmelinii*)

- curved outwards
- fewer scales
- orange twig
- hairless

	EUROPEAN LARCH		
Type	conifer, deciduous tree	**Leaves**	tuft of 30–40 on short shoots, or spirally arranged on long shoots, 2–4cm, needle-like, thin, soft, pale green, becoming darker and turning yellow in autumn; stalkless
Height	30–50m		
Habitat	forest, woodland, plantations		
Flowering	March–April		
Fruiting	September; ripens first year		
		Stipules	absent
	TRUNK AND CROWN		
Trunk	straight, not forked below		**FLOWERS AND FRUIT**
Bark	greyish brown, smooth, becomes reddish and scaly or fissured	**Flowers**	♂ and ♀ cones on same tree
		♂	small, drooping cone, yellow
		♀	upright cone, pink or red
Crown	conical, becoming broader; branches irregularly clustered	**Fruit**	egg-shaped woody cone, 2–3.5cm, with 40–50 scales; cone-scales more or less flat, round-tipped, softly hairy; bracts slightly protruding
Twigs	yellowish, hairless; long shoots and short side shoots		
	LEAVES	**Seeds**	2 per cone-scale, winged
Buds	3mm, oval, yellowish brown		

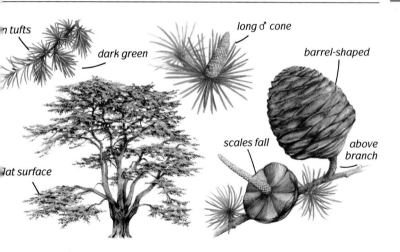

n tufts
dark green
long ♂ cone
barrel-shaped
scales fall
above branch
flat surface

Massive, spreading branches bearing flat plates of needle-like foliage make this tree easily recognizable at a distance. Bunched needles and barrel-shaped cones carried above the foliage are also distinctive. Mature stands of this tree are a rarity in the wild. *Status: introduced from south-western Asia; frequently planted for ornament.*
Similar trees: Atlas Cedar, from North Africa, is commonly planted, usually as the blue-needled variant. It has branches angled upwards and leaves in clusters of 30–45. Himalayan in origin, Deodar has a pointed crown, longer leaves and drooping young shoots.

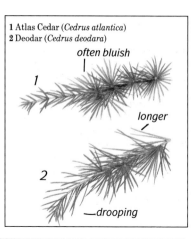

1 Atlas Cedar (*Cedrus atlantica*)
2 Deodar (*Cedrus deodara*)
often bluish
1
longer
2
drooping

	CEDAR-OF-LEBANON	Leaves	tuft of 10–20 on short shoots, spirally arranged on long shoots, 2–3cm, needle-like, pointed, stiff, dark green, hairless; stalkless
Type	conifer, evergreen tree		
Height	15–40m		
Habitat	parks, gardens		
Flowering	October–November	**Stipules**	absent
Fruiting	ripens in second or third year		
	TRUNK AND CROWN		**FLOWERS AND FRUIT**
Trunk	stout, often forked	**Flowers**	♂ and ♀ cones on same tree
Bark	brown or blackish, cracks into fine, scaly ridges	♂	cone 4–5cm, greenish yellow
		♀	cone 7–12mm, green or purplish
Crown	conical when young, becomes broad, rounded or flat-topped; stout, horizontal branches bear large, flat plates of dense foliage	**Fruit**	woody cone, 8–15cm, barrel-shaped with squarish or dimpled tip, greyish or pinkish brown, resinous, disintegrates on tree
Twigs	finely hairy, pale brown		
	LEAVES	**Seeds**	winged, 2 per cone-scale
Buds	2–3mm, egg-shaped, brown		

Scots Pine *Pinus sylvestris*

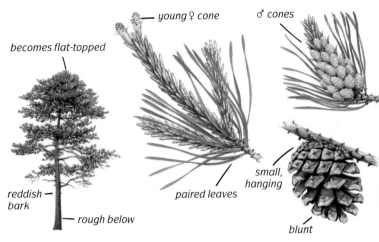

young ♀ cone

becomes flat-topped

♂ cones

reddish bark

rough below

paired leaves

small, hanging

blunt

A widespread conifer from the Atlantic coast of Europe almost to the Pacific coast of Asia. One of several pines with paired needles, it is distinguished by reddish, scaly bark on the upper trunk, relatively short, bluish needles, a small, hanging cone and small buds with scales pressed close together. *Status:* native to northern and central Europe; planted elsewhere for timber. *Similar trees:* Mountain-pine has bright green leaves and a shiny cone projecting at right-angles from the stem. Each scale has a backwardly curved point. Dwarf Mountain-pine is a similar but shorter tree or shrub, with small cones.

Mountain-pine (*Pinus mugo*)

greener leaves

small point

	SCOTS PINE		
Type	conifer, evergreen tree		hairless; stalkless; small, scale-like on long shoots
Height	20–40m	**Stipules**	absent
Habitat	forests, woods, plantations		
Flowering	May–June		**FLOWERS AND FRUIT**
Fruiting	ripens in second year	**Flowers**	♂ and ♀ cones on same tree
		♂	globular cone, yellow or sometimes red before pollen is shed
	TRUNK AND CROWN		
Trunk	straight, not normally forked	♀	1–5 cones at tip of shoot, egg-shaped, pinkish purple cones
Bark	reddish brown, scaling above, blackish brown, fissured below	**Fruit**	woody cone, 3–7cm, egg-shaped, pointed, hanging, dull, grey-brown; scales with broad, flattened end, raised in centre
Crown	conical, becomes broader or flat-topped; branches in groups at same level		
Twigs	greenish brown, hairless	**Seeds**	12–15mm, winged, 2 per scale
	LEAVES		
Buds	small, pointed, resinous		
Leaves	paired on short shoots, 3–7cm, needle-like, twisted, blue-green,		

Pinus nigra subsp. *laricio* Corsican Pine

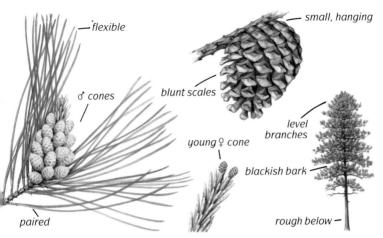

flexible

♂ cones

blunt scales

small, hanging

young ♀ cone

level branches

blackish bark

paired

rough below

From its forests in the Mediterranean region, this pine has been introduced to many parts of northern Europe, where it forms extensive plantations. It resembles Scots Pine but has darker bark and longer, more flexible and darker leaves. In colder regions, it is susceptible to disease. *Status:* native to the central Mediterranean region; planted for timber, shelter or stabilizing sand. *Similar trees:* a dark, heavy-branched tree, Austrian Pine has rigid, straight, spine-tipped leaves, regularly clustered around the stem. Bosnian Pine has similar foliage but purple young cones.

1 Austrian Pine (*Pinus nigra* subsp. *nigra*)
2 Bosnian Pine (*Pinus leucodermis*)

1

spiny

2

young cone purple

rigid

	CORSICAN PINE	
Type	conifer, evergreen tree	
Height	30–50m	
Habitat	forests, plantations	
Flowering	June	
Fruiting	ripens in second year	

TRUNK AND CROWN

Trunk	straight, rarely forked	
Bark	grey, scaling above, blackish grey, deeply fissured below	
Crown	conical or columnar, rarely becoming broader; branches in groups at same level	
Twigs	hairless, yellowish brown	

LEAVES

Buds	conical, pointed, resinous	
Leaves	paired on short shoots, 10–18cm, needle-shaped, twisted, flexible, pointed, greyish green, hairless; stalkless	
Stipules	absent	

FLOWERS AND FRUIT

Flowers	♂ and ♀ cones on same tree	
♂	clustered cones, each 8–13mm, yellow, scales purple-tipped	
♀	egg-shaped cone, *c*5mm, pink	
Fruit	woody cone, 6–8cm, egg-shaped, dull, yellowish or greyish brown; scales with broad, flattened end, with horizontal ridge and small central spine	
Seeds	2 per scale, winged	

Maritime Pine *Pinus pinaster*

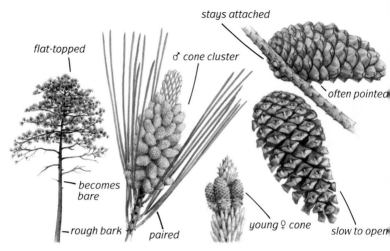

flat-topped

stays attached

♂ cone cluster

often pointed

becomes bare

rough bark

paired

young ♀ cone

slow to open

A distinctive coastal species with a high, open crown and very long needles. Glossy, woody cones can stay closed on the tree for many years before they open and fall. Resin tapped from the trunk is used in the manufacture of turpentine and for flavouring wines. *Status:* native to the western Mediterranean region; planted elsewhere for timber, shelter, sand-binding and resin. *Similar trees:* Aleppo Pine has shorter leaves and smaller cones, with rounded scales and a short stalk, which curves backwards. Calabrian Pine has leaves like the former and a cone like the latter, but with a short, straight stalk.

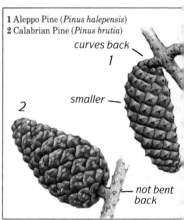

1 Aleppo Pine (*Pinus halepensis*)
2 Calabrian Pine (*Pinus brutia*)

curves back

1

smaller

2

not bent back

	MARITIME PINE		
Type	conifer, evergreen tree	**Leaves**	paired on short shoots, 10–25cm, needle-like, twisted, rigid, pointed, glossy grey-green, becoming deeper green, hairless; stalkless
Height	up to 40m		
Habitat	hot, dry, coastal areas		
Flowering	June		
Fruiting	ripens in second year	**Stipules**	absent

	TRUNK AND CROWN		FLOWERS AND FRUIT
Trunk	often twisted, becomes bare of branches below	**Flowers**	♂ and ♀ cones on same tree
Bark	reddish brown, becomes deeply fissured and ridged	♂	clustered cones, 8–10mm, yellow
Crown	conical or domed; branches in irregular wide-spaced groups	♀	groups of 3–5 cones near stem-tip, each 10–12mm, egg-shaped, deep pink
Twigs	grey or red-brown, hairless	**Fruit**	woody cones in small clusters, 8–22cm, conical, pointed, glossy brown; scales with horizontal ridges and often a broad, sharp point

	LEAVES		
Buds	10–20mm, tapered both ends, reddish brown, not resinous; scales bent back	**Seeds**	7–8mm with wing up to 30mm

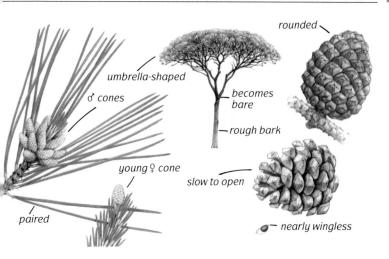

rounded

umbrella-shaped

♂ cones

becomes bare

rough bark

young ♀ cone

slow to open

paired

nearly wingless

his umbrella-shaped tree forms a istinctive element of the 1editerranean landscape and provides uch-valued shade during long, hot ımmers. Huge woody cones contain eeds differing from those of other pines ı having scarcely any wing. They are dible and eagerly sought. *Status:* ative to Portugal and the 1editerranean region to the Black Sea; ften planted as a shade-tree. *Similar ees:* Canary Island Pine is planted in he Mediterranean region for its high-uality timber. It differs in the very ong leaves, grouped in threes, and eeds with a much larger wing.

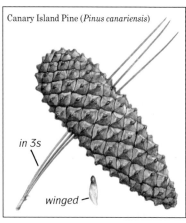

Canary Island Pine (*Pinus canariensis*)

in 3s

winged

	STONE PINE		
Type	conifer, evergreen tree	**Leaves**	paired, 10–20cm, needle-like, rather thick, often twisted, pointed, greyish green, hairless; stalkless
Height	20–30m		
Habitat	woods on light, sandy soils		
Flowering	June	**Stipules**	absent
Fruiting	ripens in third year		
	TRUNK AND CROWN		**FLOWERS AND FRUIT**
Trunk	straight, widely forked above	**Flowers**	♂ and ♀ cones on same tree
Bark	greyish or reddish brown, fissured forming flat plates	♂	cluster of cones, each 10–14mm, egg-shaped, orange-brown
Crown	broad, umbrella-shaped; branches stout, radiating	♀	solitary cone 8–12mm, yellowish green
Twigs	greyish green to orange-brown, often curved, hairless	**Fruit**	woody cone, 8–14cm, globular or slightly elongated, blunt, glossy brown; scale-tips rounded, with radiating folds
	LEAVES		
Buds	5–12mm, oval, reddish brown, not resinous; white-fringed scales curved backwards	**Seeds**	15–20mm, nut-like with hard coat and narrow, papery wing

Shore Pine *Pinus contorta*

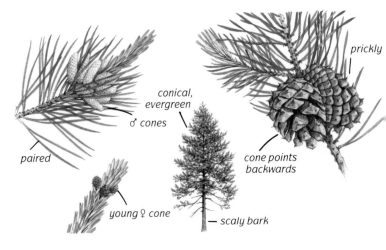

paired

conical, evergreen

♂ *cones*

prickly

cone points backwards

young ♀ cone

scaly bark

Not the most attractive of pines, this tough species survives to produce useful timber even in windswept places with very poor, waterlogged soils. It has short, paired leaves in bunches, and twisted buds. Cones remain on the tree and in nature ripen late, often after a forest fire. *Status:* introduced from the Pacific coast of North America; widely planted in central and northern Europe for timber. *Similar trees:* two other American timber trees differ in having longer leaves in threes and larger cones. Monterey Pine has very asymmetrical cones. Western Yellow-pine has symmetrical cones with strong prickles.

1 Monterey Pine (*Pinus radiata*)
2 Western Yellow-pine (*Pinus ponderosa*)

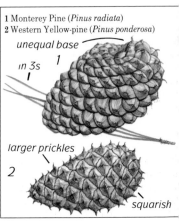

unequal base

in 3s

1

larger prickles

2

squarish

	SHORE PINE		
Type	conifer, evergreen tree	**Leaves**	paired, bunched, pointing towards branch tip, 4–7cm, needle-like, twisted, pointed, dark green, hairless; stalkless
Height	10–30m		
Habitat	plantations, often poor soils		
Flowering	April–May	**Stipules**	absent
Fruiting	ripens in 2 or more years		
	TRUNK AND CROWN		**FLOWERS AND FRUIT**
Trunk	straight, not forked	**Flowers**	♂ and ♀ on same tree
Bark	dark brown, scaly, becoming deeply fissured	♂	tiny cones crowded together at base of new shoot, yellow
Crown	slender, conical or columnar, eventually becoming domed; branches short, often twisted	♀	2–4 cones near tip of shoot, c6mm, dark red, conical
		Fruit	woody cone, pointing backwards on shoot, 2.5–7.5cm, conical, elongated, glossy yellowish brown; scale-tips angular with slender, fragile prickle
Twigs	greenish brown, becoming orange-brown, hairless, shiny		
	LEAVES		
Buds	cylindrical, often twisted, brown, resinous	**Seeds**	4–5mm, wing c8mm

♂ cones

young ♀ cone

in 5s

orange hairs

pointed scales

stays attached

narrow crown

level, turns up

scaly bark

slow to open

Arolla Pine is characterized by needles in groups of five and short cones with thin, pointed, rather than square-ended, scales. Cones ripen and fall after three years, the seeds released only as the cones are broken open by animals or eventually rot. *Status:* native to the mountains of southern and central Europe; planted further north for timber and ornament. *Similar trees:* Weymouth Pine and other five-needled pines have elongated, hanging, sticky cones and winged seeds. Two species differ in the hairless shoots. Bhutan Pine has straight cones; Macedonian Pine has shorter, curved cones.

1 Weymouth Pine (*Pinus strobus*)
2 Bhutan Pine (*Pinus wallichiana*)
3 Macedonian Pine (*Pinus peuce*)

1 sticky

2 long

hairless

shorter *3*

AROLLA PINE		
Type	conifer, evergreen tree	
Height	10–30m	
Habitat	dry slopes up to 3000m	
Flowering	May	
Fruiting	ripens in third year	

TRUNK AND CROWN

Trunk straight, sometimes forked
Bark reddish grey, smooth with resin-blisters, becoming shallowly fissured, scaly
Crown columnar to broadly conical; branches in groups at same level, tips turn upwards
Twigs with brownish orange hairs

LEAVES

Buds egg-shaped, pointed, pale brown; scales white-edged

Leaves in fives, 5–9cm, needle-like, pointed, hairless, dark green with bluish inner face; stalkless
Stipules absent

FLOWERS AND FRUIT

Flowers ♂ and ♀ on same tree
♂ cluster of cones, egg-shaped, yellow or purplish
♀ cone at stem-tip, *c*10mm, egg-shaped, dark red
Fruit woody cone, 5–8cm, broadly egg-shaped, purple-tinged when young, becoming reddish brown; scales thin, broad, pointed
Seeds 2 per scale, 12–14mm, usually wingless, shed after cones fall

Wellingtonia   *Sequoiadendron giganteum*

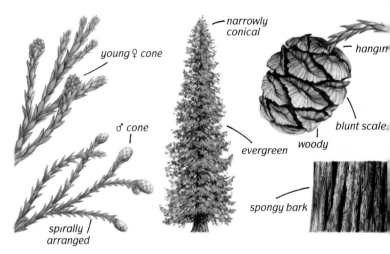

narrowly conical

young ♀ cone

hangin

♂ cone

blunt scale.

evergreen   woody

spirally arranged

spongy bark

A massive tree, though no plants in Europe come close to the true giants of western North America. They are very long-lived and may survive for around 3400 years, during which time they can reach over 90m with a buttressed trunk 7m or more across. Thick, fibrous, reddish bark acts as an insulating layer against forest fire and contributes to the longevity of the trees. *Status:* introduced from the Sierra Nevada of California; frequently planted for ornament. *Similar trees:* Japanese Red-cedar has more slender leaves but differs markedly in the smaller cones; each scale usually has five spines.

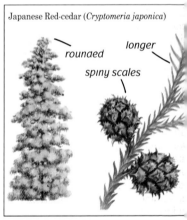

Japanese Red-cedar (*Cryptomeria japonica*)

rounaed

longer

spiny scales

stem

	WELLINGTONIA
Type	conifer, evergreen tree
Height	to 50m (85m in North America)
Habitat	parks, ornamental woodland, large gardens
Flowering	March–April
Fruiting	ripens in second year
	TRUNK AND CROWN
Trunk	straight, very broad and fluted at base
Bark	thick, fibrous, soft, reddish brown or darker brown
Crown	narrowly conical; drooping lower branches curve upwards
Twigs	stout, grey-green, covered by bases of scale-leaves
	LEAVES
Buds	small, not scaly

Leaves	spirally arranged, 4–12mm, oval to spear-shaped, rather scale-like, flattened above, pointed, hairless; stalkless, blade joins stem
Stipules	absent
	FLOWERS AND FRUIT
Flowers	♂ and ♀ on same tree
♂	cone at shoot-tip, pale yellow
♀	usually single cone at stem tip, upright, 8–10mm, green with pinkish spines
Fruit	solitary woody cone, 5–8cm, egg-shaped; 25–40 scales, square-ended, wrinkled, centre sunken with small spine
Seeds	3–7 per scale, winged

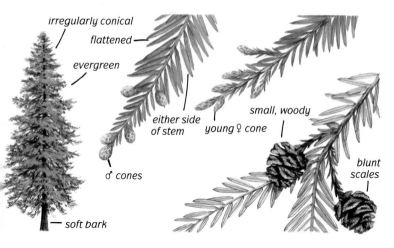

irregularly conical

flattened

evergreen

either side of stem

young ♀ cone

small, woody

blunt scales

♂ cones

soft bark

In its native environment, this species can claim the record for the tallest living thing on earth, at over 110m. Many Coast Redwoods are around 1000 years old and individuals can reach 2600 years. In the event of lightning damage to the trunk, a tree can re-grow from suckers at the base and may form a grove of trees. This ability extends the life of a plant. *Status:* introduced from western North America; widely planted, mainly in western Europe, for ornament or timber. *Similar trees:* Chinese Fir has longer, brighter leaves, clustered male cones, and fruiting cones with thin, pointed scales.

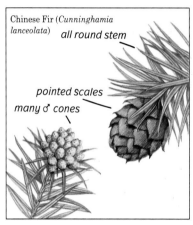

Chinese Fir (*Cunninghamia lanceolata*)

all round stem

pointed scales

many ♂ cones

	COAST REDWOOD		
Type	conifer, evergreen tree	**Leaves**	mostly in 2 rows, 6–20mm, narrowly oblong, straight or curved, flattened, pointed, hairless, dark green, 2 white bands below; base of blade joins twig; spirally arranged on leading shoot, scale-like
Height	to 45m (100m in North America)		
Habitat	parks, ornamental woodland		
Flowering	February–March		
Fruiting	ripens in second year		
	TRUNK AND CROWN	**Stipules**	absent
Trunk	straight, rarely forked, stout, suckers at base		**FLOWERS AND FRUIT**
Bark	reddish brown, thick, spongy, sometimes fissured	**Flowers**	♂ and ♀ on same tree
		♂	cone at tip of side shoot, 1.5–2mm, whitish yellow
Crown	columnar; irregular rings of branches, lower bent downwards	♀	globular, green cone with bristle-tipped scales
Twigs	green, obscured by leaf-bases	**Fruit**	woody cone at branch tip, 2–3cm, egg-shaped, hanging, reddish brown; 15–20 scales, square-ended, centre sunken
	LEAVES		
Buds	c3mm, pointed, scaly	**Seeds**	3–5 per scale, winged

Swamp Cypress *Taxodium distichum*

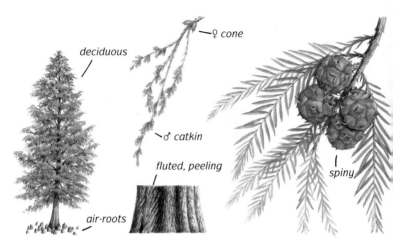

deciduous

♀ cone

♂ catkin

fluted, peeling

spiny

air-roots

An unusual deciduous conifer with pale, feathery foliage, which in autumn sheds not only leaves but entire leafy shoots. Grown by water it produces curious air-roots, which emerge from the ground as a knobbly mound and enable the roots to function when deprived of oxygen in mud. *Status:* introduced from south-eastern North America; grown for ornament in western and central Europe. *Similar trees:* discovered in China during 1941 but previously known from fossils several million years old, Dawn Redwood differs in the paired leaves, paired shoots and blunt cone-scales.

Dawn Redwood (*Metasequoia glyptostroboides*)

paired shoots

blunt scales

	SWAMP CYPRESS		
Type	conifer, deciduous tree		shoots, 1–2cm, thin, flat, pointed, pale green, 2 grey bands below, turning reddish brown in autumn; stalkless
Height	20–30m (50m in America)		
Habitat	usually planted by water		
Flowering	March–April	**Stipules**	absent
Fruiting	ripens in first year		
			FLOWERS AND FRUIT
	TRUNK AND CROWN	**Flowers**	♂ and ♀ flowers on same tree, at shoot tip
Trunk	straight, develops buttresses		
Bark	reddish brown, fibrous, peels, vertical or spiral fissures	♂	3–4 hanging catkins, 6–20cm, branched, slender, purplish, becoming yellow with pollen
Crown	conical with rounded top		
Twigs	reddish brown, slender long shoots, short side-shoots shed with leaves in autumn	♀	tiny cone, green
		Fruit	woody cone, 2–3cm, globular, ripens purplish brown, stalk 2–4mm; scales spine-tipped
	LEAVES		
Buds	rounded, small, scaly	**Seeds**	2 per scale, irregularly 3-angled, narrowly winged
Leaves	spirally placed on long shoots, on alternate sides of short		

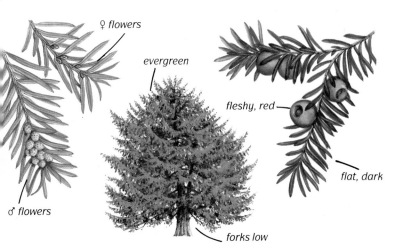

♀ flowers

evergreen

fleshy, red

flat, dark

♂ flowers

forks low

With distinctive dark foliage and red berries, Yew is a common feature of churchyards, and its strong, supple timber had many uses. Ancient trees occur, more than a thousand years old, with massive, hollow trunks. *Status:* native to most of Europe except for the extreme east and north; commonly planted for ornament. *Similar trees:* two species have longer foliage and larger, greenish fruits. California Nutmeg has branches in rings, large, conical buds, spine-tipped leaves and an egg-shaped fruit. Plum-fruited Yew has softer, brighter blue-green leaves and white-speckled fruit.

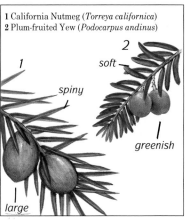

1 California Nutmeg (*Torreya californica*)
2 Plum-fruited Yew (*Podocarpus andinus*)

2

soft

spiny

greenish

large

	YEW	**Leaves**	on 2 sides of most shoots, spiral on upright shoots, 1–3cm, needle-like, flat, pointed, edge curved under, hairless, very dark green above, 2 yellowish green bands below; stalk short
Type	conifer, evergreen tree or sometimes a shrub		
Height	10–25m		
Habitat	woods, scrub, mainly on lime-rich soils, planted elswhere		
Flowering	February–April		**FLOWERS AND FRUIT**
Fruiting	August–September	**Flowers**	♂ and ♀ flowers on different trees
	TRUNK AND CROWN	♂	cones clustered beneath year-old shoots, 5–6mm, globular, turning yellow with pollen
Trunk	short, forked, sometimes twisted, stout and hollow		
Bark	light brown or reddish, thin, scaly and peeling	♀	cone, 1–2mm, green
Crown	conical or domed; branches angled upwards or spreading	**Fruit**	berry-like, 8–12mm, solitary, cup-like, red fleshy layer around woody, nut-like centre
Twigs	green, grooved	**Seeds**	solitary, 5–7mm, elongated
	LEAVES		
Buds	minute, egg-shaped, green		

Lawson Cypress *Chamaecyparis lawsoniana*

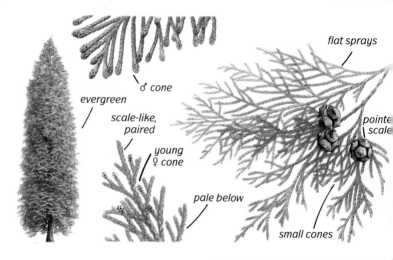

flat sprays

♂ cone

evergreen

scale-like, paired

young ♀ cone

pointed scale

pale below

small cones

Very commonly planted, this North American species is one of the most popular of all ornamental conifers. The foliage has a distinctive, parsley-like smell. Many cultivated variants exist. *Status:* introduced from western North America; planted for ornament, timber and shelter; sometimes naturalized. *Similar trees:* two cultivated species from Japan have brighter leaves, marked with white below and lacking the gland. Hinoki Cypress has blunt, often rounded leaves. Sawara Cypress has pointed leaves spread apart at the tips; the very slender shoots droop in many plants.

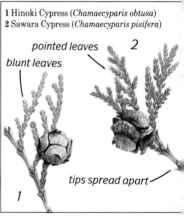

1 Hinoki Cypress (*Chamaecyparis obtusa*)
2 Sawara Cypress (*Chamaecyparis pisifera*)

pointed leaves 2

blunt leaves

tips spread apart

1

	LAWSON CYPRESS		Leaves	paired, 0.5–2mm, scale-like, diamond-shaped with central, translucent gland, pointed tip curves inwards, hairless, dark green above, paler below; stalkless; occasionally some needle-like leaves
Type	conifer, evergreen tree			
Height	up to 45m			
Habitat	plantations, parks, gardens			
Flowering	March–April			
Fruiting	September–October			
			Stipules	absent
	TRUNK AND CROWN			
Trunk	straight, sometimes forked			**FLOWERS AND FRUIT**
Bark	smooth, greyish brown, becomes cracked into vertical plates		Flowers	♂ and ♀ on same tree
			♂	cone 2–5mm, at shoot-tip, blackish scales turn red, then yellow with pollen
Crown	conical; few large branches, sometimes in irregular rings, leading shoot droops		♀	globular cone, bluish green
Twigs	forming flat sprays, often hanging at tips		Fruit	woody cone, 5–8mm, globular, often bluish, turns yellowish brown; scales in 4 pairs, wrinkled, small central spine
	LEAVES			
Buds	tiny, hidden by leaves		Seeds	usually 2–4 per scale, winged

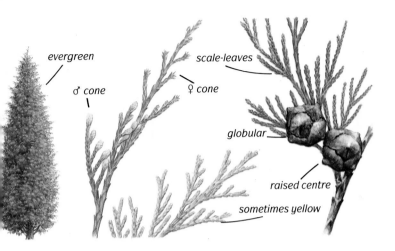

evergreen

scale-leaves

♂ cone

♀ cone

globular

raised centre

sometimes yellow

Renowned for rapid growth, this hybrid conifer is popular for hedging and wherever a screen is required quickly. It is a cross between species of two genera, the form differing slightly depending whether Nootka Cypress or Monterey Cypress was the female parent. *Status: of garden origin; very commonly planted for ornament. Similar trees: both parent species are commonly planted.* Nootka Cypress has dull green foliage, which is rough and oily smelling; small cones ripen in two years. Tolerant of salt-laden winds, Monterey Cypress becomes a large tree with flattish plates of foliage and large, lumpy cones.

1 Nootka Cypress (*Chamaecyparis nootkatenis*)
2 Monterey Cypress (*Cupressus macrocarpa*)

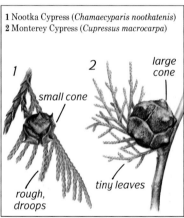

1

small cone

rough, droops

2

large cone

tiny leaves

LEYLAND CYPRESS		**Leaves**	scale-like, paired in 4 ranks, 0.5–2mm, all similar, closely pressed together, pointed, hairless, dark green or grey-green above, yellowish green below; stalkless
Type	conifer, evergreen tree		
Height	up to 35m		
Habitat	parks, gardens, plantations		
Flowering	March		
Fruiting	October	**Stipules**	absent
TRUNK AND CROWN		**FLOWERS AND FRUIT**	
Trunk	straight, sometimes forked	**Flowers**	♂ and ♀ flowers on same plant
Bark	reddish brown, forming shallow, vertical fissures	♂	cone 3–5mm, greenish, turning yellow with pollen
Crown	narrowly columnar to broadly conical; branches crowded, angled upwards, retained to base, leading shoot leans	♀	small, green, globular cone
		Fruit	woody cone, rarely produced by some trees, 2–3cm, globular, brown; few paired scales, each with blunt central spine
Twigs	slender, with old scale-leaves; forms sprays of foliage		
LEAVES		**Seeds**	rarely produced, 2–6 per scale
Buds	tiny, hidden by leaves		

Italian Cypress *Cupressus sempervirens*

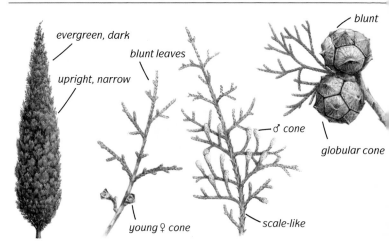

evergreen, dark

upright, narrow

blunt leaves

blunt

♂ cone

globular cone

young ♀ cone

scale-like

An unmistakable feature of many Italian landscapes, this narrowly columnar conifer is widely planted for its distinctive habit. The wild form is rarely planted as its broad, irregularly conical outline is far less striking. *Status:* native to south-eastern Europe; much planted for ornament or timber in southern Europe, often naturalized. *Similar trees:* two species with broad crowns have smaller cones of 6–8 scales. Mexican Cypress has dull green, scarcely scented foliage, spreading leaf-tips and bluish young cones. Smooth Cypress has smooth, scaling bark and blue-grey, scented, resin-flecked leaves.

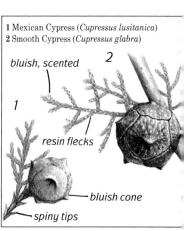

1 Mexican Cypress (*Cupressus lusitanica*)
2 Smooth Cypress (*Cupressus glabra*)

bluish, scented

2

1

resin flecks

bluish cone

spiny tips

	ITALIAN CYPRESS	
Type	conifer, evergreen tree	
Height	15–30m	
Habitat	planted mostly near houses	
Flowering	March	
Fruiting	ripens in second year	

	TRUNK AND CROWN
Trunk	straight, often forked above
Bark	grey-brown, shallow fissures and twisted, scaly ridges
Crown	narrowly columnar with upright branches or sometimes conical
Twigs	slightly 4-angled, curved upwards near tip, reddish brown

	LEAVES
Buds	tiny, hidden by leaves
Leaves	scale-like, paired in 4 ranks, pressed together, 0.5–1mm, diamond-shaped, blunt, dull, dark green, hairless; stalkless; needle-like leaves rarely on leading shoots
Stipules	absent

	FLOWERS AND FRUIT
Flowers	♂ and ♀ cones on same tree, each at tip of small shoot
♂	elliptical cone, 4–8mm, green, turning yellow with pollen
♀	oblong cone, 3–4mm
Fruit	solitary cone, 2.5–4cm, shortly oblong or globular, reddish brown to yellowish grey; 4–7 pairs of wavy-edged scales, each with broad point
Seeds	8–20 per cone scale, flattened, narrowly winged

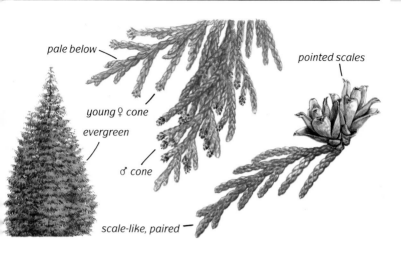

pale below

pointed scales

young ♀ cone

evergreen

♂ cone

scale-like, paired

Old, well-grown trees make magnificent specimens, with huge lower branches curved down to the ground, eventually rooting to become new trunks. Glossy, dark green foliage has a distinctive, fruity scent, and small, elongated cones have spine-tipped scales. *Status:* introduced from western North America; commonly planted for timber, ornament and hedging. *Similar trees:* White-cedar has leaves with a conspicuous gland, lacking whitish marks below, and blunt cone-scales. Chinese White-cedar has uniformly green, scentless leaves, and cones with fewer pairs of scales, each with a strong, curved spine.

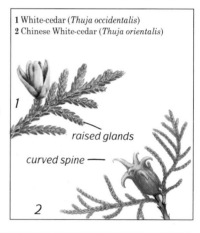

1 White-cedar (*Thuja occidentalis*)
2 Chinese White-cedar (*Thuja orientalis*)

1

raised glands

curved spine

2

	WESTERN RED-CEDAR	**Leaves**	scale-like, paired in 4 ranks, side pair larger, 1.5–3mm, oval, blunt, with tiny gland, glossy deep green above, paler below with whitish streaks, hairless; stalkless
Type	conifer, evergreen tree		
Height	up to 40m (50m in America)		
Habitat	plantations, parks, gardens		
Flowering	March		
Fruiting	October of first year	**Stipules**	absent
	TRUNK AND CROWN		**FLOWERS AND FRUIT**
Trunk	straight or forked above, fluted below; lower branches may root forming new trunks	**Flowers**	♂ and ♀ cones on same tree
		♂	cone 1–2mm, dark red, becomes pale yellow with pollen
Bark	reddish brown, soft, thick with lifting strips	♀	cone 2–5mm, yellowish green
Crown	conical or irregular; lower branches curve down, leading shoot upright	**Fruit**	woody cone, 1–1.5cm, elliptical, upright, green, turns brown; 5–6 pairs of spine-tipped scales
Twigs	reddish brown shoots form flattened sprays of foliage	**Seeds**	2–3 per scale, winged
	LEAVES		
Buds	tiny, hidden by leaves		

Juniper *Juniperus communis*

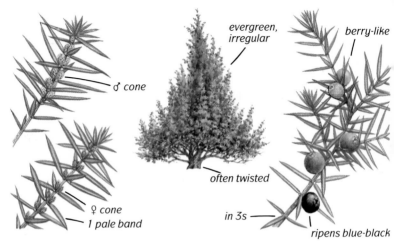

evergreen, irregular

♂ cone

berry-like

♀ cone
1 pale band

often twisted

in 3s

ripens blue-black

Squat and spiny, Juniper is a common shrub scattered on chalk downland, but also forms an understorey to pine woodland, growing to tree size. Highly variable wild plants include low-growing shrubs on sea cliffs, and narrow columns on hills inland. *Status:* native to north-western Europe, Asia and North America; planted for ornament. *Similar trees:* two Mediterranean species differ in having longer leaves with two pale bands. Syrian Juniper has much larger blue-black fruits. More widespread, Prickly Juniper has fruits ripening through yellow to dull red or purple.

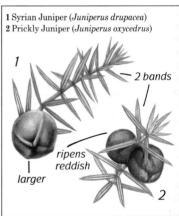

1 Syrian Juniper (*Juniperus drupacea*)
2 Prickly Juniper (*Juniperus oxycedrus*)

2 bands

larger

ripens reddish

JUNIPER

Type	conifer, evergreen shrub or sometimes a tree
Height	2–5m, rarely 15m
Habitat	grassland, scrub, woods; lime-rich soils or shallow peat
Flowering	April–June
Fruiting	after 2–3 years

TRUNK AND CROWN

Trunk	short, often twisted or bent
Bark	reddish brown, peels in strips
Crown	very variable, usually irregularly conical, sometimes low-growing or columnar
Twigs	greenish or reddish brown, hairless, the lower twigs often retain dead leaves

LEAVES

Buds	small, hidden by spiny leaves
Leaves	clusters of 3 around stem, 5–20mm, needle-like, sharply pointed, hairless, with broad, white band above, grey-green below; base jointed
Stipules	absent

FLOWERS AND FRUIT

Flowers	♂ and ♀ on different trees, solitary at leaf-base
♂	cone 6–8mm, yellow
♀	cone 2–3mm, greenish
Fruit	berry-like cone, 6–9mm, globular, solitary at leaf-base, turning black with bluish waxy layer
Seeds	3, separate, not winged

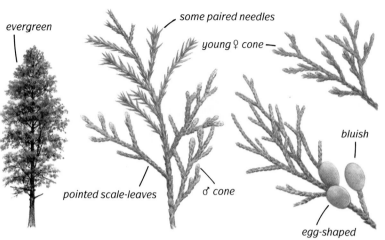

evergreen

some paired needles

young ♀ cone

pointed scale-leaves

♂ cone

bluish

egg-shaped

he tallest of the commonly grown
unipers, this slow-growing tree can
orm a remarkably narrow column. Its
oliage has a pleasant aromatic scent.
tatus: introduced from eastern North
America; much grown for ornament and
or timber in central and southern
Europe. *Similar trees:* two species have
npleasant-smelling foliage and
lobular fruits. Chinese Juniper has
ale-edged scale-leaves and larger
ruits, showing scale outlines.
pparently forming hybrids with the
atter, Savin is a native shrub with
lunt leaves, pressed together, and
mall fruits.

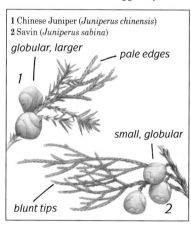

1 Chinese Juniper (*Juniperus chinensis*)
2 Savin (*Juniperus sabina*)

globular, larger

pale edges

small, globular

blunt tips

PENCIL CEDAR	

Type	conifer, evergreen tree
Height	15–30m
Habitat	parks, gardens, plantations
Flowering	March–April
Fruiting	September of first year

TRUNK AND CROWN

Trunk	straight, becomes buttressed
Bark	reddish brown, peels in long, narrow strips
Crown	conical or columnar; branches diverge narrowly
Twigs	very slender

LEAVES

Buds	tiny, concealed by leaves
Leaves	juvenile leaves needle-like, paired, 5–6mm, pointed, often at shoot-tip; adult leaves

scale-like, paired in 4 ranks, 0.5–1.5mm, pointed tips spread apart, dark green or bluish green, hairless; stalkless

Stipules	absent

FLOWERS AND FRUIT

Flowers	♂ and ♀ on different trees
♂	rounded, yellow cone, 4–5mm, at shoot tip
♀	green cone, 2–3mm, at base of leaf
Fruit	solitary, berry-like, 4–6mm, egg-shaped, ripens brownish violet with bluish waxy layer, short-stalked
Seeds	1 or 2, separate

Phoenicean Juniper *Juniperus phoenicea*

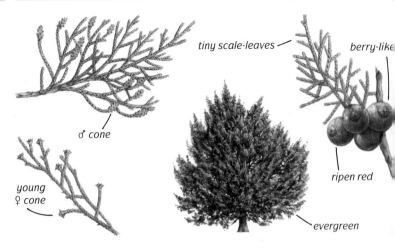

tiny scale-leaves

berry-like

♂ cone

young ♀ cone

ripen red

evergreen

The curious cord-like foliage of this Mediterranean species consists of widely branched shoots, with minute, pale-edged scale-leaves pressed tightly together. A small tree or sometimes a shrub, it also has a mat-like form that is found by the coast. Amongst the Mediterranean species, it is distinctive in having up to nine seeds in the fruit. *Status:* native to southern Europe; rarely cultivated. *Similar trees:* native to mountains of southern France and Spain, Spanish Juniper has paired leaves, which lack the pale, minutely toothed edge. Its slightly smaller fruits ripen to blackish purple.

Spanish Juniper (*Juniperus thurifera*)

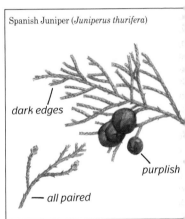

dark edges

purplish

all paired

PHOENICEAN JUNIPER

Type	conifer, evergreen tree or shrub
Height	2–8m
Habitat	dry, rocky places, often coasts
Flowering	March–April
Fruiting	ripens in second year

TRUNK AND CROWN

Trunk	irregular, short
Bark	scaly, reddish brown
Crown	broad, irregular, rarely low-growing; branches spread apart
Twigs	slender, 4-angled, scaly

LEAVES

Buds	tiny, concealed by leaves
Leaves	adult leaves scale-like, paired, in 4 ranks, closely overlapping, 0.7–1mm, oval or diamond-shaped with sunken gland, blunt or slightly pointed, yellowish green with whitish, finely toothed edge; stalkless; juvenile leaves rarely present, needle-like, groups of 3, 5–14mm, pointed, 2 whitish bands on both sides
Stipules	absent

FLOWERS AND FRUIT

Flowers	♂ and ♀ on same tree
♀	cone 4–5mm, at shoot-tip
♂	cone 2–3mm, on small shoot, blackish
Fruit	berry-like, 8–14mm, globular or egg-shaped, green with waxy layer, ripens dark red
Seeds	3–9, separate

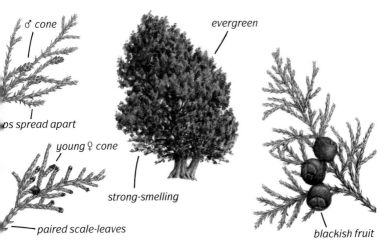

♂ cone

evergreen

ps spread apart

young ♀ cone

strong-smelling

paired scale-leaves

blackish fruit

o-called because of the strong,
isagreeable odour given off by the
oliage when lightly bruised, Stinking
uniper is largely restricted to
nountains of the Balkan Peninsula and
'rimea. A scale-leaved species with
rregularly branched, four-angled twigs,
 is identified by uniformly coloured
eaves with pointed tips spread apart.
tatus: native to south-eastern Europe;
arely cultivated elsewhere. *Similar*
rees: often confused with Stinking
uniper, Greek Juniper is a taller tree
vith slender, rounded twigs; smaller,
ess pointed scale-leaves, pressed
ogether; and fruits with 4 – 6 seeds.

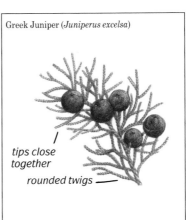

Greek Juniper (*Juniperus excelsa*)

*tips close
together*

rounded twigs

	STINKING JUNIPER		
Type	conifer, evergreen tree		gland, pointed, tips spread apart, uniformly dull, grey-green, not pale-edged, hairless; stalkless; juvenile leaves paired, rarely present
Height	up to 17m		
Habitat	mountains, rocky places		
Flowering	March–April		
Fruiting	ripens in second year	**Stipules**	absent

	TRUNK AND CROWN		FLOWERS AND FRUIT
Trunk	straight or sometimes forked	**Flowers**	♂ and ♀ on same tree or sometimes different trees
Bark	reddish brown, becoming grey and bleached, scaly	♂	cone 4–5mm, at shoot-tip
Crown	narrowly conical, becoming broad and irregular	♀	cone 2–3mm, on small shoot
		Fruit	solitary berry-like cone, 7–12mm, globular, waxy when young, ripening dark reddish brown to almost black
Twigs	c1mm thick, 4-angled, scaly, branching irregularly		

	LEAVES		
Buds	tiny, concealed by leaves	**Seeds**	usually 1 or 2, separate
Leaves	adult leaves scale-like, paired, in 4 ranks, overlapping, 1.5–2mm, oval or angular, mostly without		

White Willow *Salix alba*

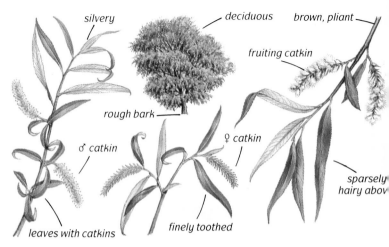

silvery · deciduous · brown, pliant · fruiting catkin · rough bark · ♂ catkin · ♀ catkin · sparsely hairy abov · leaves with catkins · finely toothed

Tall and graceful, this species is commonly found by water. It is readily identified by its leaves, which are silvery and silky, and slender with a very finely toothed edge. Near habitation many are pollarded; cut at head height they produce a regular supply of small timber. *Status:* native, common to most of Europe, but rarer in the extreme south; widely planted for ornament and stabilizing river banks. *Similar trees:* two subspecies are often cultivated. Cricket-bat Willow has purplish twigs and dull, bluish leaves becoming almost hairless. Golden Willow has orange or yellow twigs.

1 Cricket-bat Willow (*Salix alba* subsp. *coerulea*)
2 Golden Willow (*Salix alba* subsp. *vitellina*)

purplish · nearly hairless · yellow or orange · 2 · bluish · lighter above

WHITE WILLOW	
Type	deciduous tree
Height	10–25m
Habitat	rivers, damp or wet soils
Flowering	April–May
Fruiting	July

TRUNK AND CROWN

Trunk	mostly upright, often pollarded
Bark	thick ridges, dark grey-brown
Crown	young narrow; old broad; branches angled upwards
Twigs	silkily hairy, becoming smooth, pliant, greenish brown

LEAVES

Buds	egg-shaped, pointed, hairy
Leaves	on alternate side of shoot, 6–10cm, narrowly spear-shaped or elliptical, with pointed tip, small, equal teeth and tapered base, silkily hairy above becoming almost hairless, with greyish, matted hairs below; stalk 5–8mm, hairy
Stipules	very slender, soon falling

FLOWERS AND FRUIT

Flowers	♂ and ♀ catkins on separate trees, opening with leaves
♂	cylindrical catkin, 4–6cm, of tiny flowers, almost upright
Stamens	2 per ♂ flower, separate, yellow
♀	catkin 3–4cm
Stigmas	2, forked, on short style
Ovaries	1 per ♀ flower; stalkless
Fruit	catkin of small capsules, each c4mm, releasing seeds
Seeds	with tuft of cottony hairs

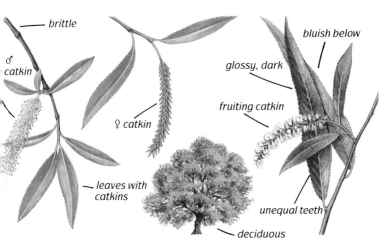

brittle

♂ catkin

♀ catkin

leaves with catkins

bluish below

glossy, dark

fruiting catkin

unequal teeth

deciduous

Similar to White Willow, this large tree is distinguished by glossy, unevenly toothed leaves. If twisted, brittle twigs crack at the base. In water, Crack Willow produces fine, red, coral-like rootlets. *Status:* native or planted, common in much of Europe. *Similar trees:* one of the hybrids between White Willow and Crack Willow, Basford Willow differs from the former by glossy leaves and short catkin scales, and the latter by reddish twigs and slender, fine-toothed leaves. Bay Willow has broad, glossy leaves, which are sticky and fragrant when young, and male flowers with five or more stamens.

1 Basford Willow (*Salix* × *rubens*)
2 Bay Willow (*Salix pentandra*)

longer

broad, glossy

2

1

small, equal teeth

many more stamens

	CRACK WILLOW		
Type	deciduous tree		fall, glossy, dark green above, bluish below; stalk 5–15mm
Height	10–18m		
Habitat	deep, moist soils, by rivers	**Stipules**	3–8mm, slender, soon falling
Flowering	April–May		
Fruiting	June–July		**FLOWERS AND FRUIT**
		Flowers	♂ and ♀ catkins on separate trees, in clusters on leafy shoots
	TRUNK AND CROWN		
Trunk	stout, often pollarded	♂	catkin 4–6cm, cylindrical; scales 2–3mm, sparsely hairy
Bark	thick ridges, dull grey		
Crown	broad, conical or domed; widely branched	**Stamens**	2, rarely 3 per ♂ flower, separate, yellow
Twigs	brittle, becoming smooth, glossy, greenish brown	♀	with larger scales than ♂
		Stigmas	2, each 2-lobed; style short
	LEAVES	**Ovaries**	1, hairless
Buds	conical, yellowish brown	**Fruit**	catkin of capsules, each 4–5mm, or commonly sterile, some releasing seeds
Leaves	9–15cm, narrowly spear-shaped with slender tip, coarse, uneven teeth, wedge-shaped base, sparse hairs that soon		
		Seeds	with cottony hairs

Goat Willow *Salix caprea*

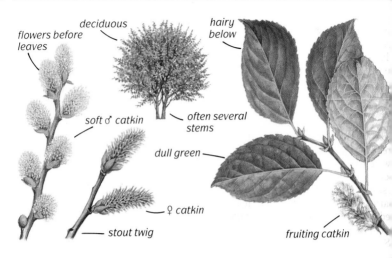

flowers before leaves

deciduous

hairy below

soft ♂ catkin

often several stems

dull green

♀ catkin

stout twig

fruiting catkin

More commonly a shrub than a tree, this broad-leaved plant is most distinctive in spring, when leafless shoots are smothered with short, soft catkins. Stripped twigs have distinct raised lines. *Status:* native and common to much of Europe. *Similar trees:* Grey Willow has dark brown twigs and narrower, more oblong leaves, which are grey-green above and whitish grey with short hairs below. It is common through much of Europe except for the west, where it is replaced by Rusty Willow. This has rougher leaves, which are glossy and dark green above with reddish hairs below.

1 Grey Willow (*Salix cinerea* subsp. *cinerea*)
2 Rusty Willow (*Salix cinerea* subsp. *oleifolia*)

dark, glossy

whitish hairs

1

2

narrower

reddish hairs

	GOAT WILLOW	
Type	deciduous shrub or tree	
Height	rarely more than 10m	
Habitat	hedgerows, woods, scrub	
Flowering	March–April	
Fruiting	May–June	
	TRUNK AND CROWN	
Trunk	often several	
Bark	fissured, greyish brown	
Crown	broad, rather open branches mostly angled upwards	
Twigs	thick, stiff	
	LEAVES	
Buds	egg-shaped, blunt, glossy	
Leaves	5–12cm, oval, elliptical or oblong, with tip shortly pointed, edge often wavy, toothed, base wedge-shaped or rounded, dull green above with sparse hairs, grey-green below with thick, soft hairs; stalk 1–2.5cm, stiff, hairy	
Stipules	8–12mm, ear-shaped, toothed	
	FLOWERS AND FRUIT	
Flowers	♂ and ♀ catkins on separate trees, near twig tip, before leaves	
♂	catkins 15–25mm, egg-shaped or shortly cylindrical; scales broadly oval, blackish with silvery grey hairs	
Stamens	2 per ♂ flower, yellow	
♀	catkins similar to ♂	
Stigmas	2, each often 2-lobed	
Ovaries	1, 4–5mm, densely hairy	
Fruit	catkins of small capsules, each capsule c10mm, splitting to release seeds	
Seeds	with cottony hairs	

Salix daphnoides Violet Willow

An ornamental species, Violet Willow has dark, reddish twigs overlaid with a bluish, waxy layer, which gradually rubs off. Crimson buds open as large, softly hairy catkins before the narrow leaves appear. It is often grown for winter colour. *Status:* native, scattered across northern and central Europe; widely planted for ornament. *Similar trees: S. acutifolia* has more slender twigs, and narrower leaves with a long point and more veins. Almost invariably a shrub, Purple Willow has mostly paired leaves; each male flower has two red stamens fused as one. The hybrid between Violet and Purple Willows (*S. × calliantha*) makes a small tree.

♂ catkin / softly hairy / ♀ catkin / catkins before leaves / deciduous / glossy, dark / bluish below / unequal teeth / red buds / bluish coating / fruiting catkin

1 *Salix acutifolia*
2 Purple Willow (*Salix purpurea*)

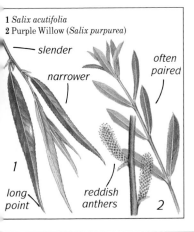

slender / narrower / often paired / long point / reddish anthers / **1** / **2**

VIOLET WILLOW

Type	deciduous shrub or tree
Height	6–8m (max 12m)
Habitat	damp places
Flowering	February–March
Fruiting	May–June

TRUNK AND CROWN

Trunk	often several
Bark	rather smooth, greyish brown
Crown	rounded; branches upright or spreading
Twigs	glossy, dark reddish brown with bluish waxy covering

LEAVES

Buds	pointed, flattened, dark red
Leaves	on alternate sides of stem, 7–12cm, oblong or oval, leathery, shortly pointed, edge toothed, base wedge-shaped, slightly woolly but becoming hairless, glossy dark green above, bluish below; stalk 7–20mm, grooved above
Stipules	5–12mm, oval, toothed

FLOWERS AND FRUIT

Flowers	♂ and ♀ catkins on separate trees, before the leaves
♂	catkin 2–4cm, cylindrical, stalkless; scales *c*2mm, oval, blackish, silkily hairy
Stamens	2, separate; anthers yellow
♀	catkin smaller than ♂
Stigmas	2 per ♀ flower
Ovaries	1 per ♀ flower, hairless
Fruit	catkin of small, narrowly egg-shaped capsules, each *c*4mm
Seeds	with tuft of cottony hairs

Osier *Salix viminalis*

Commonly lining rivers and streams, this willow forms a large shrub or tree. Plants are cut annually to provide slender shoots, which are stripped of bark for basket-weaving. Male plants are attractive in spring when covered with furry, yellow catkins. *Status:* native mainly to central and western Europe; widely planted elsewhere. *Similar trees:* Hoary Willow has even narrower leaves with matt white, felted hairs below, curved catkins and a smooth ovary. Though easily distinguished by broader, toothed leaves, the fragrant Almond Willow is grown like Osier, as is the hybrid (*S. × mollissima*) between these species.

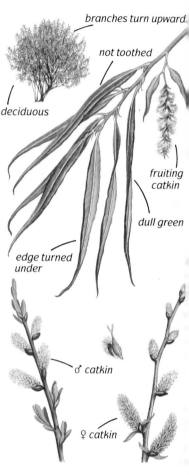

branches turn upward

not toothed

deciduous

fruiting catkin

dull green

edge turned under

♂ catkin

♀ catkin

1 Hoary Willow (*Salix elaeagnos*)
2 Almond Willow (*Salix triandra*)

very narrow

broader, toothed

curved

long catkin

	OSIER	
Type	deciduous shrub or tree	
Height	3–6m, rarely 10m	
Habitat	usually near water	
Flowering	February–April	
Fruiting	May–June	

TRUNK AND CROWN

Trunk	sometimes several	
Bark	fissured, greyish brown	
Crown	usually narrow, top rounded; branches mostly upright	
Twigs	long, pliant, hairy, becoming glossy yellowish brown	

LEAVES

Buds	3–7mm, egg-shaped, often blunt, hairy, becoming smooth	
Leaves	on alternate sides of stem, 10–18cm, narrow with long tip, edge not toothed but turned under and often wavy, base wedge-shaped, dull green with few hairs above, silky, silvery hairs below; stalk rarely more than 1cm	
Stipules	5–10mm, slender, soon falling	

FLOWERS AND FRUIT

Flowers	♂ and ♀ catkins on different plants, before leaves appear	
♂	catkin 15–30mm, egg-shaped or cylindrical; scales *c*2mm, oval, blunt, reddish brown, hairy	
Stamens	2 per ♂ flower, yellow	
♀	catkin similar to ♂	
Stigmas	2, undivided; style slender	
Ovaries	1, densely hairy	
Fruit	catkin of small, egg-shaped capsules, each to 6mm, releasing many seeds	
Seeds	with tuft of cottony hairs	

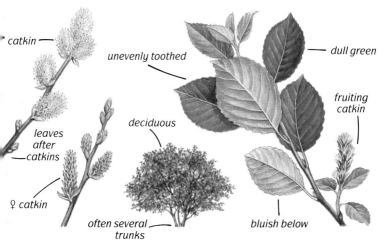

catkin

unevenly toothed

dull green

fruiting catkin

deciduous

leaves after catkins

♀ catkin

often several trunks

bluish below

This very variable willow is more often a low, broad shrub than a small tree. It belongs to a group of species mainly of northern regions and occurs in mountains, though not at the highest altitudes. Like other willows, this species is food for larvae of many butterflies and moths. *Status:* native to northern and central Europe. *Similar trees:* Tea-leaved Willow has glossy brown, usually hairless twigs, tougher leaves, which are glossy green above, smaller stipules, and the ovary is hairy. Catkins are usually produced with the leaves. It forms hybrids (*S. × tetrapla*) with Dark-leaved Willow.

Tea-leaved Willow (*Salix phylicifolia*)

leaves with catkins

tougher, glossy

glossy, hairless

	DARK-LEAVED WILLOW
Type	deciduous shrub or small tree
Height	1–4m
Habitat	by streams, pools, in mountains
Flowering	April–May
Fruiting	July–August

TRUNK AND CROWN

Trunk	often several, slender
Bark	slightly fissured, dark grey
Crown	broad; rather widely branched
Twigs	slender, usually with whitish hairs, dull brownish green

LEAVES

Buds	blunt, shortly hairy
Leaves	alternating on stem, 2–6.5cm, oval or elliptical, shortly pointed, unevenly toothed, base wedge-shaped or rounded, sparsely hairy to hairless, dull green above, bluish below; stalk usually less than 1cm
Stipules	rather large, ear-shaped

FLOWERS AND FRUIT

Flowers	♂ and ♀ catkins on separate trees, produced before leaves
♂	catkin 15–40mm, cylindrical; scales 1–2.5mm, dark, thinly hairy
Stamens	2 per ♂ flower, separate, yellow
♀	catkin less compact than ♂
Stigmas	2 mostly forked; style slender
Ovaries	1 per ♀ flower, hairless
Fruit	catkin of small, tapered capsules, each 5–7mm, releasing seeds
Seeds	many, each with long hairs

Golden Weeping-willow

Salix × sepulcralis
nv. *chrysocoma*

A graceful weeping tree, so commonly planted that at times it appears native. It is easily distinguished from other willow species by its pendulous shoots, yellow twigs and bright, yellowish green leaves. For a long time it was treated as a variant of White Willow but it is a hybrid between the golden form of that species and the following Chinese species. Largely sterile, it is propagated by cuttings. *Status:* cultivated origin; widely grown for ornament. *Similar trees:* Chinese Weeping-willow has brown twigs and short, almost stalkless catkins. Relatively tender and short-lived in western Europe, it is much less planted.

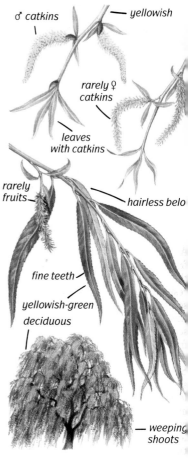

♂ catkins — yellowish

rarely ♀ catkins

leaves with catkins

rarely fruits

hairless belo

fine teeth

yellowish-green

deciduous

weeping shoots

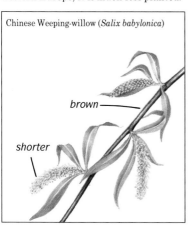

Chinese Weeping-willow (*Salix babylonica*)

brown

shorter

	GOLDEN WEEPING-WILLOW		
Type	deciduous tree		even, base wedge-shaped, sparsely hairy, becoming hairless, bright, yellowish green above, paler below; stalk up to 8mm, rather stout
Height	8–22m		
Habitat	mainly wet places		
Flowering	April		
		Stipules	small, toothed, soon falling
	TRUNK AND CROWN		
Trunk	stout, upright		**FLOWERS AND FRUIT**
Bark	network of fissures and ridges, pale greyish brown	**Flowers**	usually ♂ catkins only, with leaves
Crown	broad, domed; branches mostly angled upwards	♂	catkins 3–6cm, slender, cylindrical, pendulous, yellow; scales *c*2mm, oblong or oval, thinly hairy
Twigs	slender, weeping, greenish yellow; sparse hairs soon fall		
		Stamens	2 per ♂ flower, separate
	LEAVES	♀	sometimes a few ♀ catkins
Buds	slender, pointed, brown, more or less hairless	**Stigmas**	2, each forked; style short
		Ovaries	1, stalkless, hairless
Leaves	on alternate sides of stem, 7–12cm, narrowly spear-shaped with slender tip, teeth fine and	**Fruit**	usually sterile

Western Balsam-poplar
Populus trichocarpa

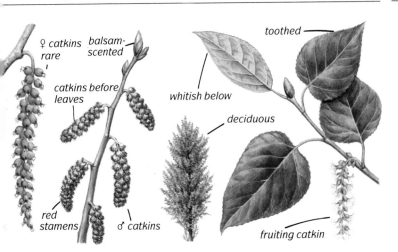

♀ catkins rare
balsam-scented
catkins before leaves
toothed
whitish below
deciduous
red stamens
♂ catkins
fruiting catkin

After a spring shower, the balsamic fragrance of Balsam-poplars pervades the air for many metres around; thick resin exuded by opening buds is the source of this scent. Of rapid growth, this handsome tree soon makes a useful screen or shelter. *Status:* introduced from northern North America; widely planted for ornament and timber. *Similar trees:* several other poplars have scented buds and are white beneath the leaves. Eastern Balsam-poplar produces many suckers; their oval leaves have a rounded base, and the stalk is up to 7cm long. Balm-of-Gilead has a more slender tip and a heart-shaped base to the leaf.

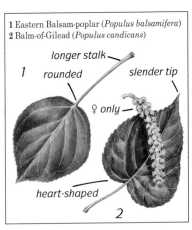

1 Eastern Balsam-poplar (*Populus balsamifera*)
2 Balm-of-Gilead (*Populus candicans*)

longer stalk
rounded
1
slender tip
♀ only
heart-shaped
2

WESTERN BALSAM-POPLAR		
Type	deciduous tree	
Height	to 35m (60m in North America)	
Habitat	roadsides, plantations	
Flowering	March–April	
Fruiting	May–June	

TRUNK AND CROWN

Trunk	upright or angled upwards
Bark	smooth, greenish grey, dark greyish brown below, fissured
Crown	narrow, conical; many main branches, angled upwards
Twigs	angular or rounded, becoming smooth, yellowish grey

LEAVES

Buds	mostly 10–15mm, egg-shaped, pointed, glossy, reddish brown, very sticky, fragrant
Leaves	on alternate sides of stem, 5–15cm (max. 23cm), oval, thick-textured, shortly pointed with shallow, blunt teeth, base broadly wedge-shaped or squarish, dark, glossy green above, whitish beneath; stalk 1.5–4cm, stout, grooved above

FLOWERS AND FRUIT

Flowers	♂ and ♀ catkins on separate trees, produced before leaves
♂	catkin 5–9cm, red, scales 3–5mm, fringed, sparsely hairy
Stamens	20–60 per ♂ flower
♀	catkin 6–10cm, green, rarely produced in western Europe
Stigmas	2, broad, irregularly lobed
Ovaries	1, egg-shaped, hairy
Fruit	catkin 15–20cm, of small capsules, each splitting open
Seeds	many, each with tuft of hairs

White Poplar *Populus alba*

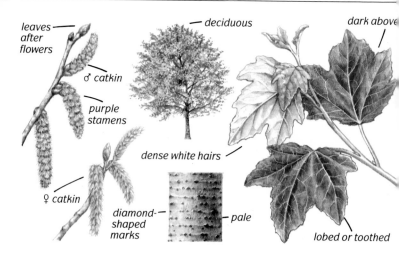

leaves after flowers

♂ catkin

purple stamens

♀ catkin

diamond-shaped marks

pale

deciduous

dense white hairs

dark above

lobed or toothed

Easily recognized by the dark leaves which flash white beneath in the breeze, and the pale grey bark of the upper trunk handsomely marked with blackish diamonds. Leaves of strong, sucker shoots are maple-like and lobed, though other leaves have irregular teeth. *Status:* mainly central and eastern Europe; commonly planted in the west for ornament and shelter. *Similar trees:* Grey Poplar is generally considered to be a hybrid between White Poplar and Aspen, though some regard it as a species. The leaves are grey beneath, becoming hairless, and the edge has blunt, wavy teeth.

Grey Poplar (*Populus* × *canescens*)

grey below

mostly ♂

irregularly toothed

	WHITE POPLAR	
Type	deciduous tree	
Height	15–25m	
Habitat	mainly wet places, sometimes in sandy coastal areas	

| | **Flowering** | February–March |
| | **Fruiting** | May–June |

TRUNK AND CROWN

Trunk often leaning; sucker shoots
Bark pale greyish brown, marked with blackish diamonds, base blackish and coarsely fissured
Crown irregular, broadest near top
Twigs densely hairy, gradually becoming smooth and brown

LEAVES

Buds *c*5mm, egg-shaped, pointed, hairy at base becoming smooth
Leaves on alternate sides of stem, 3– 9cm, broadly oval, blunt with irregular, blunt lobes, those of sucker shoots often deeply lobed, thinly hairy becoming smooth and dark green above, white with thick hairs below; stalk 5–6cm, rounded, hairy

FLOWERS AND FRUIT

Flowers ♂ and ♀ catkins on separate trees, before leaves
♂ catkin 4–7cm; scales oval, toothed, pale brown
Stamens 5–10 per ♂ flower, purple
♀ catkin 3–5cm
Stigmas 2, each divided into 2 lobes
Ovaries 1, egg-shaped, hairless
Fruit catkin 8–10cm, of small capsules, each *c*3mm, shortly stalked, releasing seeds
Seeds many, with cottony hairs

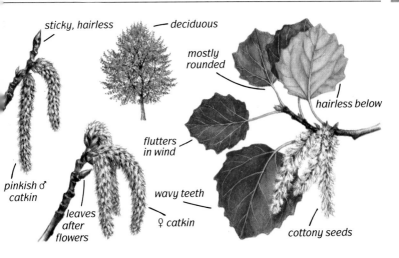

sticky, hairless — deciduous

mostly rounded

hairless below

flutters in wind

pinkish ♂ catkin

leaves after flowers

wavy teeth

♀ catkin

cottony seeds

Fluttering ceaselessly in the breeze, leaves of Aspen make a curious clattering sound. It is a remarkably widespread species, from western Europe to Japan and the tree limit of the tundra to the Mediterranean region. *Status:* native, most of Europe. *Similar trees:* two North American species are cultivated. Big-toothed Aspen has leaves with a squarish or wedge-shaped base and large, sharper teeth and greyish hairs on the buds, young twigs, and beneath the young leaves. American Aspen has finely toothed leaves and yellower bark; its hybrid with Aspen is sometimes grown.

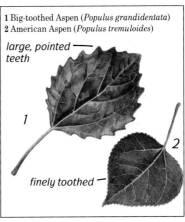

1 Big-toothed Aspen (*Populus grandidentata*)
2 American Aspen (*Populus tremuloides*)

large, pointed teeth

1

2

finely toothed

ASPEN

Type	deciduous tree
Height	up to 20m
Habitat	near water, often on mountains
Flowering	February–March
Fruiting	May

TRUNK AND CROWN

Trunk	slender, often several
Bark	smooth, greyish brown above; darker, fissured towards base
Crown	usually broad, much-branched
Twigs	with raised leaf-scars, grey-brown, becoming hairless

LEAVES

Buds	most c5mm, flower-buds larger, egg-shaped, hairless, glossy brown, slightly sticky
Leaves	alternately arranged, 1.5–8cm, rarely 15cm, oval to nearly circular, blunt with irregular, blunt teeth, base squarish to almost heart-shaped, dark green, paler beneath, turning clear yellow in autumn; stalk 4–7cm, flattened

FLOWERS AND FRUIT

Flowers	♂ and ♀ catkins on separate trees, before leaves
♂	catkin 5–8cm cylindrical; scales 5–6mm, broad, fringed, dark brown, with white hairs
Stamens	5–12 per ♂ flower, purplish
♀	catkin like ♂
Stigmas	2, cut into irregular lobes
Ovaries	1, egg-shaped, rough
Fruit	catkin up to 12cm, of small capsules, each c4mm, short-stalked, releasing seeds
Seeds	many, with cottony hairs

Black-poplar *Populus nigra*

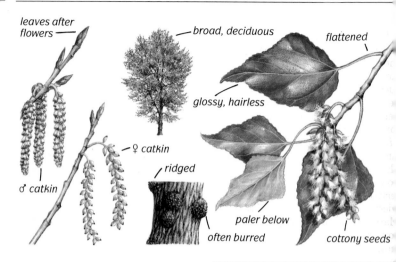

leaves after flowers

broad, deciduous

flattened

glossy, hairless

♀ catkin

♂ catkin

ridged

paler below

often burred

cottony seeds

Typically broad and rounded, this tree is better known as its narrowly columnar variant, the Lombardy Poplar. Both trees have leaves which are triangular or shaped like an ace-of-spades. *Status:* native to central and southern Europe; widely planted for shelter and timber. *Similar trees:* Lombardy Poplar has a very slender crown; typically male, trees with female catkins or a broader crown are probably crosses with Black Poplar. Berlin Poplar, a hybrid between Lombardy Poplar and *P. laurifolia*, has angular twigs, and leaves with a whiter underside, a wedge-shaped base and a rounded stalk.

1 Lombardy Poplar (*Populus nigra* cv. 'Italica')
2 Berlin Poplar (*Populus × berolinensis*)

narrow column
mostly ♂

2

not flattened

wedge-shaped

1

	BLACK-POPLAR
Type	deciduous tree
Height	20–35m
Habitat	damp soils of river valleys; grown by roads, in plantations
Flowering	March–April
Fruiting	May–June

	TRUNK AND CROWN
Trunk	often with swellings and burrs
Bark	grey-brown, coarsely fissured
Crown	broad, irregular; branches often curve downwards
Twigs	more or less hairless, rounded, yellowish brown

	LEAVES
Buds	to 10mm, egg-shaped, pointed, glossy brown, sticky
Leaves	on alternate sides of stem, 4–10cm, triangular or broadly oval with slender point, edge with small, rounded teeth, base squarish or broadly wedge-shaped, hairless, dark, glossy green above, paler below; stalk 3–7cm, flattened

	FLOWERS AND FRUIT
Flowers	♂ and ♀ catkins on separate trees, before leaves
♂	catkin 3–5cm, cylindrical; scales 1–2mm, fringed, green or brownish, soon falling
Stamens	12–30 per ♂ flower, red
♀	catkins more slender than ♂
Stigmas	2 per ♀ flower, each 2-lobed
Ovaries	1, egg-shaped, hairless
Fruit	catkin 9–15cm, of capsules, each 5–6mm, releasing seeds
Seeds	many, each with tuft of cottony hairs

Populus × canadensis Hybrid Black-poplar

... large, fast-growing hybrid, so ...ommonly planted that it often replaces ...he native Black Poplar. That and an ...merican species have produced several ...uch hybrids, one of the most widespread ...eing 'Serotina', a male tree illustrated ...ere. *Status:* of garden origin; planted ...or ornament, shelter and pulp-wood. *...imilar trees:* Cottonwood is the ...merican parent. The leaves have small ...lands and hairy, sharp teeth; male ...owers have up to 60 stamens. Two ...emale hybrids are widely grown. With ...ider branching and a rounded crown, ...laryland Poplar produces masses of ...ottony seeds. Railway Poplar has ...ostly sterile fruit.

leaves after flowers

broad

deciduous

only ♂ catkins

1 Cottonwood (*P. deltoides*); **2** Maryland Poplar (*P. × canadensis* cv. 'Marilandica'); **3** Railway Poplar (*P. × canadensis* cv. 'Regenerata')

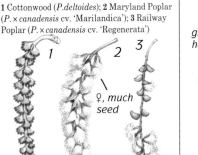

1

2

3

♀, much seed

♂, more stamens

♀, many sterile

paler below

glossy, hairless

blunt teeth

	HYBRID BLACK-POPLAR	**Leaves**	point, glossy greenish brown, sticky
Type	deciduous tree		on alternate sides of stem, 6– 10cm, almost triangular, sharply pointed, with distinct, blunt teeth, base squarish or slightly heart-shaped, sometimes rounded, hairless, bright, glossy green above, paler below, young leaves tinged reddish brown; stalk 4–10cm, flattened sideways
Height	often more than 30m		
Habitat	roadsides, parks, plantations		
Flowering	March–April		
	TRUNK AND CROWN		
Trunk	usually with long, unbranched base		
Bark	coarsely fissured, without burrs, greyish brown		
Crown	broadest above, flattish topped; lower branches heavy, angled upwards, diverging rather narrowly		**FLOWERS AND FRUIT**
Twigs	smooth, glossy greenish grey, often angular	**Flowers** ♂	catkins, before leaves
		♂	catkin 3–6cm, cylindrical; scales 4–5mm, broad, fringed, purplish-tipped
	LEAVES		
Buds	10–20mm, narrowly egg-shaped, tapered to slender	**Stamens**	20–25 per ♂ flower, anthers crimson
		Fruit	not produced

Alder *Alnus glutinosa*

A waterside tree, Alder is identified by woody, cone-like, fruiting catkins, which persist for much of the year. Production of new shoots from suckers often results in bushy growth. Alder has the rare ability to turn nitrogen from the air into valuable plant food, thanks to root nodules containing bacteria. *Status:* native to most of Europe; sometimes planted. *Similar trees:* lacking sticky twigs, Grey Alder has grey, smooth bark, pointed leaves that are grey below, and stalkless female catkins. Italian Alder has leaves with shallow, rounded teeth and a solitary female flower or rarely up to 3 in a cluster.

stalked

blunt

small ♀ catkin

old cone

stalked

long ♂ catkin

deciduous

toothed

blunt or notched

clustered

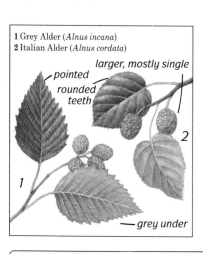

1 Grey Alder (*Alnus incana*)
2 Italian Alder (*Alnus cordata*)

pointed

rounded teeth

larger, mostly single

2

1

grey under

	ALDER		
Type	deciduous tree		of veins, hairless where main veins diverge, dark green above and below; stalk 2–3.5cm
Height	up to 20m (rarely 35m)		
Habitat	mainly wet places	**Stipules**	soon falling
Flowering	February–March		
Fruiting	October–November		**FLOWERS AND FRUIT**
		Flowers	♂ and ♀, before leaves
	TRUNK AND CROWN	♂	3–6 catkins in cluster, each 2–6cm, opening yellow; 3 flowers to each bract
Trunk	often several		
Bark	dark brown, fissured		
Crown	conical or rounded, open	**Stamens**	4 per ♂ flower
Twigs	sticky when young, hairless, turning purplish brown	♀	cluster of 3–5 catkins, each 5–7mm, purplish, stalked; 2 tiny flowers to each bract
	LEAVES		
Buds	5–7mm, blunt; stalked	**Stigmas**	2 per ♀ flower
Leaves	on alternate sides of stem, 4–10cm, elliptical to almost circular, blunt or notched, doubly toothed, base wedge-shaped or rounded, 5–8 pairs	**Ovaries**	1 per ♀ flower
		Fruit	cluster of 3–5 woody, cone-like catkins, each 10–30mm, egg-shaped, green, turning brown; stalked; scales 5-lobed
		Seeds	nut-like, with narrow wing

Alnus viridis Green Alder

A shrub that only occasionally reaches tree proportions, this is usually much smaller than the more widespread European species. Common in the Alps, Green Alder often forms extensive thickets. It is a variable species and several subspecies are sometimes distinguished by leaf characters. *Status:* native in mountains of central and south-eastern Europe; planted elsewhere. *Similar trees:* another small alder, introduced from North America and often naturalized, Smooth Alder produces catkins before its leaves and has sticky twigs, with up to 10 fruiting catkins in a head, the upper of which are stalkless.

♀ catkin

leaves with catkins

long ♂ catkin

often several stems

deciduous

pointed — stalked

clustered

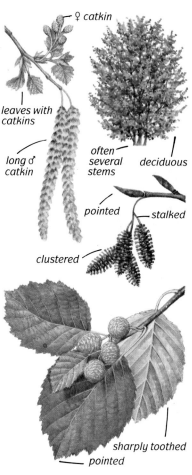

Smooth Alder (*Alnus rugosa*)

reddish hairs

stalkless cones

sharply toothed

pointed

	GREEN ALDER		
Type	deciduous shrub or tree		variably pointed, sharply, doubly toothed, base wedge-shaped or notched, usually with tufts of hairs below; stalk 8–12mm
Height	1–5m		
Habitat	wet places		
Flowering	March–April	**Stipules**	small, soon falling
Fruiting	September–October		**FLOWERS AND FRUIT**
	TRUNK AND CROWN	**Flowers**	♂ and ♀ together, with leaves
		♂	small cluster of long catkins, each 5–12cm, yellowish
Trunk	often several		
Bark	rough, brown	**Perianth**	usually 4-lobed
Crown	irregular, rounded	**Stamens**	4 per ♂ flower
Twigs	greenish brown or reddish brown, sometimes minutely hairy	♀	cluster of 3–5 catkins, each 6–10mm, reddish, stalked
		Stigmas	1 per ♀ flower
	LEAVES	**Ovaries**	2 per ♀ flower
Buds	12–15mm, conical, pointed, glossy reddish brown; stalkless	**Fruit**	cluster of 3–5 woody, cone-like catkins, each 8–15mm, egg-shaped, stalked, blackish
Leaves	on alternate sides of stem, sticky when young, 3–9cm, elliptical to almost circular,	**Seeds**	nut-like with papery wing

63

Silver Birch *Betula pendula*

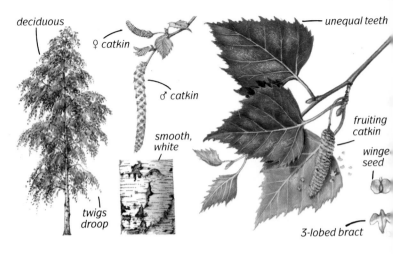

deciduous

♀ catkin

♂ catkin

smooth, white

twigs droop

unequal teeth

fruiting catkin

winged seed

3-lobed bract

Silver Birch's graceful form is best seen in spring, when the slender, silvery trunk and boughs are barely concealed by a filigree of pale green. A colonizer of treeless wastes, it was important in establishing northern Europe's forests after the last Ice Age. *Status:* native to most of Europe; planted for ornament. *Similar trees:* Downy Birch has hairy, stiffer twigs, leaves with more equal teeth, catkin scales with side-lobes angled forwards, and narrowly winged nutlets. Paper-bark Birch has papery, creamy-white or pink bark, larger leaves with unequal teeth, and catkin scales with narrowly diverging lobes.

1 Downy Birch (*Betula pubescens*)
2 Paper-bark Birch (*Betula papyrifera*)

equal teeth

1

narrow wing

2

peeling, papery bark

	SILVER BIRCH	
Type	deciduous tree	
Height	up to 30m	
Habitat	light soils, often where forest is cleared or wasteland	
Flowering	April–May	
Fruiting	July–August	
	TRUNK AND CROWN	
Trunk	slender, forked above	
Bark	smooth, silvery-white, black lenticels above, often peeling, blackish and fissured below	
Crown	narrow or broad, light; branches gradually arch down	
Twigs	slender, hanging, brown, with resin-glands	
	LEAVES	
Buds	long, pointed, not sticky	
Leaves	alternating along stem, 2–7cm, triangular, thin, pointed, sharply, doubly toothed, base squarish, yellow in autumn, almost hairless; stalked	
Stipules	small, soon falling	
	FLOWERS AND FRUIT	
Flowers	♂ and ♀ flowers on same plant	
♂	2–4 catkins at tip of twig, 3–6cm, purplish brown, becoming yellow with pollen	
Stamens	2 per ♂ flower	
♀	catkin at leaf-base, brownish	
Stigmas	2 per ♀ flower	
Ovaries	1 per ♀ flower, 2-celled	
Fruit	catkin 15–35mm; scales 3-lobed, middle lobe narrow, side lobes curving backwards and outwards	
Seeds	seed-like nutlet with 2 wings 2–3 times as broad as nutlet	

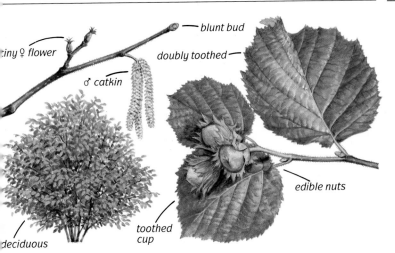

tiny ♀ flower
blunt bud
doubly toothed
♂ catkin
edible nuts
toothed cup
deciduous

At its most striking in late winter when the bright yellow catkins are a welcome sight, Hazel is more often a shrub than a tree. It is frequently coppiced, and the pliant poles and rods were formerly used in building. Large, edible nuts are sought by squirrels, mice, jays and pheasants. *Status:* native to most of Europe except the extreme north; planted for hedging, fruit or ornament. *Similar trees:* usually a tree, Turkish Hazel has more lobed leaves and the cup beneath the nut has narrower, spiky lobes. Filbert is grown for its larger, edible nuts, which are enclosed by a longer cup.

1 Turkish Hazel (*Corylus colurna*)
2 Filbert (*Corylus maxima*)

spiky lobes
more lobed
longer

HAZEL

Type	deciduous shrub or sometimes tree
Height	2–6m (rarely 8m)
Habitat	woods, hedgerows, scrub
Flowering	January–March
Fruiting	September–October

TRUNK AND CROWN

Trunk	often several
Bark	brown, smooth, slightly peeling
Crown	broad, branches slender
Twigs	dull green or brown, with reddish, gland-tipped hairs

LEAVES

Buds	c4mm, egg-shaped, blunt
Leaves	alternating on stem, 5–12cm, nearly circular, narrowly pointed, doubly toothed, sometimes slightly lobed, base notched, 6–8 pairs of veins, slightly hairy, especially below; stalk 8–15mm, stickily hairy
Stipules	oblong, blunt, soon falling

FLOWERS AND FRUIT

Flowers	♂ and ♀ flowers, before leaves
♂	slender, hanging catkin, 2–8cm, turning yellow with pollen, 1 flower per bract
Stamens	3–5 per ♂ flower
♀	small cluster, bud-like, 4–5mm
Stigmas	2 per ♀ flower, bright red
Ovaries	1 per ♀ flower, 2-celled
Fruit	1–4 rounded, brown, woody-shelled nuts, each 15–20mm, in greenish cup about equalling nut, cut to middle into irregularly toothed lobes

Hornbeam *Carpinus betulus*

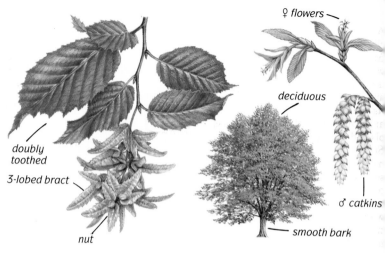

♀ flowers

deciduous

doubly toothed

3-lobed bract

nut

♂ catkins

smooth bark

A graceful tree, with smooth, grey bark, upswept branches and dark, toothed foliage; it is easily identified by distinctive three-lobed bracts in the fruiting head. In hedges, it responds well to clipping and keeps leaves in winter, much like Beech. Hornbeam is sometimes pollarded or coppiced, and has a hard, fine-grained timber. *Status:* native; widespread except in much of northern and western Mediterranean region; planted for timber, shelter or ornament. *Similar trees:* Eastern Hornbeam from south-eastern Europe is a smaller tree with the bract around the nut toothed, not lobed.

Eastern Hornbeam (*Carpinus orientalis*)

small, many veins

bract toothed

	HORNBEAM	
Type	deciduous tree	
Height	up to 30m	
Habitat	woods, hedges; planted in streets and parks	
Flowering	March–May	
Fruiting	October–November	

TRUNK AND CROWN

Trunk	often twisted, fluted below
Bark	greyish brown, smooth, becomes deeply fissured below
Crown	broad, tapered above; branches angled upwards, sinuous
Twigs	slender, hairy, greyish brown

LEAVES

Buds	6–7mm, slender, sharp-pointed, brown, hairy, against twig
Leaves	on alternate sides of stem, 4–10cm, oval, pointed, sharply and doubly toothed, base rounded, hairy beneath on veins, dark green, turning yellow in autumn, *c*15 pairs of veins; stalk *c*10mm, reddish
Stipules	small, soon falling

FLOWERS AND FRUIT

Flowers	♂ and ♀ on same tree
♂	catkin 25–50mm, yellowish, scales red-tipped
♀	drooping catkin, 20–30mm, 2 flowers per 3-lobed bract, green with pink stigmas
Fruit	nut 6–8mm, 1–2 at base of 3-lobed bract, *c*35mm long, in cluster 5–15cm long
Seeds	1 per fruit, not released

A small, deciduous tree, with glossy, ribbed leaves. It is easily distinguished from all other native trees by the whitish, hop-like fruits. Hop-hornbeam is occasionally planted for ornament and, in southern Europe, it is used for its hard timber. *Status:* native to central and eastern parts of southern Europe; planted elsewhere for ornament.

Similar trees: Eastern Hop-hornbeam is native to eastern North America, but is sometimes cultivated in Europe for ornament. It differs in the larger, less ribbed leaves, which are downy beneath with hairy stalks; the twigs with gland-tipped hairs; and the fruits with longer, hairier stalks.

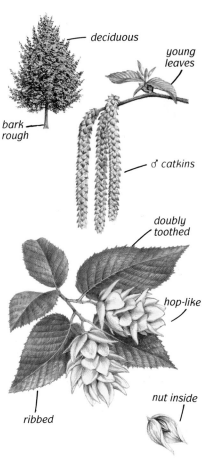

deciduous

young leaves

bark rough

♂ catkins

doubly toothed

hop-like

nut inside

ribbed

Eastern Hop-hornbeam (*Ostraya virginiana*)

longer stalk

hairier below

longer

	HOP-HORNBEAM	
Type	deciduous tree	
Height	15–18m	
Habitat	woods, hedges, parks	
Flowering	April	
Fruiting	September–October	

TRUNK AND CROWN

Trunk	sometimes several
Bark	brown, scales fall leaving lighter patches, smooth, becoming fissured
Crown	conical, becoming rounded; branches angled upwards
Twigs	reddish brown, hairy, with tiny pores

LEAVES

Buds	egg-shaped, pointed, shiny
Leaves	on alternate sides of stem, 5–12cm, oval, pointed, sharply and doubly toothed, base wedge-shaped, hairy, becoming smooth, shiny dark green above, paler below, 12–15 pairs of veins; stalk 3–4mm, softly hairy
Stipules	small, soon falling

FLOWERS AND FRUIT

Flowers	♂ and ♀ on same tree
♂	♂ catkin 3.5–10cm, hanging, yellow; 1 flower per bract
♀	♀ catkin 20–30mm, drooping; 2 greenish flowers at bract base
Fruit	nut *c*5mm, at bract base, in hanging, white or pale brown head, 3–5cm long; elliptical bracts, 15–20mm, hairy, pointed
Seeds	1 per fruit, not released

Beech *Fagus sylvatica*

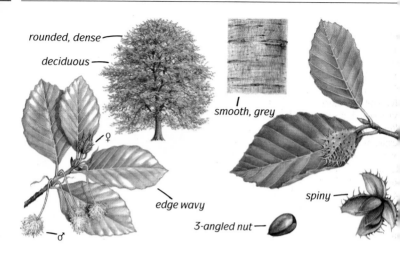

rounded, dense

deciduous

smooth, grey

♀

edge wavy

spiny

3-angled nut

♂

Sunlight streaming through chinks in the sombre canopy, illuminating massive, smooth, grey trunks and arched boughs, brings a cathedral-like atmosphere to a mature stand of Beech. In the deep shade, spring-flowering bulbs grow in the litter of fallen leaves and fruits. *Status:* native mainly to western and central Europe; planted for ornament, shelter and timber. *Similar trees:* Copper Beech is a common variant with deep purplish foliage. Oriental Beech, from eastern Europe, has larger leaves, with up to 12 pairs of veins, and blunt lower spines on the fruit.

1 Copper Beech (*Fagus sylvatica* cv. 'Purpurea')
2 Oriental Beech (*Fagus orientalis*)

broadest above middle

purplish

broader spines

	BEECH	
Type	deciduous tree	
Height	20–30m (rarely 50m)	
Habitat	well-drained soils, especially on chalk hillsides	
Flowering	April–May	
Fruiting	September–October	

TRUNK AND CROWN

Trunk	stout below, forked above
Bark	smooth, grey
Crown	broad, rounded, dense
Twigs	brownish grey

LEAVES

Buds	1–2cm, slender, pointed at both ends, reddish brown
Leaves	on alternate sides of stem, 4–9cm, elliptical or oval, pointed, edge not toothed, often wavy, with fine hairs, base wedge-shaped or rounded, 5–9 pairs of veins, pale green becoming dark, glossy green, turning orange or brown in autumn; stalk 5–15mm; young plants often with dead leaves over winter
Stipules	brown, papery, soon fall

FLOWERS AND FRUIT

Flowers	♂ and ♀ on same plant
♂	tiny, many, in tassel-like head on stalk 5–6cm long
Perianth	bell-shaped, with 4–7 lobes
Stamens	8–16 per ♂ flower
♀	usually 2 enclosed by stalked, cup-like structure of 4 bracts
Stigmas	3 per ♀ flower
Ovaries	1 per ♀ flower
Fruit	3-angled nut, 12–18mm, brown, 1 or 2 in spiny, woody casing, which splits into 4

Introduced from South America, this distant relative of the Beech is becoming popular both for ornament and timber. It is one of the so-called 'Southern Beeches' from the Southern Hemisphere, most of which are evergreen but some are deciduous. *Status:* introduced from Chile and Argentina; planted in western Europe, for ornament and timber. *Similar trees:* Raoul has stouter shoots with longer, pointed buds, finely toothed leaves with 14–18 pairs of veins, and bark with vertical fissures. Antarctic Beech is a shorter tree with smaller leaves usually having 4 pairs of veins.

1 Raoul (*Nothofagus procera*)
2 Antarctic Beech (*Nothofagus antarctica*)

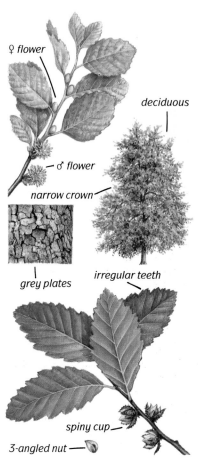

♀ flower

— ♂ flower

deciduous

narrow crown

grey plates

irregular teeth

spiny cup

3-angled nut

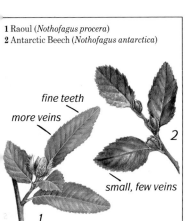

fine teeth

more veins

small, few veins

1

2

	ROBLE BEECH			
Type	deciduous tree			light brown, close to twig
Height	20–30m		**Leaves**	on alternate sides of stem, 5–
Habitat	grown in small plantations, also parks and gardens			8cm, oval to almost oblong, blunt, sharply and irregularly toothed, base slightly unequal, 7–11 pairs of veins, hairless, dark green above, paler below, turning yellow or red in autumn; stalk 4–7mm
Flowering	May			
Fruiting	September			
	TRUNK AND CROWN			
Trunk	forked above		**Stipules**	crinkled, soon falling
Bark	greenish grey, smooth, becoming cracked into small, squarish plates			**FLOWERS AND FRUIT**
Crown	rather narrow, open; branches arch outwards		**Flowers**	♂ and ♀ flowers on same plant
Twigs	slender, with sparse, short hairs, regularly branching to either side		♂	solitary, stalked
			Stamens	♂ with 30–40
	LEAVES		♀	tiny, pale green, at leaf-base
Buds	4–6mm, egg-shaped, blunt,		**Stigmas**	3 per ♀ flower
			Ovaries	1 per ♀ flower
			Fruit	nut, 5–10mm, 3 in cup-like, shortly spiny casing which splits into 4

Evergreen Oak *Quercus ilex*

Characteristic of the Mediterranean region, this tree has been taken to many other countries where it survives frost and keeps its dense foliage in winter. Usually like a small laurel, it has remarkably variable leaves, which are holly-like on sucker shoots. The tannin-rich bark was used by Ancient Greeks and Romans for tanning leather. *Status:* native to the Mediterranean region; much planted elsewhere for ornament and shelter. *Similar trees:* Cork Oak has toothed leaves with a wavy midrib and longer scales on the acorn cup. Rarely reaching tree size, Kermes Oak has spiny, hairless leaves and spiny scales on the acorn cup.

thick

ơ catkin

evergreen

grey below

broad, dense

small plates

greyish-hairy

scales pressed together

some leaves spiny

1 Cork Oak (*Quercus suber*)
2 Kermes Oak (*Quercus coccifera*)

very thick bark

spiny

pointed scales

toothed

longer scales

EVERGREEN OAK

Type	evergreen tree
Height	up to 25m
Habitat	forest, woodland; left in fields for shade; street tree
Flowering	May–June
Fruiting	September–October

TRUNK AND CROWN

Trunk	stout
Bark	dark grey, cracking into small, squarish plates
Crown	broad, domed, dense
Twigs	grey-hairy, becoming hairless

LEAVES

Buds	egg-shaped, hairy
Leaves	2–9cm, variable, oval to oblong, thick, edge unbroken or spiny-toothed on sucker shoots, base tapered or rounded, straight midrib with 7–11 pairs of veins, glossy, dark green above, greyish-hairy below; stalk 6–15mm
Stipules	narrow, hairy, soon falling

FLOWERS AND FRUIT

Flowers	♂ and ♀ flowers on same plant
♂	drooping catkins, 3–5cm
Perianth	tiny, with 4–7 pointed lobes
Stamens	6–12 per ♂ flower
♀	spike of 1–4 flowers
Stigmas	3–4 per ♀ flower
Ovaries	1 per ♀ flower, 3-celled
Fruit	nut (acorn) ripening in first year, 2–4cm, egg-shaped; cup greyish-hairy, covering less than half of fruit, scales oval, pressed closely together

A robust, stately tree with large, lobed leaves, deeply fissured bark, and acorns that are situated on the leafless part of the twig. The timber was once used extensively for panelling walls. *Status:* native to central and southern Europe; planted elsewhere for ornament and shelter. *Similar trees:* Valonia Oak has smooth leaves with bristle-tipped lobes and a larger acorn cup with long, broad scales. Macedonian Oak has glossy, short-stalked leaves and an acorn cup with short, radiating scales. A cultivated hybrid of Turkey Oak and Cork Oak, Lucombe Oak resembles the former but has mostly evergreen leaves and thicker bark.

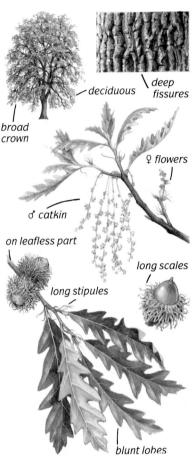

deciduous

deep fissures

broad crown

♀ flowers

♂ catkin

on leafless part

long scales

long stipules

blunt lobes

1 Valonia Oak (*Quercus macrolepis*)
2 Macedonian Oak (*Quercus trojana*)
3 Lucombe Oak (*Quercus × hispanica*)

bristle tip
wide scales

1

3

2

glossy, evergreen
shorter scales

	TURKEY OAK		
Type	deciduous tree		rough above, paler below, minutely hairy; stalk 8–25mm
Height	20–35m	**Stipules**	to 25cm, very slender, prominent, remaining attached
Habitat	mainly on acid soils		
Flowering	May		**FLOWERS AND FRUIT**
Fruiting	September–October	**Flowers**	♂ and ♀ flowers on same tree
		♂	catkin, 5–8cm
	TRUNK AND CROWN	**Perianth**	tiny, 4–7 lobes
Trunk	stout, forked above	**Stamens**	4 per ♂ flower
Bark	dark grey, deeply fissured	♀	cluster of up to 5 flowers
Crown	broad, domed; branches stout	**Stigmas**	4 styles per ♀ flower
Twigs	brown, rough, sparsely hairy	**Ovaries**	1 per ♀ flower, 3-celled
		Fruit	nut (acorn), ripens in second year, 2–3.5cm, rarely 5cm, oblong, reddish brown, broad cup covers $\frac{1}{2}$ nut, scales to 1cm, slender, spreading or bent back; stalk to 2cm
	LEAVES		
Buds	oval, blunt, shortly hairy		
Leaves	alternate along stem, variable, 5–10cm, rarely 18cm, oblong or oval, pointed, 7–9 pairs of unequal, oval, blunt lobes, greyish-hairy becoming dull green, almost hairless but		

Pedunculate Oak *Quercus robur*

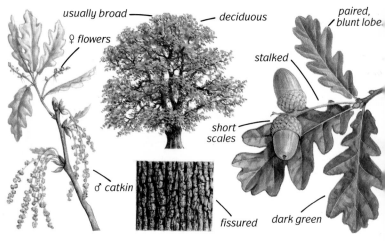

usually broad — deciduous — paired, blunt lobe

♀ flowers

stalked

short scales

♂ catkin

fissured — dark green

Renowned throughout Europe as a symbol of durability and longevity, this tree can survive for a thousand years. Light brown with silvery, close grain, the hard timber is valuable commercially; formerly it was exploited for architecture and ship-building. *Status:* native to much of Europe except for the extreme north and parts of the Mediterranean region; planted for shelter, timber and ornament. *Similar trees:* native to south-eastern Europe, *Q. pedunculiflora* differs in having bluish green leaves with yellowish grey hairs below and warty acorn cups with yellowish hairs.

Quercus pedunculiflora

yellowish hairs

greyish hairs

bluish green

	PEDUNCULATE OAK
Type	deciduous tree
Height	20–35m, rarely 45m
Habitat	woodland, especially lowland on heavy, fertile soils
Flowering	April–May
Fruiting	September–October
	TRUNK AND CROWN
Trunk	stout, often short and burred
Bark	fissured, brownish grey
Crown	usually broad, branches stout, wide-spreading, often sinuous
Twigs	grey-brown, usually hairless
	LEAVES
Buds	2–5mm, oval, blunt, hairless
Leaves	alternate along stem, 5–12cm, more or less oblong, blunt, 4–7 pairs of blunt, unequal lobes, base with 2 ear-like lobes, dull

green, hairless above, paler and usually hairless below; stalk 1–5mm

Stipules	slender, soon falling
	FLOWERS AND FRUIT
Flowers	♂ and ♀ flowers on same tree
♂	clustered catkins, 2–4cm
Perianth	tiny, 4–7 lobes
Stamens	6–8, rarely 12 per ♂ flower
♀	1–5 flowers in stalked head
Stigmas	3 per ♀ flower
Ovaries	1 per ♀ flower, 3-celled
Fruit	nut (acorn) ripens first year, 1.5–4cm, oblong or elliptical, brown; cup 1.5–2cm wide, $\frac{1}{3}$–$\frac{1}{2}$ covers nut; scales small, oval, flat, closely overlapping, shortly hairy; stalk 2–8cm

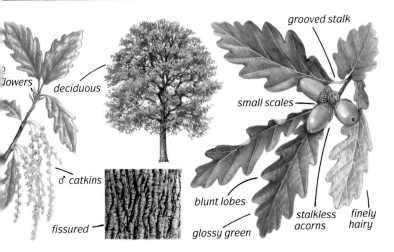

Quercus petraea Sessile Oak

flowers
deciduous
grooved stalk
small scales
♂ catkins
blunt lobes
stalkless acorns
finely hairy
fissured
glossy green

majestic tree but one which tends to e overlooked as it is often confused vith Pedunculate Oak, from which it iffers by the stalkless acorns. As they re less often attacked by insects, the ark, glossy, distinctly stalked leaves re more ornamental. *Status:* native xcept in the extreme north and the 1editerranean region; planted for imber, shelter and ornament. *Similar rees:* native to south-eastern Europe, *). dalechampii* has hairless leaves nd acorns with a warty, greyish, ractically hairless cup. Hungarian)ak has hairy twigs and leaves with up o ten, deep, wavy-edged lobes.

1 *Quercus dalechampii*
2 Hungarian Oak (*Quercus frainetto*)
many wavy lobes
1
warty, hairless
hairless below
short stalk
2

	SESSILE OAK		
Type	deciduous tree		finely hairy below with brownish tufts at base of veins; stalk 1.8–2.5cm, grooved
Height	20–40m		
Habitat	woodland, mainly acid soils	**Stipules**	soon falling
Flowering	April–May		
Fruiting	September–October		**FLOWERS AND FRUIT**
		Flowers	♂ and ♀ flowers, with leaves
	TRUNK AND CROWN	♂	clustered, hanging catkins
Trunk	stout, often straight and unbranched below	**Perianth**	tiny, 4–7 lobes, usually 6
		Stamens	6–12 per ♂ flower
Bark	brownish grey, fissured	♀	bud-like, within hairy scales
Crown	rather narrowly domed	**Stigmas**	3 per ♀ flower, stalkless
Twigs	hairless	**Ovaries**	1 per ♀ flower, 3-celled
	LEAVES	**Fruit**	2–6 nuts (acorns), ripening first year, 1.5–3cm, oblong; cup with oval, closely overlapping scales, finely hairy; almost stalkless
Buds	5–6mm, many scales, hairy		
Leaves	alternate along stem, 7–12.5cm, oval, broadest above, 5–8 pairs of rounded lobes, base tapered, rather glossy, dark green above,		

Downy Oak *Quercus pubescens*

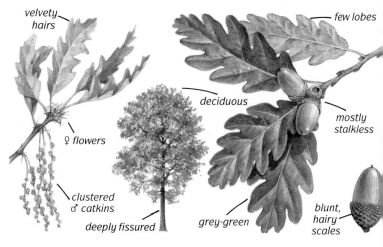

velvety hairs

few lobes

deciduous

♀ flowers

mostly stalkless

clustered ♂ catkins

deeply fissured

grey-green

blunt, hairy scales

A rather small tree or sturdy shrub, distinguished by grey-green, shallowly lobed leaves, covered with velvety hairs when young. Winter buds and acorn cups are also hairy. *Status:* native mainly to southern and western Europe; rarely planted for ornament. *Similar trees:* two species have longer leaf-stalks and looser scales on the acorn cup. Confined mainly to the eastern half of the Mediterranean region, *Q. virgiliana* has leaves with broad, often wavy-edged lobes, and the scales of the acorn cup have a slender, upright tip. Pyrenean Oak from south-western Europe has narrower, blunt scales on the acorn cup.

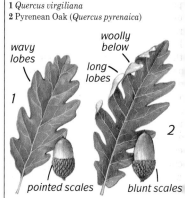

1 *Quercus virgiliana*
2 Pyrenean Oak (*Quercus pyrenaica*)

wavy lobes

woolly below

long lobes

pointed scales

blunt scales

DOWNY OAK	
Type	deciduous tree or large shrub
Height	15–25m
Habitat	dry, usually lime-rich soils
Flowering	May
Fruiting	October

TRUNK AND CROWN

Trunk	sometimes very short
Bark	dark grey, finely and deeply fissured, forming rough plates
Crown	domed, branches swollen at junction with trunk
Twigs	brown, densely grey-hairy

LEAVES

Buds	4–7mm, reddish brown, hairy
Leaves	alternate along stem, 4–13cm, variable, 4–8 pairs of broad, shallow, forward-pointing lobes, base rounded or broadly tapered, grey-green, densely hairy when young, becoming hairless above; stalk 2–15mm
Stipules	soon falling

FLOWERS AND FRUIT

Flowers	♂ and ♀ flowers, with leaves
♂	clustered catkins
Stamens	6–12 per ♂ flower
Perianth	tiny, with 4–7 lobes
♀	1–3, each within cup of scales
Stigmas	3 per ♀ flower, deep red
Ovaries	1 per ♀ flower, 3-celled
Fruit	nut (acorn), ripens first year, 2–4cm; cup 1–1.5cm wide, $\frac{1}{4}$–$\frac{1}{3}$ covers nut, scales oval, usually blunt, pressed together, grey-woolly; stalkless or short-stalked

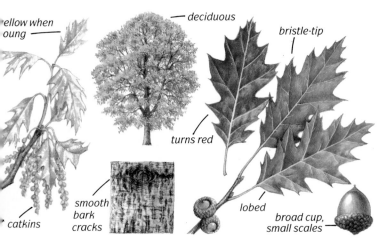

yellow when young

deciduous

bristle-tip

turns red

smooth bark cracks

catkins

lobed

broad cup, small scales

pectacular when a cold snap in autumn turns its leaves fiery shades of range and scarlet, Red Oak is widely lanted for ornament. Like several ther introduced North American pecies, it has relatively large leaves ith pointed lobes and teeth. *Status:* ntroduced from eastern North merica; commonly planted for rnament, timber and shelter. *Similar rees:* two American species have more eeply divided leaves and short, squat corns. Scarlet Oak's glossy leaves lack airs below at the base of the veins. Pin ak has leaves with tufts of hairs eneath, and a narrow acorn cup.

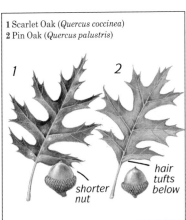

1 Scarlet Oak (*Quercus coccinea*)
2 Pin Oak (*Quercus palustris*)

1

2

hair tufts below

shorter nut

	RED OAK	
Type	deciduous tree	
Height	20–35m	
Habitat	planted on most soils	
Flowering	April–May	
Fruiting	October	

TRUNK AND CROWN

Trunk	straight below
Bark	silvery grey, smooth above, with brown fissures below
Crown	broad-domed, branches straight
Twigs	stout, reddish brown, hairless

LEAVES

Buds	5–7mm, oval, reddish brown
Leaves	alternating, 12–25cm, oval or elliptical, variable, cut $\frac{1}{2}$ way into 7–11 pairs of lobes, few bristle-tipped teeth, only few hairs in

angles of veins below, yellow, becoming dull green, turning orange, red or brown in autumn; stalk 2.5–3cm

Stipules	soon falling

FLOWERS AND FRUIT

Flowers	♂ and ♀ flowers, with leaves
♂	catkins, 5–8cm, yellow
Perianth	tiny, with 4–7 lobes
Stamens	6–12 per ♂ flower
♀	tiny, at leaf-base, red
Stigmas	3–4 per ♀ flower
Ovaries	1 per ♀ flower, 3-celled
Fruit	nut (acorn), ripens second year, 2–3cm, oblong, reddish brown; cup 2–2.5cm wide, covers $\frac{1}{3}$ nut, scales oval, pressed closely together, finely hairy; stalk 8–10mm

Sweet Chestnut *Castanea sativa*

A strikingly attractive tree, with bold, toothed leaves, bunches of long, pale yellow catkins and a stout, deeply fissured trunk, which often has a curious spiral pattern. Long-lived, the trunk may attain a girth of 13m or more, with the crown misshapen from lightning damage or branches shed in high wind. It is grown widely for its edible nuts. *Status:* native to southern Europe; widely planted and naturalized elsewhere. *Similar trees:* an ornamental species from western North America, Golden Chestnut is an evergreen with untoothed, leathery leaves, golden beneath, and fruits which mature in 2 years.

ridges often spiral

often massive

deciduous

♀ flower

♂ catkins

sharp teeth

many veins

large leaf

spiny

large, edible nut

Golden Chestnut (*Chrysolepis chrysophylla*)

slow ripening

yellowish below   *evergreen*   *not toothed*

SWEET CHESTNUT

Type	deciduous tree
Height	20–30m
Habitat	well-drained soils, in woods
Flowering	June–July
Fruiting	September–October

TRUNK AND CROWN

Trunk	often massive and gnarled
Bark	brown, vertically or spirally fissured and ridged
Crown	broad, irregular; massive old branches taper abruptly
Twigs	greenish brown, sometimes grooved, with lenticels

LEAVES

Buds	4–5mm, egg-shaped
Leaves	on alternate sides of stem, 10–25cm, narrowly oval to oblong, pointed, regularly toothed, teeth point forwards with slender tip, base tapered or rounded, *c*20 pairs of veins, glossy, dark green above, paler below, turning yellow or brown in autumn; stalk 0.5–3cm
Stipules	papery, soon falling

FLOWERS AND FRUIT

Flowers	♂ and ♀ flowers on same plant
♂	catkins, 12–30cm, pale yellow
Stamens	10–20 per ♂ flower
♀	2–3 in spiny bracts, in short ♀ catkin or below ♂ catkin
Stigmas	7–9 per ♀ flower
Ovaries	1 per ♀ flower, 6-celled
Fruit	1–3 nuts in husk with branched spines, splits into 2–4; nuts 20–35mm, hemispherical or angular, glossy, reddish brown

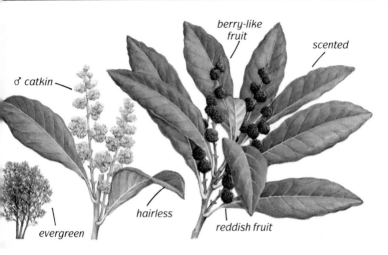

♂ catkin

berry-like fruit

scented

hairless

evergreen

reddish fruit

...strongly aromatic shrub or small tree, ...lated to the shrubby Bog-myrtle (*M. ...ale*) of north-western Europe. Faya is ...und mainly in broad-leaved evergreen ...rests of the western Atlantic islands, ...mnants of a forest type widespread in ...e Mediterranean region 30 million ...ears ago. *Status:* native to the Azores, ...adeira and the Canary Islands; ...ultivated and naturalized in southern ...urope; possibly native to Portugal. *...imilar trees:* Bayberry is a deciduous ...rub, rarely tree-sized, with leaves ...overed by glossy, yellow glands, ...nbranched catkins and small, whitish ...uits. It is sometimes naturalized.

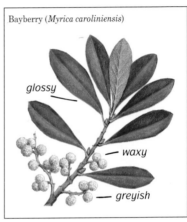

Bayberry (*Myrica caroliniensis*)

glossy

waxy

greyish

FAYA

Type	evergreen tree or shrub
Height	2–10m
Habitat	woodland, scrub
Flowering	April–May
Fruiting	September

TRUNK AND CROWN

Trunk	short, forked
Bark	smooth, brown
Crown	rounded, irregular
Twigs	with small, reddish, tack-shaped hairs

LEAVES

Buds	egg-shaped, pointed
Leaves	on alternate sides of stem, 4–12cm, spear-shaped, broadest above middle, edge unbroken, turned under, base wedge-shaped, hairless; stalkless

Stipules	absent

FLOWERS AND FRUIT

Flowers	♂ and ♀ catkins on different plants, among leaves
♂	in branched catkins on growth of current year
♀	usually in unbranched catkins, each flower with 2 or more scales at the base
Perianth	absent
Stamens	2–16 per ♂ flower
Stigmas	2, slender, on short style
Ovaries	1, 1-chambered
Fruit	berry-like, slightly fleshy, reddish to black, with rough, waxy surface

English Elm *Ulmus procera*

A prominent tree of the landscape with a billowy crown formed by the domed masses of foliage from each main branch. The roots often produce suckers, so that an old tree is ringed by its younger progeny. In recent years, millions of trees have died from Dutch Elm disease, but young suckers often survive and offer hope for regeneration. *Status:* native to western and southern Europe; planted for shelter and timber. *Similar trees:* from central and south-eastern Europe, European White-elm has long-stalked flowers and fruit, the latter fringed with hairs. The leaves may have long, soft hairs below.

purplish stamens

before leaves

different-sized teeth

uneq... bo...

bristly

broad

encircl... w...

irregular crown

deciduous

rarely produced

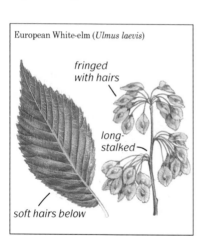

European White-elm (*Ulmus laevis*)

fringed with hairs

long-stalked

soft hairs below

	ENGLISH ELM
Type	deciduous tree
Height	20–35m
Habitat	woodland, hedgerows
Flowering	February–March
Fruiting	April–June

TRUNK AND CROWN

Trunk	straight, forked above, suckers around base
Bark	brown, rough, fissured
Crown	irregularly domed; often few large, spreading branches
Twigs	rather stout, shortly hairy

LEAVES

Buds	small, pointed, brown, hairy
Leaves	alternate along stem, 4.5–9cm, oval to almost circular, pointed, doubly toothed, base unequal, longer side rounded, not overlapping short stalk, dark green, turning yellow in autumn, rough with stiff hairs to almost hairless above, 10–12 pairs of veins
Stipules	small, soon falling

FLOWERS AND FRUIT

Flowers	☿, before leaves, 5–9mm, clustered, greenish
Perianth	4–5 joined lobes, bell-shaped
Stamens	4–5, purplish red
Stigmas	1, forked
Ovaries	1, flattened
Fruit	rarely produced, nut-like with circular wing notched at tip, 10–17mm, seed above middle
Seeds	1, not released from fruit

Ulmus minor **Small-leaved Elm**

variable species, especially in Britain,
here it is often split into several
arieties, subspecies or even species.
mall-leaved Elm is common in
ontinental Europe, though its numbers
ave been decimated by Dutch Elm
isease. Smooth, glossy leaves and an
liptical fruit with the seed above the
iddle distinguish it from other
ommon elms. *Status:* native to much of
urope; planted for timber, shelter and
nament. *Similar trees:* Grey-leaved
lm has young shoots densely covered
ith white hairs, and leaves downy grey
low. Chinese Elm is an ornamental
ecies planted for its delicate sprays of
uch smaller, dark green leaves.

Grey-leaved Elm (*Ulmus canescens*)
Chinese Elm (*Ulmus parvifolia*)

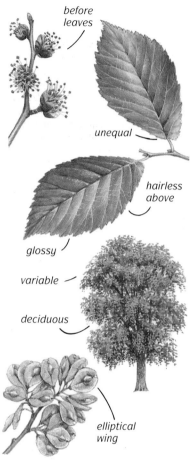

before leaves

unequal

hairless above

glossy

variable

deciduous

elliptical wing

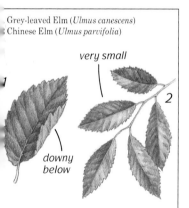

very small

downy below

	SMALL-LEAVED ELM	
Type	deciduous tree	
Height	15–30m	
Habitat	hedgerows, woodland	
Flowering	February–March	
Fruiting	May–July	

TRUNK AND CROWN

Trunk	straight, suckers around base
Bark	greyish brown, fissured
Crown	variable, domed or conical; few main branches
Twigs	slender, often hanging, pale brown, becoming smooth

LEAVES

Buds	c5mm, egg-shaped, red, downy
Leaves	alternate along twig, 6–8cm, oval, broadest towards slender tip, sharply, doubly toothed, base unequal, squarish long side not overlapping stalk, shiny dark green, turning yellow in autumn, hairless above, downy tufts below, 7–12 pairs of veins; stalk c5mm, downy
Stipules	small, soon falling

FLOWERS AND FRUIT

Flowers	♂, before leaves, clustered, each 5–8mm, purplish
Perianth	4–5 joined lobes, bell-shaped
Stamens	4–5, purple anthers
Stigmas	1, forked, white
Ovaries	solitary, flattened
Fruit	nut-like with notched, elliptical wing, 7–18mm, seed above middle
Seeds	1, not released from fruit

Wych Elm *Ulmus glabra*

A handsome, densely-canopied tree, with large, bristly, lop-sided leaves. There is a rounded lobe at the base of each leaf, which usually overlaps the short stalk. Weeping forms are grown, with twisted, pendulous branches. Fruits are enclosed centrally within a broad, oval wing. *Status:* native to much of Europe except parts of the Mediterranean region; often planted by fields, in parks or churchyards. *Similar trees:* also large-leaved are the hybrids with Small-leaved Elm, distinguished from Wych Elm by their smooth leaves. Dutch Elm has corky ridges on the crooked shoots. Huntingdon Elm has straight, scarcely corky shoots.

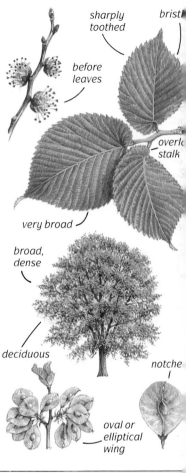

sharply toothed

brist[l]

before leaves

overl[ap] stalk

very broad

broad, dense

deciduous

notche[d]

oval or elliptical wing

1 Dutch Elm (*Ulmus × hollandica* var. *hollandica*); **2** Huntingdon Elm (*Ulmus × hollandica* var. *vegeta*)

1 corky, smooth

2

smooth

WYCH ELM

Type	deciduous tree
Height	25–40m
Habitat	often by water
Flowering	February–March
Fruiting	May–June

TRUNK AND CROWN

Trunk	stout, with burrs and suckers
Bark	grey to brown, smooth becoming cracked and ridged
Crown	rounded, dense; branches angled upwards, twisted, sometimes bent down to ground
Twigs	stout, bristly, become smooth

LEAVES

Buds	stout, with reddish hairs
Leaves	alternate along stem, 8–18cm, broad, almost circular to oval, slender tipped, sharply, doubly toothed, base unequal, longer, rounded side overlaps stalk, bristly, dark green above, paler below, turning deep yellow in autumn, 12–18 pairs of veins; stalk 2–5mm, thick, hairy
Stipules	small, soon falling

FLOWERS AND FRUIT

Flowers	♀, before leaves, clustered, each 7–8mm, purplish red
Perianth	4–5 joined lobes, bell-shaped
Stamens	4–5, anthers purplish red
Stigmas	with 2 styles
Ovaries	1, flattened
Fruit	nut-like, central within oval or elliptical, notched wing, 1.5–2.5cm; stalk 2–3mm
Seeds	1, not released

An attractive tree with dark green leaves edged by large, rounded teeth. The smooth, scaly bark has rounded, orange patches. Some cultivated trees have many stout, almost upright branches arising near the base, forming a dense crown that is oval in outline. *Status:* introduced from the Caucasus; unfrequently planted for ornament. *Similar trees:* Keaki is a Japanese ornamental tree with sharply toothed leaves turning yellow, red or orange. *Zelkova abelicea* is an uncommon native species from the mountains of Crete, and is sometimes cultivated. It differs in the small leaves with few, rounded teeth, and white, scented flowers.

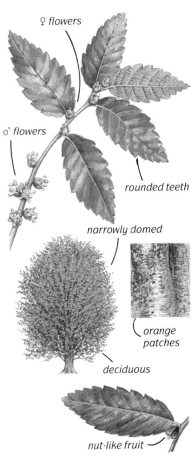

♀ flowers

♂ flowers

rounded teeth

narrowly domed

orange patches

deciduous

nut-like fruit

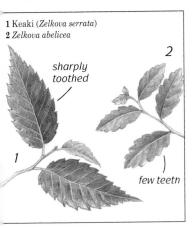

1 Keaki (*Zelkova serrata*)
2 *Zelkova abelicea*

sharply toothed

few teeth

CAUCASIAN ELM	
Type	deciduous tree
Height	20–35m
Habitat	parks, gardens, rarely hedges
Flowering	April–May
Fruiting	August–September

TRUNK AND CROWN

Trunk	often short, becomes buttressed; suckers at base
Bark	yellowish grey, smooth, scaling leaving orange patches
Crown	narrowly domed; branches angled upwards
Twigs	slender, greyish brown, downy

LEAVES

Buds	small, blunt, reddish, downy
Leaves	alternate along stem, 5–10cm, oval or elliptical, pointed, with rounded teeth, base rounded or squarish, slightly unequal, dark green above, turning orange-brown in autumn, dull or shiny, often with scattered, stiff hairs, veins 6–12 pairs; stalk 1–2mm
Stipules	small, soon falling

FLOWERS AND FRUIT

Flowers	♂ and ♀ flowers on different plants, with leaves
♂	on lower part of twig
♀	solitary at leaf-base
Perianth	5 joined lobes
Stamens	5, yellow, upright
Stigmas	2 on slender styles
Fruit	nut-like, solitary, 4–5mm, rounded, ridged
Seeds	1, not released

Southern Nettle-tree *Celtis australis*

This graceful tree differs from the related elms by the narrow, nettle-like leaves drawn out into a long, slender point. Berry-like fruits are sweet-tasting with an edible nut-like centre, and were important in the diet of Stone Age people. *Status:* native to southern Europe; planted elsewhere for ornament and shade. *Similar trees: Celtis tournefortii* is a native shrub or small tree with oval, bluntly toothed leaves. The fruit has a 4-ridged, nut-like centre. Hackberry, a cultivated species from eastern North America, has rough bark and leaves with fewer, long, whiskered teeth. The orange or purple ripe fruit has a shorter stalk.

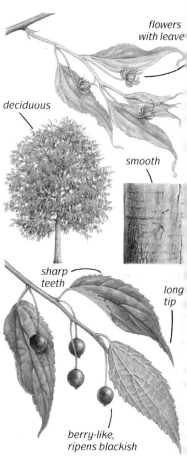

flowers with leave

deciduous

smooth

sharp teeth

long tip

berry-like, ripens blackish

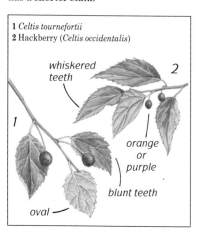

1 *Celtis tournefortii*
2 Hackberry (*Celtis occidentalis*)

whiskered teeth

2

1

orange or purple

blunt teeth

oval

SOUTHERN NETTLE-TREE

Type	deciduous tree
Height	10–25m
Habitat	woodland, scrub, roadsides
Flowering	May
Fruiting	August

TRUNK AND CROWN

Trunk	straight below, forked above
Bark	grey-brown, smooth with rows of lenticels, some fissured
Crown	domed
Twigs	slender, downy, reddish brown

LEAVES

Buds	small, downy
Leaves	alternate along stem, 4–15cm, narrowly oval, with long, slender, sometimes twisted point, edge often wavy, sharply toothed, base rounded or shallowly notched, dark green, turning yellow in autumn, stiffly hairy above, downy below with white hairs, 3 main veins from base; stalk 1–3.5cm
Stipules	small, soon falling

FLOWERS AND FRUIT

Flowers	♂ and ♀ on same tree, with leaves, 7–10mm, yellowish, long-stalked
Perianth	4–5 separate lobes
Stamens	4–5, yellow
Stigmas	2, on slender styles
Ovaries	1, rounded
Fruit	berry-like, solitary, 9–12mm, globular, smooth, blackish brown, long-stalked
Seeds	pitted, nut-like centre to fruit retains single seed

Morus nigra **Black Mulberry**

♀ flowers

heart-shaped

ripen blackish

wny low

toothed

flowers

deciduous

sometimes lobed

White Mulberry (*Morus alba*)

pale

glossy

almost hairless

ommonly a short, broad, gnarled tree, ack Mulberry has been cultivated for s sweet-and-sour fruit in Europe since eek and Roman times. The exact igin of this species is unknown since l trees are apparently cultivated or turalized from cultivation. *Status:* troduced, probably from central Asia; dely grown for fruit in southern rope, often naturalized. *Similar trees:* troduced from China, White Mulberry the food plant for silk-worms and els the silk industry. It differs in the ossy, almost hairless leaves and alked, white or pale purplish fruit.

	BLACK MULBERRY	
Type	deciduous tree	
Height	3–16m	
Habitat	fields, gardens	
Flowering	April–May	
Fruiting	August–September	

TRUNK AND CROWN

Trunk	short, often leaning
Bark	dark orange-brown, rough, scaling, fissured, with burrs
Crown	low, domed; branches stout, rough, twisted
Twigs	stout, become reddish brown

LEAVES

Buds	stout, conical, glossy brown
Leaves	alternate along stem, 6–20cm, broadly oval or heart-shaped, sharply pointed, toothed, sometimes deeply lobed, base notched, dark green, roughly hairy above, paler, downy below; stalk 1.5–2.5cm, stout, hairy
Stipules	soon falling

FLOWERS AND FRUIT

Flowers	♂ and ♀ flowers on same tree, in short spikes
♂	2–2.5cm, yellowish green
Stamens	4, yellow
♀	1–1.5cm
Perianth	4 lobes, joined at base
Stigmas	2, slender
Ovaries	1 per ♀ flower
Fruit	at leaf-base, 2–2.5cm, many berry-like segments, deep red to blackish purple, almost stalkless, becomes sweet
Seeds	1 per fruit segment

Osage Orange *Maclura pomifera*

This small, thorny tree is most easily distinguished by its orange-sized, yellowish fruit, with milky white, inedible flesh. When trimmed, the plant forms an impenetrable hedge and is used as such in southern Europe. *Status:* introduced from North America; planted for ornament and hedges; naturalized in southern Europe. *Similar trees:* Paper Mulberry has hairy, toothed leaves, which are sometimes deeply lobed. Male flowers are in hanging catkins; female flowers form globular, woolly heads, which turn into spiky, globular fruits. From eastern Asia, it is naturalized in southern Europe.

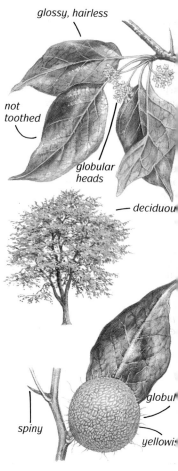

glossy, hairless

not toothed

globular heads

deciduou

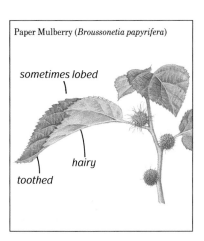

Paper Mulberry (*Broussonetia papyrifera*)

sometimes lobed

hairy

toothed

spiny

globul

yellowi

	OSAGE ORANGE		
Type	deciduous tree		hairless above, paler below; stalk 5–8mm, shortly hairy
Height	up to 14m	**Stipules**	soon falling
Habitat	hedges, street tree, parks		
Flowering	June		**FLOWERS AND FRUIT**
Fruiting	October–November	**Flowers**	♂ and ♀ on different trees
		♂	greenish yellow, in broad, stalked heads, 1.5–2.5cm
	TRUNK AND CROWN	**Stamens**	4, yellowish
Trunk	often forked, slender	♀	many in globular head, 2–2.5cm, green
Bark	rough, orange-brown	**Perianth**	4-lobed
Crown	irregular, domed; branches twisted	**Stigmas**	2, on slender styles
Twigs	spiny, downy becoming hairless	**Ovaries**	1 per ♀ flower
		Fruit	10–14cm, globular, green, turning yellow or orange, with white, stringy flesh
	LEAVES	**Seeds**	not released
Buds	small, brown		
Leaves	alternate along stem, 5–12cm, oval, pointed, edge unbroken, base wedge-shaped or rounded, glossy dark green,		

...ıch cultivated in the Mediterranean
...gion for its delicious fruit, which is
...ten fresh or dried. Though these
...ible figs are an exception, fruits of
...st fig species are pollinated by tiny
...ısps that enter a hole at the fruit tip
...d lay eggs in specialized flowers.
...atus: native to southern Europe;
...ltivated for fruit, ornament and shade.
...milar trees: two evergreens with
...athery leaves, grown as street trees in
...e south, have curious roots sprouting
...om branches. Indian Rubber-tree, with
... long leaves, is grown as a pot plant in
...rthern Europe. Banyan Tree has
...oad, wavy-edged leaves.

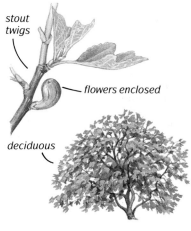

stout twigs

flowers enclosed

deciduous

Indian Rubber-tree (*Ficus elastica*)
Banyan Tree (*Ficus benghalensis*)

unbroken edge

thick

2

wavy edge

toothed

most lobed

ripens brownish purple

FIG

Type	deciduous tree or shrub
Height	up to 10m
Habitat	fields, orchards, parks, gardens, naturalized by roads
Flowering	September–November
Fruiting	July–October, following year

TRUNK AND CROWN

Trunk	usually short, often forked
Bark	pale grey with darker streaks, smooth or uneven
Crown	domed, wide-spreading; branches twisted
Twigs	stout, with large leaf-scars

LEAVES

Buds	conical, pointed
Leaves	alternate along stem, 7–30cm, most with 3–5 deep, blunt lobes, thick, leathery, irregularly toothed, base notched, glossy dark green, roughly hairy; stalk 5–10cm, stout
Stipules	broad, soon falling leaving circular scar around twig

FLOWERS AND FRUIT

Flowers	♂ and ♀ tiny, inside hollow structure that becomes fruit
Perianth	2–6 tiny segments
Stamens	♂ flowers with 4
Stigmas	♀ flowers with 2, slender
Ovaries	1 per ♀ flower
Fruit	5–8cm, pear-shaped, green to brownish purple, hollow structure containing individual tiny fruits
Seeds	retained within tiny fruits

Sweet-gum *Liquidambar styraciflua*

A magnificent tree in autumn, when the whole crown can turn bright shades of red, purple or yellow. Similar to maples, it is easily distinguished by the alternate leaves and globular, spiky fruit. Where it is native in North America, it is the source of scented gum, and the fine-grained timber is used for furniture. *Status:* introduced from North America; frequently planted in northern Europe for ornament, especially for autumn colour. *Similar trees:* Oriental Sweet-gum, from south-west Asia, has smaller, more deeply lobed, dull green leaves with coarser, irregular teeth.

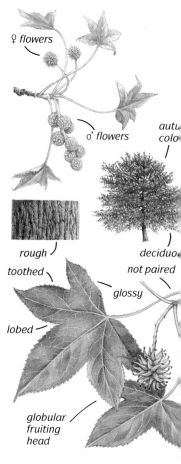

♀ *flowers*

♂ *flowers*

autu colo

rough

deciduo

toothed

not paired

glossy

lobed

globular fruiting head

Oriental Sweet-gum (*Liquidambar orientalis*)

dull green

deeper lobes

irregularly toothed

	SWEET-GUM	
Type	deciduous tree	
Height	5–30m (45m in North America)	
Habitat	parks, gardens, street tree	
Flowering	May	
Fruiting	October–November	

TRUNK AND CROWN

Trunk	usually short and broad
Bark	pale grey to brown, rough
Crown	conical to broadly domed; branches widely spreading
Twigs	slender, downy becoming hairless

LEAVES

Buds	conical, glossy green
Leaves	alternate along stem, 8–15cm, with 3–7 lobes, pointed, finely toothed, glossy green above, turning red, purple or orange in autumn, reddish hairs in tufts below; stalk 10–15cm, grooved
Stipules	small, soon falling

FLOWERS AND FRUIT

Flowers	♂ and ♀ flowers on different plants
♂	yellow, globular heads clustered into spike, 5–10cm
♀	in globular head, 1–1.5cm, solitary or sometimes paired
Stamens	many in ♂ head
Stigmas	1 per ♀ flower
Ovaries	1 per ♀ flower
Fruit	globular, spiny head, 2–3.5cm, of many slender capsules, each 6–8mm, stalk 4–6cm
Seeds	each capsule with 1 or 2 seeds

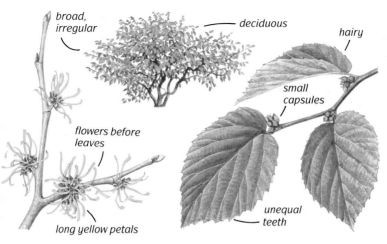

broad, irregular

deciduous

hairy

small capsules

flowers before leaves

long yellow petals

unequal teeth

Flowering in mid-winter, this ornamental species is valued for the colour and scent of its flowers. The commonest of several cultivated species, it is usually a shrub though some species and cultivars form small trees. An extract is used for treating bruises and inflammation. *Status:* introduced from China; commonly planted for ornament. *Similar trees:* Virginian Witch-hazel, from North America, flowers in the autumn. Persian Ironwood is a small tree with scarcely toothed leaves, small, purplish flowers and smooth grey bark flaking to reveal pink or yellow patches.

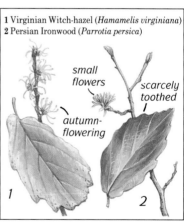

1 Virginian Witch-hazel (*Hamamelis virginiana*)
2 Persian Ironwood (*Parrotia persica*)

small flowers

scarcely toothed

autumn-flowering

1

2

	WITCH-HAZEL	
Type	deciduous shrub, rarely reaching tree size	
Height	2.5–4m	
Habitat	parks, roadsides near towns	
Flowering	December–March	
Fruiting	August–September	
	TRUNK AND CROWN	
Trunk	often several, forked	
Bark	smooth, greyish brown	
Crown	broad, irregular; branches angled upwards, twisted	
Twigs	slender, pale grey	
	LEAVES	
Buds	conical, pointed	
Leaves	alternate along stem, 7–12cm, broadly oval or rounded, long-pointed, doubly toothed, base	

rounded or wedge-shaped, softly hairy, yellow or orange in autumn; stalk short

Stipules large, soon falling

FLOWERS AND FRUIT

Flowers ♂, before leaves, few in compact, short-stalked cluster, 3–4cm long, deep yellow

Petals 4, long, narrow; sepals 4, rounded, reddish

Stamens 4, purplish

Ovaries single

Fruit oblong capsule, splits lengthwise

Seeds 2, black, shiny

London Plane *Platanus × hybrida*

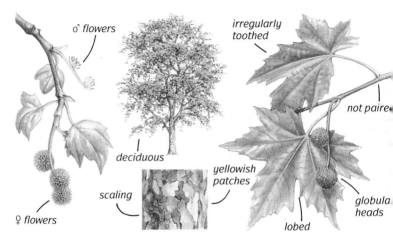

o' flowers

irregularly toothed

not paired

deciduous

yellowish patches

scaling

♀ flowers

globular heads

lobed

Tolerant of pollution, this tree is common in towns of southern and western Europe. Of rapid growth, it makes a huge tree with lobed leaves, globular, spiky fruits and scaly bark revealing large patches of creamy white. Of obscure origin, it is considered to be a hybrid between Oriental Plane and American Plane (*P. occidentalis*). *Status:* of garden origin; widely planted for ornament, shade and timber. *Similar trees:* Oriental Plane has more deeply lobed leaves with a narrower base, and fruiting heads in clusters of 3–6. Native to south-eastern Europe, it is also planted elsewhere.

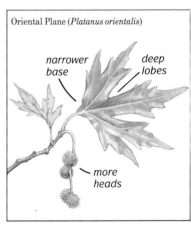

Oriental Plane (*Platanus orientalis*)

narrower base

deep lobes

more heads

	LONDON PLANE	
Type	deciduous tree	
Height	up to 45m	
Habitat	parks, roadsides	
Flowering	April–June	
Fruiting	February–April	

TRUNK AND CROWN

Trunk	long, straight
Bark	grey-brown, scaling leaving whitish yellow patches, becomes fissured at base
Crown	domed; branches often twisted
Twigs	slender, often hanging

LEAVES

Buds	6–8mm, reddish brown
Leaves	alternate along stem, 8–24cm, variably 5-lobed, pointed, irregularly toothed, base squarish or notched, glossy, bright green above, paler below, veins woolly; stalk long, broad-based
Stipules	oval, toothed, usually falling

FLOWERS AND FRUIT

Flowers	♂ and ♀ on same tree, in globular heads
♂	2–6 yellowish heads in cluster 4–8cm long
Perianth	4–6 lobes
Stamens	4–6 per ♂ flower
♀	2–5 reddish heads on stalk
Ovaries	3–6 per ♀ flower, surrounded by long hairs at base
Fruit	usually 2 globular heads on stalk, breaks into segments, each with tuft of hairs
Seeds	1 per segment, not released

...is puzzling tree looks superficially
...e some sort of cypress from afar, but
...has very slender twigs and scale-like
...ves resembling a Horsetail
...quisetum). Originally from New
...uth Wales, it is remarkably resistant
...drought and tolerant of salt, making
...deal for stabilizing sand dunes. The
...rd wood is so dense that it sinks in
...ter. *Status:* introduced from
...ustralia; planted in the Mediterranean
...gion for ornament, shelter or
...bilizing sand. *Similar trees:* Drooping
...e-oak has much longer male flower-
...ads and larger fruiting heads. It is
...ore tolerant of frosts.

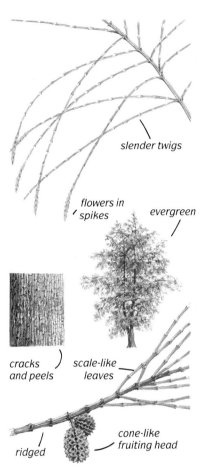

slender twigs

flowers in spikes

evergreen

...rooping She-oak (*Causuarina stricta*)

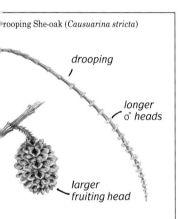

drooping

longer ♂ heads

larger fruiting head

cracks and peels

scale-like leaves

ridged

cone-like fruiting head

	HORSETAIL SHE-OAK		unbroken, base broad, hairless, grey-green; stalkless	
Type	evergreen tree			
Height	5–20m	**Stipules**	absent	
Habitat	well-drained, light soils			
Flowering	February–March		**FLOWERS AND FRUIT**	
Fruiting	September–October	**Flowers**	♂ and ♀ on same tree, minute, in heads at shoot-tip	
	TRUNK AND CROWN	♂	in dense spike 1–1.5cm long, brownish, each flower formed by 1 stamen	
Trunk	upright, forked above			
Bark	grey-brown, peels in long strips	**Stamens**	1 per ♂ flower	
Crown	conical or columnar; branches slender, angled upwards	♀	compact, reddish head, 3–4mm	
Twigs	very slender, wiry, ridged, drooping	**Stigmas**	2, on short style	
		Ovaries	1 per ♀ flower	
	LEAVES	**Fruit**	cone-like head, 1–1.5cm, cylindrical, of tiny, woody scales, fruit nut-like with short wing	
Buds	minute			
Leaves	in rings of 6–8 around twigs, scale-like, sharply pointed, edge	**Seeds**	1 per fruit, not released	

Caucasian Wing-nut *Pterocarya fraxinifolia*

An impressive tree with huge leaves composed of paired leaflets. Suckers at the base can grow into new trees, forming a dense, impenetrable clump if left untended. In fruit the tree is easily recognized, as it has long clusters of broadly winged nuts. *Status:* introduced from south-western Asia; grown mainly for ornament in Europe. *Similar trees:* Chinese Wing-nut differs in the hairy shoots and leaves with a flattened wing either side of the central stalk. The hybrid between these two species is also grown, distinguished by its intermediate leaves and great vigour.

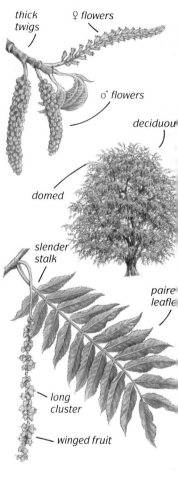

thick twigs

♀ flowers

♂ flowers

deciduous

domed

slender stalk

paired leaflet

long cluster

winged fruit

Chinese Wing-nut (*Pterocarya stenoptera*)

winged stalk

	CAUCASIAN WING-NUT		
Type	deciduous tree		turning bright yellow in autumn; central stalk rounded
Height	up to 35m	**Stipules**	absent
Habitat	woods, parks, often near water		
Flowering	April–May		**FLOWERS AND FRUIT**
Fruiting	September–October	**Flowers**	♂ and ♀ catkins on same tree, with leaves
	TRUNK AND CROWN	♂	on year-old twigs, 5–12cm, thick, hanging, many yellowish green flowers
Trunk	often clumped, with suckers		
Bark	grey-brown, fissured, ridged	**Stamens**	many
Crown	domed; branches spreading	♀	on new growth, 10–15cm, hanging, many greenish flowers
Twigs	stout, smooth		
	LEAVES	**Stigmas**	2 on single style, pink
Buds	stalked, slender, not scaly	**Ovaries**	1 per ♀ flower
Leaves	alternate along stem, up to 60cm, with 5–15 pairs of oblong, pointed, sharply toothed leaflets, often overlapping, leaflet at tip, glossy green above, paler below,	**Fruit**	nut with rounded or oblong wing *c*2cm wide, in cluster 25–50cm long
		Seeds	1 per nut, not released

A magnificent tree with a rugged grey trunk and large, scented leaves bearing paired leaflets. The large fruit is best known as a nut after the spongy outer wall has been removed. Immature fruits are also pickled whole. The timber is hard and beautifully marked, especially when cut from burrs. *Status:* native to south-eastern Europe; often planted for fruit, timber or ornament, and widely naturalized. *Similar trees:* Black Walnut is a North American species grown mainly for timber. It has many sharply toothed leaflets, and shortly hairy fruits containing a ridged, very hard nut.

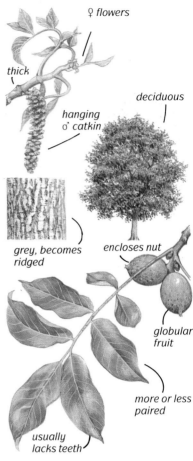

♀ *flowers*

thick

hanging ♂ catkin

deciduous

grey, becomes ridged

encloses nut

globular fruit

more or less paired

usually lacks teeth

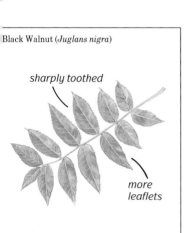

Black Walnut (*Juglans nigra*)

sharply toothed

more leaflets

	WALNUT		
Type	deciduous tree		elliptical leaflets, leaflet at tip, each leaflet 6–15cm, pointed, edge almost unbroken, downy when young, becoming hairless; stalked
Height	up to 30m		
Habitat	woodland, fields, parks		
Flowering	May–June		
Fruiting	September–October	**Stipules**	absent
	TRUNK AND CROWN		**FLOWERS AND FRUIT**
Trunk	stout, often short	**Flowers**	♂ and ♀ on same tree
Bark	grey, young smooth, becomes deeply fissured and ridged	♂	catkins on year-old twigs, 5–15cm, hanging, green
Crown	broad, domed; branches spreading, twisted	**Stamens**	♂ flowers with many
		♀	few flowers, on new growth
Twigs	stout, hairless, pith with separate cavities	**Stigmas**	2 on single style
		Ovaries	1 per ♀ flower
	LEAVES	**Fruit**	solitary or few, 4–5cm, globular, green, hairless, spongy wall around large, wrinkled nut
Buds	c6mm, broad, scaly, blackish		
Leaves	alternate along stem, mostly with 3–4 pairs of oval or	**Seeds**	1 per nut, not released

Bitternut *Carya cordiformis*

A tall, narrowly domed tree with leaves similar to the related Walnut, but the fruit differs in having a thin husk, which splits to release a bitter, inedible nut. In winter it has distinctive bright yellow buds. Bitternut and several related species are grown in North America and Europe for the very tough but flexible timber. *Status:* introduced from eastern North America; planted for ornament and timber. *Similar trees:* Pignut-tree has dark buds with more scales, fewer leaflets and a smoothly rounded fruit. Shagbark Hickory has very scaly bark, larger buds and large leaves with the end leaflet stalked.

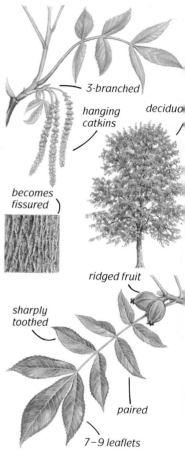

3-branched

hanging catkins

deciduo

becomes fissured

ridged fruit

sharply toothed

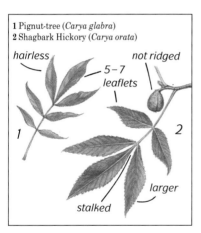

1 Pignut-tree (*Carya glabra*)
2 Shagbark Hickory (*Carya orata*)

hairless

not ridged

5–7 leaflets

1

2

larger

stalked

paired

7–9 leaflets

	BITTERNUT		
Type	deciduous tree		stalkless leaflet at tip, leaflets pointed, sharply toothed, downy below when young, becoming hairless, golden-yellow in autumn
Height	up to 30m		
Habitat	parks, gardens, plantations		
Flowering	May–June		
Fruiting	October	**Stipules**	absent

	TRUNK AND CROWN		FLOWERS AND FRUIT
Trunk	stout, usually straight	**Flowers**	♂ and ♀ on same tree
Bark	grey-brown, smooth becoming scaly and fissured	♂	3-branched catkins, 5–7.5cm, hanging, green
Crown	conical to narrowly domed; branches angled upwards	♀	2–3, tiny, on new growth
		Stamens	many
Twigs	rather slender, hairless	**Stigmas**	2 on single style
	LEAVES	**Ovaries**	1 per ♀ flower
Buds	bright yellow, slender, 4–6 scales	**Fruit**	2–4cm, almost globular, 4-ridged, shortly hairy, tough husk enclosing nut
Leaves	alternate along stem, 20–30cm, usually with 4 pairs of oval leaflets, each 5–15cm,	**Seeds**	1 per nut, not released

Commonly grown as an ornamental tree or for hedging in southern Europe, White Holly's tough leaves resist scorching by the Mediterranean sun, and its fragrant, white flowers scent the evening air. *Status:* introduced from south-eastern Australia; widely planted for ornament in the Mediterranean region and western Europe, sometimes naturalized. *Similar trees:* Karo has thick, blunt leaves and red flowers. Pittosporum has blackish stems, thin, glossy, crinkled leaves and purplish, honey-scented flowers. It is commonly used with cut flowers; variegated cultivars are also grown for ornament.

white
fragrant
glossy
unbroken edge
wavy
evergreen
globular, ripens orange

1 Karo (*Pittosporum crassifolium*)
2 Pittosporum (*Pittosporum tenuifolium*)

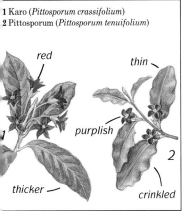

red
thin
purplish
2
thicker
crinkled

	WHITE HOLLY		
Type	evergreen tree or large shrub		pointed, edge unbroken, rather wavy, base wedge-shaped, hairless, dark, glossy green; stalk short
Height	up to 20m		
Habitat	parks, gardens, street tree		
Flowering	May–June	**Stipules**	absent
Fruiting	September		
	TRUNK AND CROWN		**FLOWERS AND FRUIT**
Trunk	usually short, forked	**Flowers**	♀, rather few in broad, branched heads, white, fragrant
Bark	grey-brown, smooth, becomes fissured	**Petals**	5, equal, oval, pointed; sepals 5, slender
Crown	pyramidal or domed; branches spreading	**Stamens**	5, yellow
Twigs	green, rather stout	**Stigmas**	1
	LEAVES	**Fruit**	almost globular capsule, 1–1.2cm, ripens orange, hairless, leathery wall splits into 2, releasing seeds
Buds	small, inconspicuous		
Leaves	alternate along stem, 7–20cm, oval or narrowly oval, sharply	**Seeds**	many, in sticky substance

Evergreen Magnolia   *Magnolia grandiflora*

A spectacular species with large, glossy leaves and huge flowers, the size of dinner plates. White flowers open a few at a time over a long period; later flowers are damaged by frosts and blotched brown. In cooler areas, it is most often grown against a wall. *Status:* introduced from south-eastern North America; commonly grown in western Europe for ornament. *Similar trees:* a taller tree, flowering in the spring before the leaves, Campbell's Magnolia has deep pink flowers that gradually fade. Hybrid Magnolia is shorter, with smaller flowers, which are white inside and tinged purplish outside.

glossy — leathery — white — edge unbroken — huge flowers — hairy — evergreen — shor — fleshy segments

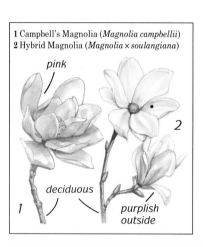

1 Campbell's Magnolia (*Magnolia campbellii*)
2 Hybrid Magnolia (*Magnolia × soulangiana*)

pink — deciduous — 1 — 2 — purplish outside

	EVERGREEN MAGNOLIA		
Type	evergreen tree or shrub		green above, thickly covered with reddish brown hairs below; stalk 2–2.5cm, stout
Height	to 10m (30m in North America)		
Habitat	parks, large gardens	**Stipules**	large, soon falling
Flowering	June–October		
Fruiting	September–November		**FLOWERS AND FRUIT**
	TRUNK AND CROWN	**Flowers**	♂, single at shoot tip, 20–25cm, bowl-shaped, creamy white, scented
Trunk	usually short, forked		
Bark	smooth, dark grey	**Petals**	almost equal, separate to base, thick; no distinct sepals
Crown	narrow; branches spread apart		
Twigs	stout, with reddish hairs	**Stamens**	many, arranged spirally
	LEAVES	**Stigmas**	1 per ovary
Buds	8–15mm, conical	**Ovaries**	many, in narrow cone
Leaves	alternate along stem, 8–16cm, elliptical or oval, broadest above middle, thick, leathery, edge unbroken, sometimes wavy, hairless, glossy deep	**Fruit**	4–6cm, conical, composed of separate fleshy segments,
		Seeds	each fruit-segment with large seed on slender thread

pectacular tree when fully grown,
h a massive, straight trunk leading
to a tall, narrow crown. Four-lobed
ves are quite unlike those of other
es, and curious, cup-shaped, green
l orange flowers bear a faint
emblance to tulips. Only two species
ulip-tree are known, one in North
erica and the other in Asia. *Status:*
roduced from eastern North
erica; widely planted for ornament
l timber. *Similar trees:* Chinese Tulip-
e has unfolding, coppery leaves with
nore deeply divided, narrowly lobed
de and a reddish stalk.

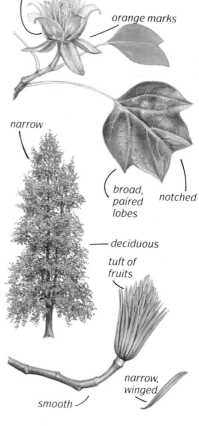

greenish

orange marks

narrow

broad, paired lobes

notched

deciduous

tuft of fruits

smooth

narrow, winged

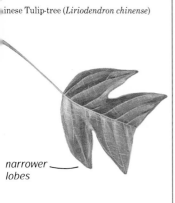

inese Tulip-tree (*Liriodendron chinense*)

narrower lobes

TULIP-TREE

Type	deciduous tree
Height	to 40m (60m in North America)
Habitat	parks, gardens, plantations
owering	June–July
Fruiting	September

TRUNK AND CROWN

Trunk	straight, oldest buttressed
Bark	grey, smooth, becoming ridged
Crown	narrow; most branches angled upwards, lower bent down
Twigs	smooth, green or reddish brown

LEAVES

Buds	5–12mm, oblong, flattened
Leaves	alternate along stem, 7–16cm, broad with 2 or 4 oval or triangular lobes, tip squarish or notched, hairless, glossy green above, paler below, turning yellow or orange in autumn; stalk 5–10cm
Stipules	large, oblong or elliptical, blunt, eventually falling

FLOWERS AND FRUIT

Flowers	♀, at stem-tip, cup-shaped, 6–8cm wide, whitish green, inner marked with orange
Perianth	6 petal-like parts, 4–5cm, equal, separate; 3 smaller, sepal-like parts fold back
Stamens	many, long, spirally arranged
Stigmas	1 per ovary
Ovaries	many in central spike
Fruit	tuft of brown fruits from each flower, each 4–5cm, narrow, flattened with long wing
Seeds	1 per fruit, not released

Sweet Bay *Laurus nobilis*

A small evergreen with tough, leathery leaves emitting a wonderful spicy aroma if lightly crushed. Dried leaves are widely used for flavouring food. Plants in towns are often trimmed to shape. *Status:* native to the Mediterranean region; widely cultivated for ornament, shelter, or as a herb; often naturalized. *Similar trees:* planted in the Mediterranean region, Avocado has larger leaves and elongated clusters of flowers, each of which have 6 lobes to the perianth. The large, edible fruit is pear-shaped and rough-skinned with soft, creamy-textured, yellowish flesh.

spicy aroma

compact head

♂ flowers

evergreen

♀ flowers

tough leaves

wavy edge

blackish berries

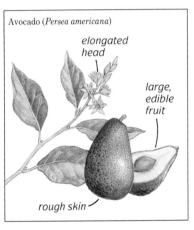

Avocado (*Persea americana*)

elongated head

large, edible fruit

rough skin

	SWEET BAY		
Type	evergreen tree or shrub		with glands, hairless, paler below; stalk 4–6mm, red
Height	2–20m	**Stipules**	absent
Habitat	woodland, scrub, parks		
Flowering	April–June		**FLOWERS AND FRUIT**
Fruiting	September–October	**Flowers**	♂ and ♀ on same tree
		♂	in short-stalked, compact head, each 7–10mm, dull whitish yellow
	TRUNK AND CROWN		
Trunk	usually short, forked	♀	2–6 in head, greenish white, with 2–4 sterile stamens
Bark	grey, smooth or fissured below		
Crown	broadly conical; branches angled upwards	**Perianth**	4-lobed, petal-like
		Stamens	8–12 per ♂ flower
Twigs	slender, hairless, green or reddish	**Stigmas**	1 on short style
		Ovaries	1 per ♀ flower
	LEAVES	**Fruit**	small cluster of almost globular berries, each 8–15mm, black, stalk 3–4mm
Buds	2–3mm, conical, reddish brown		
Leaves	5–10cm, narrowly oval or oblong, tough, pointed, edge wavy, dark green above, dotted	**Seeds**	1 per fruit

nost curious and distinctive feature
older trees of Phytolacca is that the
ea where the base of the trunk adjoins
e roots becomes greatly enlarged at
l level. It is as though the trunk had
elted and flowed across the ground. It
y spread for a metre or more from the
nk in each direction and is most
ticeable on a bank or where the soil
s been washed away. Phytolacca's
ccculent, berry-like fruits hang in long
usters. Related species occurring in
rope are all herbaceous plants, and
e sometimes used for their edible
ung leaves or berries. *Status:*
troduced from South America;
anted in the Mediterranean region for
nament and shade; naturalized in
aces. *Similar trees:* none.

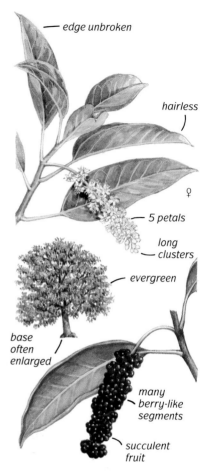

edge unbroken

hairless

♀

5 petals

long clusters

evergreen

base often enlarged

many berry-like segments

succulent fruit

	PHYTOLACCA	**Stipules**	absent
Type	evergreen tree		**FLOWERS AND FRUIT**
Height	3–8m	**Flowers**	♂ and ♀ on different trees, in hanging clusters, mostly at stem-tip
Habitat	towns, street tree		
Flowering	June–August		
Fruiting	September–October	♂	clusters 8–15cm, greenish white, stalk 1–1.5cm
	TRUNK AND CROWN	♀	slightly larger than ♂
Trunk	short, stout, enlarged base	**Perianth**	5 petal-like, oblong lobes
Bark	smooth, grey-brown	**Stamens**	many per ♂ flower
Crown	broadly domed; branches stout, spreading	**Stigmas**	1 per ovary
		Ovaries	7–10 per ♀ flower
Twigs	stout, rather succulent, hairless	**Fruit**	long clusters of fruits, each with globular berry-like segments, 5–7.5mm, purplish black
	LEAVES		
Buds	small, green	**Seeds**	each fruit segment with single seed
Leaves	alternate along stem, 5–12cm, oval or elliptical, pointed, edge unbroken, base wedge-shaped, bright green, hairless; stalked		

Quince *Cydonia oblonga*

deciduous

often thorny

pink

smooth above

woolly below

not toothed

fragrant

hard

Introduced in ancient times from Asia, the Quince is nowadays widespread in Europe. In northern and western regions it is most often planted as an ornamental shrub. In southerly areas it is grown for its edible fruits, which have a delightful fragrance and are extremely hard. *Status:* native to south-western and central Asia; cultivated and naturalized in much of Europe. *Similar trees:* two species with similar fruits are widely cultivated shrubs with toothed leaves and red flowers. Flowering Quince has larger flowers and leaves than Dwarf Quince.

1 Flowering Quince (*Chaenomeles speciosa*)
2 Dwarf Quince (*Chaenomeles japonica*)

1

toothed

small

2

red or orange

	QUINCE
Type	deciduous tree or shrub
Height	1.5–7.5m
Habitat	hedges and copses
Flowering	April–May
Fruiting	September

TRUNK AND CROWN

Trunk	slender, usually short
Bark	grey-brown, smooth
Crown	often very broad, spreading
Twigs	woolly, becoming smooth, spiny

LEAVES

Buds	2–3mm, reddish-brown, hairy
Leaves	alternate, 5–10cm, oval, blunt, green and smooth above, greyish and woolly below; stalkless

Stipules	small, usually falling very early

FLOWERS AND FRUIT

Flowers	♂, single in angles of leaves, 3.8–5cm, bowl-shaped, pink, rarely white
Petals	5, broad, blunt or slightly notched at the tip, tapered at base; sepals 5, smaller, very hairy, persistent on fruit, toothed
Stamens	15–25
Stigmas	5, styles woolly towards base
Ovaries	1, in base of flower
Fruit	fleshy but extremely hard, 2.5–3.5cm, rarely 12cm, globular or pear-shaped, ripening yellow, very fragrant
Seeds	many, brown to blackish

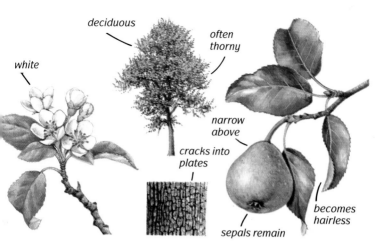

white

deciduous

often thorny

narrow above

cracks into plates

becomes hairless

sepals remain

is widespread tree is a hybrid of
…mplex and obscure origin. Wild trees
…ve small, sour fruit; orchard trees,
…ich produce the familiar large, sweet-
…ting fruit, belong to var. *culta*. The
…es often seen in hedgerows or on field
…rgins may be escapes from
…tivation, but sometimes represent
…e remains of old orchards. *Status:*
…tivated throughout Europe, except
… the far north and far south, often on
…arge scale. *Similar trees:* Plymouth
…ar is native to Atlantic Europe. It has
…oad leaves and small, speckled fruits,
…ich ripen red and lack sepals.

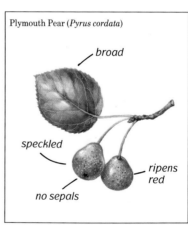

Plymouth Pear (*Pyrus cordata*)

broad

speckled

no sepals

ripens red

	COMMON PEAR		Leaves	alternate, 5–8cm, oval to elliptical, pointed, base rounded, finely short-toothed, hairy, becoming smooth; stalkless
Type	deciduous tree			
Height	up to 20m			
Habitat	orchards, hedges, often as isolated trees		**Stipules**	soon falling
owering	April–May			**FLOWERS AND FRUIT**
Fruiting	September–October		**Flowers**	♂, 5–9 in clusters with leaves, white, stalks up to 1cm
	TRUNK AND CROWN		**Petals**	5, 12–14mm, broadly oval, tapering abruptly at base; sepals 5, 6–8mm, narrow, persistent on fruit
Trunk	straight, often suckering			
Bark	blackish, cracking into small plates		**Stamens**	20–30, red
Crown	broadly pyramidal; branches angled upwards on young trees, spreading on old trees		**Stigmas**	5, free, often hairy at base
			Ovaries	1, in base of flower
Twigs	stout, reddish brown, soon smooth and shiny, often spiny		**Fruit**	fleshy, firm, gritty-textured, 6–16cm, pear-shaped, oblong or almost globular, ripening green or yellowish
	LEAVES			
Buds	5mm, yellowish brown, smooth, egg-shaped, pointed		**Seeds**	several, black

Wild Pear *Pyrus pyraster*

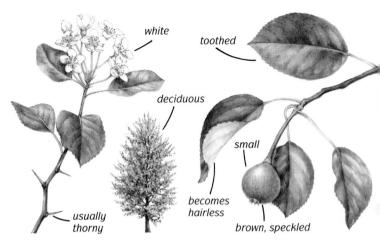

white

toothed

deciduous

small

becomes
hairless

usually
thorny

brown, speckled

Often confused with Common Pear,
Wild Pear can be distinguished by its
more bushy and spiny growth, and by
the much smaller, hard and tart fruit.
Status: native throughout much
of Europe, absent from some
Mediterranean islands and parts of the
far north. *Similar trees:* two species
with narrower leaves are Sage-leaved
Pear, from central Europe; and Almond-
leaved Pear, from France and Spain
eastwards. The former has leaves with
unbroken edges, and larger fruits. The
latter usually has a few teeth towards
the leaf-tip.

1 Sage-leaved Pear (*Pyrus salvifolia*)
2 Almond-leaved Pear (*Pyrus amygdaliformis*)

no teeth

grey-woolly

1

narrower

larger

few teeth

WILD PEAR	
Type	deciduous tree
Height	8–20m
Habitat	thickets, open woodland
Flowering	April–May
Fruiting	September–October
TRUNK AND CROWN	
Trunk	straight, short
Bark	rough, cracked
Crown	round-headed; branches spreading or angled upwards
Twigs	grey to brown, usually spiny
LEAVES	
Buds	small, brown, scales 5–8
Leaves	alternate, 2.5–7cm, elliptical, oval or circular, pointed, base wedge-shaped, rounded or heart-shaped, finely toothed, hairy but soon smooth; stalkless

Stipules	soon falling
FLOWERS AND FRUIT	
Flowers	♀, in clusters, white
Petals	5, 10–17mm, elliptical to circular, slightly crinkled, tapered at base; sepals 5, 3–8mm, persistent on fruit
Stamens	20–30, red
Stigmas	5, styles often hairy at base
Ovaries	1, 5-chambered, in base of flower
Fruit	1–3.5cm, fleshy, firm, gritty-textured, globular or top-shaped, ripening yellow, brown or black, with conspicuous lenticels
Seeds	several, black

silvery

deciduous

not toothed

becomes green

often weeping

hard, sour

white, clustered

ripens brown

slender, elegant shape and silvery
[lea]ves make Willow-leaved Pear an
[att]ractive tree of parks and gardens; the
[w]eeping cultivar 'Pendula' is common.
[Th]e small fruits do not always develop
[ful]ly, and are unsuitable for eating.
[Sta]tus: native to Asia from the
[Cau]casus mountains and Iran to
[Sib]eria; widely cultivated in Europe.
[Si]milar trees: two species have broader
[lea]ves, toothed towards the tip.
[P.] elaeagrifolia, from south-eastern
[Eu]rope, has woolly leaves and styles
[th]at are hairy up to the middle.
[P.] nivalis has leaves that become
[ha]irless above, and larger fruits.

1 *Pyrus elaeagrifolia*
2 *Pyrus nivalis*

woolly

spiny

broader

larger

toothed

1

2

	WILLOW-LEAVED PEAR		
Type	deciduous tree		smooth and glossy green above; stalkless
Height	up to 10m	**Stipules**	soon falling
Habitat	deciduous woods		
Flowering	April		**FLOWERS AND FRUIT**
Fruiting	October	**Flowers**	♂, in tight clusters, white, opening with the emerging leaves, stalks downy
	TRUNK AND CROWN	**Petals**	5, *c*10mm, rounded or notched at tip, tapering at base; sepals 5, woolly, persistent on fruit
Trunk	slender, straight		
Bark	dark silver-grey, smooth		
Crown	domed; main branches horizontal	**Stamens**	15–30, red
Twigs	drooping, densely white-woolly	**Stigmas**	2–5, styles woolly at base
		Ovaries	1, in base of flower
	LEAVES	**Fruit**	2.5cm, fleshy, firm, gritty-textured, sour, pear-shaped, top-shaped or cylindrical, ripening brown, stalk white, woolly
Buds	4–6mm, pyramidal, brown, downy		
Leaves	alternate, 3.5–9cm, narrow, pointed, grey-green and silvery downy on both sides, becoming		
		Seeds	several

Crab-apple *Malus sylvestris*

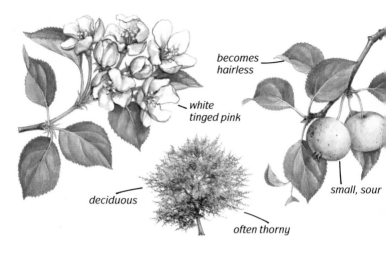

becomes hairless

white tinged pink

deciduous

often thorny

small, sour

The sour-fruited Crab-apple was once cultivated for fruit. Truly wild trees are spiny and have white flowers. Descendants of domesticated trees which have escaped back into the wild are unarmed and have pink-tinged flowers. *Status:* native to most of Europe and western Asia. *Similar trees: Malus dasyphylla* has woolly young twigs and occurs in the Balkan Peninsula and Danube basin. Cultivated Apple is a hybrid with leaves that are hairy below, and large, sweet fruit. It is the most widely grown orchard fruit, with more than one thousand cultivars recorded.

1 *Malus dasyphylla*
2 Cultivated Apple (*Malus domestica*)

woolly when young

large fruit

hairy below

	CRAB-APPLE	
Type	deciduous tree	
Height	2–10m	
Habitat	woods, hedges, in hilly, chalky areas	
Flowering	April–June	
Fruiting	September–October	
	TRUNK AND CROWN	
Trunk	short, often branching low down	
Bark	brown, cracking	
Crown	spreading, often dense; branches large and twisted	
Twigs	reddish brown, numerous short shoots, sometimes thorny	
	LEAVES	
Buds	4mm, reddish, hairy	
Leaves	alternate, 3–11cm, oval, elliptical or nearly circular, pointed, wedge-shaped or rounded at base, finely toothed, hairy but soon becoming smooth; stalkless	
Stipules	soon falling	
	FLOWERS AND FRUIT	
Flowers	☿, in few-flowered clusters, 3–4cm, white tinged pale pink	
Petals	5, oval, widest above middle, tapered at base; sepals 5, 3–7mm, hairy on inside, persistent on fruit	
Stamens	15–50, yellow	
Stigmas	2–5, styles joined and sometimes hairy at base	
Ovaries	1, in base of flower	
Fruit	fleshy, firm, 2.5–3cm, globular, ripening yellowish green tinged with red, sour	
Seeds	several, brown to blackish	

Malus × floribunda **Japanese Crab-apple**

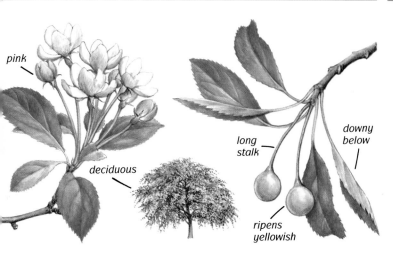

pink

deciduous

long stalk

downy below

ripens yellowish

Wreathing the branches in spring, the pink and white flowers of this small tree are produced in great profusion. One of the most popular ornamental species of all time, it probably arose as a garden hybrid in Japan, from where it was introduced to many countries. *Status: exact origin unknown but probably Japan; widely planted in Europe for ornament. Similar trees:* two widely grown ornamentals from China are Siberian Crab-apple, with white flowers and red fruits; and Purple Crab-apple, a garden hybrid with purplish flowers and fruits.

1 Siberian Crab-apple (*Malus baccata*)
2 Purple Crab-apple (*Malus × purpurea*)

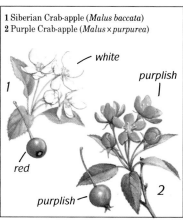

white

purplish

red

purplish

	JAPANESE CRAB-APPLE		beneath but becoming smooth; stalkless
Type	deciduous tree		
Height	6–9m	**Stipules**	small, soon falling
Habitat	parks and gardens		**FLOWERS AND FRUIT**
Flowering	April–May	**Flowers**	♀, 4–7 in clusters, 2.5–3cm across, deep pink in bud, opening pale pink, fading white, fragrant
Fruiting	October		
	TRUNK AND CROWN		
Trunk	short, straight, tapering		
Bark	grey-brown	**Petals**	5, 13–15mm, oblong, blunt, base abruptly tapered; sepals 5, short, triangular, hairy within, soon falling
Crown	rounded, dense; branches numerous		
Twigs	reddish when young, drooping, hairy		
		Stamens	15–50, yellow, pink at base
	LEAVES	**Stigmas**	2–5, styles joined at base
Buds	2–4mm, dark red-brown, pointed	**Ovaries**	1, in base of flower
		Fruit	fleshy, firm, 2.5cm, globular, ripening bright yellow
Leaves	alternate, 4–8cm, oblong to oval, pointed, sharply toothed, sometimes lobed, downy	**Seeds**	several, brown

Rowan *Sorbus aucuparia*

A small, attractive tree, with paired leaflets, broad heads of white flowers followed by red berries and, in colder areas, autumn colour. Berries are eagerly sought by fruit-eating birds and, rich in Vitamin C, the fruit can be made into a jelly. Cv. 'Beissneri' is planted for its orange-pink bark and more intense autumn colour. *Status:* native; common in much of Europe; planted for ornament in streets and parks. *Similar trees:* Hupeh Rowan is a Chinese ornamental species differing in the white or purplish fruits. Native in southern Europe and planted elsewhere, Service-tree is a larger tree with much larger, brownish green fruits.

white

broad heads

paired leaflets

smooth bark

deciduous

1 Hupeh Rowan (*Sorbus hupehensis*)
2 Service-tree (*Sorbus domestica*)

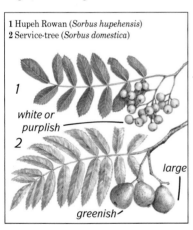

1

white or purplish

2

greenish

large

autumn colour

red

	ROWAN		Leaves	on alternate sides of stem, up to 25 × 12cm; 5–9 pairs of oblong leaflets 3–6cm long, pointed, sharp-toothed, hairy, becoming smooth, dark green above, paler below, turning yellow or red in autumn; stalk 2–4mm
Type	deciduous tree			
Height	up to 20m			
Habitat	mountainous areas, lowland on light soils			
Flowering	May – June		Stipules	small, soon falling
Fruiting	August–September			
	TRUNK AND CROWN			**FLOWERS AND FRUIT**
Trunk	slender, sometimes forked		Flowers	♀, many, in branched heads, 8–10mm, creamy white
Bark	smooth, rarely slightly ridged, greyish brown		Petals	5, *c*3.5mm, equal; sepals 5, triangular, hairy
Crown	irregularly rounded, open		Stamens	many
Branches	angled upwards		Stigmas	3–4
Twigs	hairy becoming smooth, purplish brown		Ovaries	3–4, in base of flower
	LEAVES		Fruit	many, in broad head, berry-like, almost globular, each 6–9mm, ripening bright red
Buds	10–17mm long, narrow, egg-shaped, tip curved, purplish, hairy		Seeds	several, not released

Sorbus torminalis **Wild Service-tree**

An unusual relative of the Rowan and Whitebeam, with distinctive, maple-like leaves and brown, speckled fruits resembling those of the Service-tree. Also like some maples, the foliage turns deep red in the autumn. Acid until late in ripening, the fruit eventually becomes sweet enough to eat. *Status:* native to most of Europe except parts of the north; occasionally planted for ornament. *Similar trees:* two related plants are often regarded as hybrids. Broad-leaved Whitebeam has slightly lobed leaves with grey hairs beneath. Bastard Service-tree, from Scandinavia, has a few pairs of leaflets at the leaf-base and red fruit.

1 Broad-leaved Whitebeam (*Sorbus latifolia*)
2 Bastard Service-tree (*Sorbus hybrida*)

branched head

white

triangular lobes

bark fissured

deciduous

purplish in autumn

brown fruit

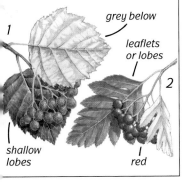

1

grey below

leaflets or lobes

2

shallow lobes

red

	WILD SERVICE-TREE
Type	deciduous tree
Height	up to 25m
Habitat	woods, often lime-rich soils
Flowering	May–June
Fruiting	September

	TRUNK AND CROWN
Trunk	slender, sometimes forked
Bark	shallowly fissured, forming squarish scales, dark, greyish brown
Crown	conical to broadly rounded
Branches	spreading
Twigs	woolly, soon becoming smooth, dark brown

	LEAVES
Buds	4–5mm, globular, green, smooth
Leaves	on alternate sides of stem, 5–9cm, oval with 3–5 pairs of triangular lobes, pointed, sharply toothed, base rounded or heart-shaped, green above and below, turning purplish red in autumn, hairy below, becoming smooth, 4–6 pairs of veins; stalk 15–40mm
Stipules	small, soon falling

	FLOWERS AND FRUIT
Flowers	☿, in loose, branched heads, 10–15mm, white; stalk hairy
Petals	5, equal, rounded; sepals 5, triangular, hairy
Stamens	many
Stigmas	2
Ovaries	2, in base of flower
Fruit	berry-like, egg-shaped to globular, each 12–18mm, brown, speckled
Seeds	several, not released

Common Whitebeam *Sorbus aria*

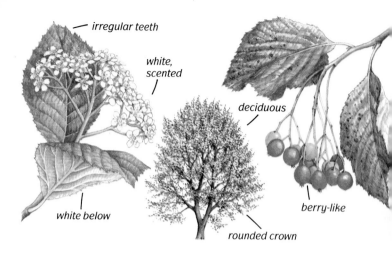

irregular teeth

white, scented

deciduous

white below

rounded crown

berry-like

Silvery white as they unfold in spring, the leaves of this tree gradually turn green on the upper surface as their pale hairs are shed; the lower leaf surface remains densely hairy. It is a characteristic tree of chalk downland. *Status:* native to most of Europe; several cultivars are commonly planted street trees. *Similar trees:* two rather shrubby species have more or less globular fruits. Greek Whitebeam has leathery leaves, which are greenish-woolly below and have rounded teeth; fruits have white spots. Rock Whitebeam has leaves with symmetrical teeth and fruits with many spots.

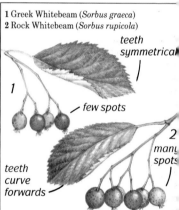

1 Greek Whitebeam (*Sorbus graeca*)
2 Rock Whitebeam (*Sorbus rupicola*)

teeth symmetrical

few spots

teeth curve forwards

many spots

COMMON WHITEBEAM

Type	deciduous tree
Height	up to 15m
Habitat	chalky soils
Flowering	May–June
Fruiting	September

TRUNK AND CROWN

Trunk	well-defined
Bark	grey, smooth, becoming flaky and fissured
Crown	conical in young trees, later broadly domed; branches angled upwards
Twigs	olive brown, hairy, becoming smooth

LEAVES

Buds	green, egg-shaped, often hairy
Leaves	alternate, 8cm, variable in shape but usually broadly oval, edges sharply toothed and sometimes shallowly lobed, densely silvery-hairy, the upper surface eventually becoming smooth and green; stalkless
Stipules	small, soon falling

FLOWERS AND FRUIT

Flowers	☿, many in loose, branched clusters at tips of shoots, each 1.5cm across, white
Petals	5, *c*6mm, equal; sepals 5, triangular, hairy
Stamens	many, cream or pink
Stigmas	2
Ovaries	2, in base of flower, hairy
Fruit	berry-like, 8mm, usually longer than broad, ripening scarlet with many small lenticels
Seeds	2

Sorbus intermedia Swedish Whitebeam

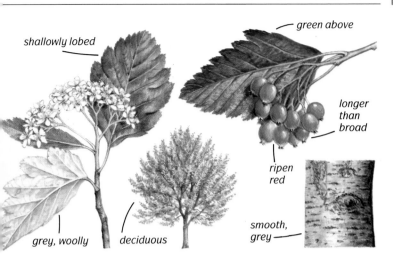

shallowly lobed

green above

longer than broad

ripen red

grey, woolly

deciduous

smooth, grey

Shallow-lobed leaves felted below with yellowish grey hairs identify Swedish Whitebeam. Red fruits are dotted with a few pale lenticels. It flowers more intensively than most other whitebeams, and is often used as an ornamental tree. *Status:* native to the Baltic region; planted elsewhere; sometimes naturalized. *Similar trees:* *S. austriaca* has leaves with whitish grey wool below. Those of *S. mougeotii* are also grey-woolly below but less deeply lobed. Both are mountain species. *S. umbellata*, from the Balkan region, has deeply lobed, white-woolly leaves and yellow fruits.

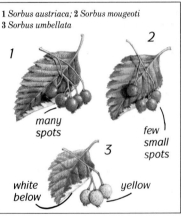

1 *Sorbus austriaca;* 2 *Sorbus mougeoti* 3 *Sorbus umbellata*

many spots

few small spots

white below

yellow

	SWEDISH WHITEBEAM
Type	deciduous tree
Height	up to 15m
Habitat	hills and mountains
Flowering	May
Fruiting	September

	TRUNK AND CROWN
Trunk	short
Bark	grey, smooth with wide, shallow cracks
Crown	dense, broadly domed
Twigs	grey to purplish, very hairy, becoming smooth

	LEAVES
Buds	8mm, egg-shaped, green or brown, with grey hairs
Leaves	alternate, 8–12cm, elliptic, shallowly lobed, the lobes reaching one-third of the way to midrib but more pronounced towards base of leaf, edge sharply toothed, smooth and green above, densely yellow-grey woolly below; stalkless
Stipules	small, soon falling

	FLOWERS AND FRUIT
Flowers	☿, many, in branched clusters in angles of leaves, each 12–20mm across, white, leaf stalk smooth
Petals	5, *c*6mm, equal; sepals 5, narrowly triangular
Stamens	many, cream
Stigmas	2, styles joined at base
Ovaries	2, in base of flower, hairy
Fruit	berry-like, 12–15mm, much longer than broad, ripening red, dotted with few small lenticels
Seeds	2

Loquat *Eriobotrya japonica*

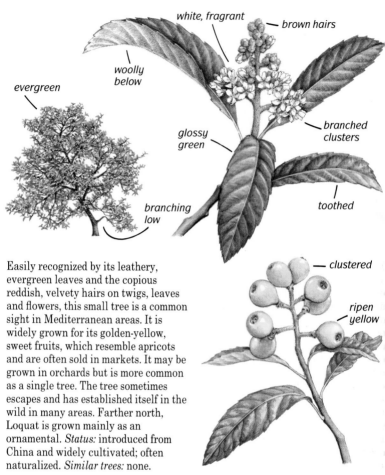

white, fragrant — **brown hairs**

woolly below

evergreen

glossy green

branched clusters

branching low

toothed

clustered

ripen yellow

Easily recognized by its leathery, evergreen leaves and the copious reddish, velvety hairs on twigs, leaves and flowers, this small tree is a common sight in Mediterranean areas. It is widely grown for its golden-yellow, sweet fruits, which resemble apricots and are often sold in markets. It may be grown in orchards but is more common as a single tree. The tree sometimes escapes and has established itself in the wild in many areas. Farther north, Loquat is grown mainly as an ornamental. *Status:* introduced from China and widely cultivated; often naturalized. *Similar trees:* none.

	LOQUAT	
Type	evergreen tree	
Height	up to 10m	
Habitat	dry, light soils	
Flowering	October–February	
Fruiting	April–June	
	TRUNK AND CROWN	
Trunk	very slender, often branching near base	
Bark	grey, slightly rough	
Crown	irregular but usually narrow	
Twigs	velvety-hairy	
	LEAVES	
Buds	c4mm, pointed, very hairy	
Leaves	alternate, 12–25cm, elliptical or oval and widest above middle, sharply toothed, leathery, conspicuously veined, dark glossy green above, densely woolly with reddish brown hairs below; stalkless	
Stipules	very narrow	
	FLOWERS AND FRUIT	
Flowers	☿, in branched, pyramidal clusters, c1cm, creamy-white, almost hidden by dense brown hair, fragrant	
Petals	5, oval or nearly circular, tip notched, base tapered; sepals 5, persisting on fruit	
Stamens	20	
Stigmas	2–5, styles joined at base	
Ovaries	1, in base of flower	
Fruit	fleshy, sweet, 3–6cm, elliptical to pear-shaped, ripening deep yellow	
Seeds	1–several, each 1–1.5cm	

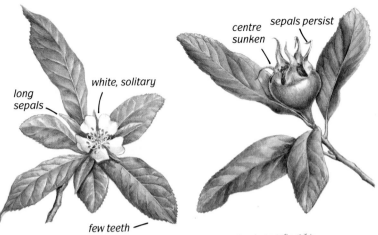

long sepals

white, solitary

few teeth

centre sunken

sepals persist

deciduous

often short

cracks into plates

Dull and rather dowdy for much of the year, the Medlar is often a shrub, at best making only a small tree. The large, solitary flowers have sepals that are longer than the white petals and are followed by distinctive fruits, most nearly resembling huge, brown rose-hips, with the narrow persistent sepals forming a crown. The fruits are edible, but only after they are 'bletted' – softened by overripening or being frosted. *Status:* native to south-eastern Europe but often cultivated as a fruit tree and naturalized in many central and western parts as far north as southern Britain. *Similar trees:* none.

	MEDLAR	
Type	deciduous tree or shrub	
Height	up to 6m	
Habitat	hedgerows, woods	
Flowering	May–June	
Fruiting	October–November	

TRUNK AND CROWN

Trunk	slender, often short
Bark	grey-brown, cracking into oblong plates
Crown	spreading, dense and tangled
Twigs	densely white-hairy, becoming smooth and black

LEAVES

Buds	1–2mm, brown, hairy
Leaves	alternate, 5–15cm, crinkled, narrowly oval, widest above or below the middle, tip broadly pointed, base wedge-shaped, edges with tiny teeth near tip, dull yellowish-green above, dense white hairs below; stalk *c*2mm
Stipules	falling early

FLOWERS AND FRUIT

Flowers	♀, single, in angle of leaf stalks, 3–6cm, white
Petals	5, 12mm; sepals 5, 1–1.6cm, narrowly triangular, persistent on fruit
Stamens	30–40, red
Stigmas	5, each on a long style
Ovaries	1, in base of flower
Fruit	fleshy but hard, roughly globular, ripening brown and remaining on tree
Seeds	10

Juneberry *Amelanchier lamackii*

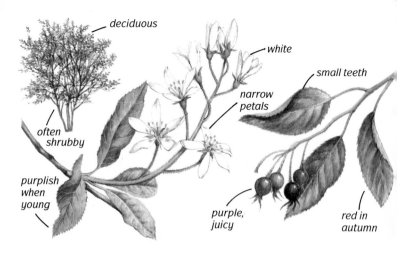

deciduous

white

often shrubby

narrow petals

small teeth

purplish when young

purple, juicy

red in autumn

The contrast of white blossom against coppery young leaves makes this tree a striking sight in spring; leaves also produce rich autumn colours. Of uncertain origin and perhaps a hybrid, it has been established in the wild in Britain for over one hundred years. *Status:* possibly native to eastern North America; introduced and naturalized in northern Europe; often planted for ornament. *Similar trees:* the only European native is the less showy Snowy Mespil. It has more coarsely toothed leaves, whitish woolly below, and blackish fruit.

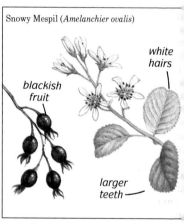

Snowy Mespil (*Amelanchier ovalis*)

white hairs

blackish fruit

larger teeth

	JUNEBERRY
Type	deciduous tree or shrub
Height	up to 10m
Habitat	woods and scrub on acid soil
Flowering	April–May
Fruiting	September–October

	TRUNK AND CROWN
Trunk	slender, short, often several
Bark	pale grey-brown
Crown	open and spreading
Twigs	shaggy white-hairy, becoming smooth

	LEAVES
Buds	7–11mm, reddish, narrow, pointed
Leaves	alternate, oval-oblong to elliptical, shortly pointed, base rounded to heart-shaped, edges curled upwards, young leaves coppery red, silky beneath, turning green, rich yellow and red in autumn; stalk hairy, becoming smooth
Stipules	small, soon falling

	FLOWERS AND FRUIT
Flowers	☿, 6–12 in loose, often drooping clusters with the leaves, white, flower-tube bell-shaped, stalks 1.5–2.5cm, hairy
Petals	5, 9–14mm, narrow, widest above middle, blunt; sepals 5, 3–5mm, hairy within, persistent on fruit
Stamens	about 20
Stigmas	5, on a single style
Ovaries	1, in base of flower
Fruit	berry-like, ripening purple-black, sweet-tasting
Seeds	4–10

Himalayan Tree-cotoneaster

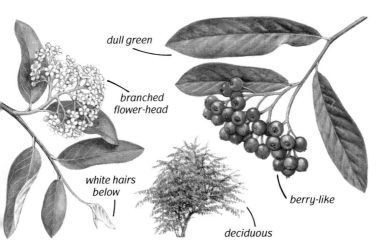

dull green

branched
flower-head

white hairs
below

berry-like

deciduous

One of the few cotoneasters to form a tree, this species is deciduous. The berries remain on the tree through the winter, showing conspicuously against the bare boughs. It is widely planted as an ornamental and has become naturalized in hedgerows and woods. *Status:* native to the Himalayas; widely cultivated; occasionally naturalized in various parts of Europe. *Similar trees:* Waterer's Cotoneaster forms a large, evergreen shrub or small tree with narrow leaves. It produces larger clusters of red or orange fruits. *C. bullatus* reaches tree size and has broader, corrugated leaves.

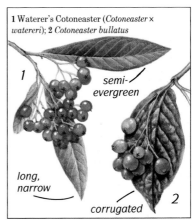

1 Waterer's Cotoneaster (*Cotoneaster ×
watereri*); **2** *Cotoneaster bullatus*

semi-
evergreen

long,
narrow

corrugated

2

	HIMALAYAN TREE-COTONEASTER
Type	deciduous tree
Height	20m
Habitat	parks, gardens, hedges, woods
Flowering	June
Fruiting	September–October
	TRUNK AND CROWN
Trunk	short, slender, often several
Bark	grey-brown, smooth
Crown	broad, domed; branches arching
Twigs	greenish, ridged
	LEAVES
Buds	small, lacking scales, hairy
Leaves	alternate, 6–16cm, elliptical to oval and widest above the middle, bluntly pointed, base wedge-shaped, dark green above, densely white hairy below; stalkless
Stipules	falling early
	FLOWERS AND FRUIT
Flowers	☿, 20–40 in flat, branched clusters, white, fragrant
Petals	5, broadly oval, widest above middle, blunt, tapering at base; sepals 5, persistent on fruit
Stamens	20
Stigmas	2, on free styles
Ovaries	1, 2-chambered, in base of flower
Fruit	berry-like, 5mm, globular, ripening bright red, remaining on tree through winter
Seeds	2, stony

Common Hawthorn · *Crataegus monogyna*

small, deciduous

dark red

scented

thorny

white

rough, scaly

deep lobes

When left to grow undisturbed, Common Hawthorn forms a densely-crowned tree. However, if cut or trimmed regularly, it soon makes a dense thorny barrier ideal for enclosing fields and fencing in animals. It is very variable in leaf shape and lobing, and in fruit colour. *Status:* native throughout Europe and much of Asia, widely used for hedging. *Similar trees:* Midland Hawthorn and *C. calycina*, both native to woodlands in northwestern and central Europe, have finely toothed leaf-lobes and stipules. Midland Hawthorn also has two stigmas and two seeds per fruit.

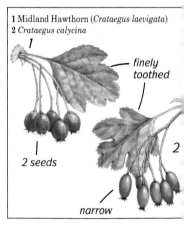

1 Midland Hawthorn (*Crataegus laevigata*)
2 *Crataegus calycina*

finely toothed

2 seeds

narrow

	COMMON HAWTHORN	
Type	deciduous tree or shrub	
Height	18m but often less	
Habitat	woods, hedges, especially on chalky soils	
Flowering	May–June	
Fruiting	September–October	

TRUNK AND CROWN

Trunk	fluted, often branching near base
Bark	silvery grey, cracking to show orange or pink beneath
Crown	variable, usually dense
Twigs	brown, thorns up to 15mm

LEAVES

Buds	2mm, rounded
Leaves	alternate, 1.5–4.5cm, oval to diamond-shaped in outline, 3–5 deep lobes, toothed near tips, leathery, dark, shiny green above, paler and dull below; stalk dark pink, grooved
Stipules	small, curved, sometimes toothed

FLOWERS AND FRUIT

Flowers	♂, 9–18, in loose, branched clusters, 8–15mm, white, rarely pink, sickly sweet-scented, stalks woolly
Petals	5, 4–6mm, oval, widest above the middle; sepals 5, triangular, persistent on fruit
Stamens	typically 20, pink or purple
Stigmas	1, on a short style
Ovaries	1, sunk into base of fruit
Fruit	berry-like, 7–14mm, globose or egg-shaped, ripening scarlet to maroon
Seeds	1, rarely 2, stony

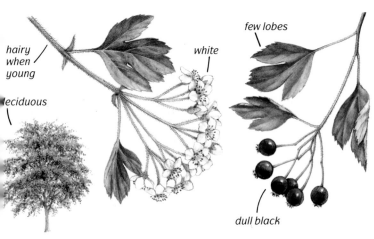

hairy when young

deciduous

white

few lobes

dull black

The most common of several eastern hawthorns with black fruits, this species is distinguished by the cobwebby hairs on the undersides of the young leaves and by the flowers, which have four or five stigmas. As the name suggests, the fruits commonly have five seeds. *Status:* native to east-central Europe, south to the northern Balkan peninsula and east to Russia. *Similar trees:* Hungarian Hawthorn occurs in woodlands in the Danube basin. It has leaves that are woolly on both sides, with up to 11 lobes, few flowers and tiny fruits.

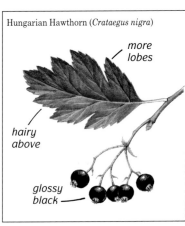

Hungarian Hawthorn (*Crataegus nigra*)

more lobes

hairy above

glossy black

	FIVE-SEEDED HAWTHORN
Type	deciduous tree or shrub
Height	up to 8m
Habitat	woodland margins
Flowering	May–June
Fruiting	August

TRUNK AND CROWN

Trunk	short, straight
Bark	pale brown
Crown	irregularly domed; upper branches arching
Twigs	with sparse, long hairs, soon smooth, grey-brown, occasional stout spines 10mm

LEAVES

Buds	2mm, brown, globular
Leaves	alternating, 2–5cm, oval in outline, leathery, dark olive-green and smooth above, paler below with cobweb-like hairs which eventually disappear, 3–7 deep lobes, the lowest spreading, toothed; stalk 1.5–3cm, hairy
Stipules	narrow, curved, toothed

FLOWERS AND FRUIT

Flowers	☿, many in loose clusters, 12–15mm, white, stalks downy
Petals	5, oval, widest above middle; sepals 5, tiny, triangular, soon falling
Stamens	20
Stigmas	4–5, styles free
Ovaries	1, in base of flower, downy
Fruit	berry-like, 10–15mm, elliptical to globular, ripening dull black or dark purplish black
Seeds	4–5, stony

Azarole *Crataegus azarolus*

Azarole owes its present fairly widespread distribution to its edible fruits, which taste somewhat of apple. They are sufficiently large and fleshy to be worth gathering, and the tree was taken from its eastern Mediterranean home to other areas, notably France and Italy, as a fruit tree. *Status:* native to Crete; cultivated and naturalized in southern Europe. *Similar trees:* Oriental Hawthorn, from the Balkan Peninsula and parts of eastern Europe, has leaf-lobes with few teeth, compact flower clusters, four or five stigmas and globular fruits.

deciduous

most not toothed

few thorns

deeply cut

felted

large red berries

Oriental Hawthorn (*Crataegus laciniata*)

hairy above

smaller

narrow, toothed

	AZAROLE	
Type	deciduous tree or shrub	
Height	up to 8m	
Habitat	humid scrubland	
Flowering	March – April	
Fruiting	June – September	

TRUNK AND CROWN

Trunk	short, slender	
Bark	pale grey-brown	
Crown	rounded, bushy; branches spreading	
Twigs	downy, becoming smooth; few, stout spines up to 10mm	

LEAVES

Buds	3–4mm, rounded, red-brown
Leaves	alternate, 3–5cm, oval to triangular in outline, base wedge-shaped and extending onto stalk, 3–5 deep lobes, sometimes with a few teeth, downy on both sides; stalk 3–8mm
Stipules	curved, coarsely toothed

FLOWERS AND FRUIT

Flowers	☿, 3–18 in compact clusters, 12–18mm, white, stalks woolly
Petals	5, oval, widest above middle; sepals 5, short-pointed, persistent on fruit
Stamens	15–20
Stigmas	1–2, rarely 3, styles thick
Ovaries	1, in base of fruit
Fruit	berry-like, 20–25mm, roughly globular with longitudinal, rounded ridges, ripening yellow or orange-red
Seeds	1–3, stony

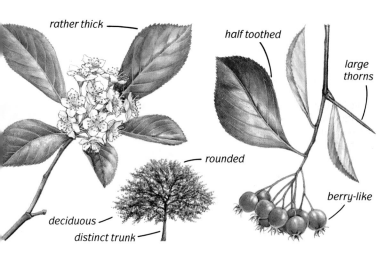

rather thick

half toothed

large thorns

rounded

berry-like

deciduous

distinct trunk

Ferociously armed with numerous long thorns, Cockspur Hawthorn is found wild in North America. In Europe, its popularity as an ornamental tree derives from the unusual rich, bright range of the autumn foliage. *Status:* native to north-eastern North America; planted in Europe for ornament and as a street tree. *Similar trees:* two hybrids between Cockspur Hawthorn and other American species are grown. Broad-leaved Cockspur Hawthorn has shorter spines, hairy flower clusters and broad leaves. Hybrid Cockspur Hawthorn has downy twigs and flower clusters, and narrow leaves.

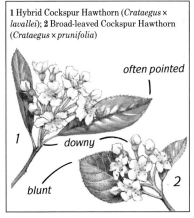

1 Hybrid Cockspur Hawthorn (*Crataegus × lavallei*); **2** Broad-leaved Cockspur Hawthorn (*Crataegus × prunifolia*)

often pointed

downy

blunt

COCKSPUR HAWTHORN

Type	deciduous tree
Height	10m
Habitat	meadows, woodland margins
Flowering	May
Fruiting	October

TRUNK AND CROWN

Trunk	slender, unbranched
Bark	grey to brown, smooth, becoming finely fissured
Crown	flat-topped, spreading
Twigs	purplish brown, smooth; numerous spines 7–10mm

LEAVES

Buds	small, rounded
Leaves	alternate, 5–8cm, oval, widest above the middle, blunt at tip, base wedge-shaped, edges finely sharp-toothed, smooth, dark, shiny green, turning bright orange in autumn; stalk 5–15mm
Stipules	toothed

FLOWERS AND FRUIT

Flowers	☿, in small, loose clusters, 1.5cm, white, stalks smooth
Petals	5, oval, widest above middle; sepals 5, persistent on fruit
Stamens	10, pink
Stigmas	2, rarely 1 or 3, styles free
Ovaries	1, in base of flower
Fruit	berry-like, 10–12mm, globose, ripening red, remaining on tree through winter
Seeds	2, stony

Peach *Prunus persica*

Prized for its succulent, downy fruits, the Peach was brought from China and is now widely grown in southern Europe. In harsher northern climes, fruit production is less reliable. This tree is also planted for ornament and in places has established itself in the wild. Nectarine is a smooth-fruited variety of Peach, cultivated on a commercial scale. *Status:* native to China; cultivated in fields and gardens; naturalized in some parts of southern Europe. *Similar trees:* Apricot has pale pink flowers and smaller fruits.

deciduous

most deep pink

large, furry

fine toothe

nectarine is smooth

Apricot (*Prunus armeniaca*)

most paler

broad

smaller

	PEACH		
Type	deciduous tree	**Stipules**	glandular
Height	6m		narrow, papery, falling early
Habitat	gardens, orchards, parks, woods, thickets		**FLOWERS AND FRUIT**
Flowering	March–May	**Flowers**	♂, single or paired, appearing before the leaves, deep pink, rarely pale pink or white, flower-tube bell-shaped; stalk short
Fruiting	June–July		
	TRUNK AND CROWN	**Petals**	5, 10–20mm, equal, broadly oval, widest above middle, tapered at base; sepals 5, 6–8mm
Trunk	straight, slender		
Bark	grey-brown, finely cracked		
Crown	rounded, bushy	**Stamens**	20–30, red when young
Twigs	smooth, reddish, angular	**Stigmas**	1, 2-lobed, style long and slender
	LEAVES		
Buds	6mm, oval, greenish brown with white hairs	**Ovaries**	1, downy
		Fruit	berry-like, 4–8cm, globular, ripening greenish or yellow tinged with red, sweet-tasting
Leaves	alternate, 5–15cm, narrowly oval-oblong to elliptical, long-pointed, edges with small, sharp teeth, smooth; stalk 1.5cm,	**Seeds**	1, in a grooved stone

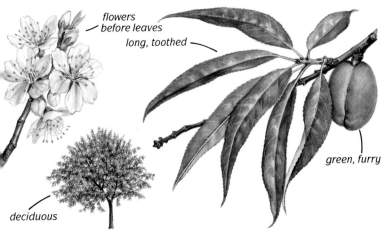

flowers before leaves

long, toothed

green, furry

deciduous

One of the first trees to flower in spring, Almond can turn hillsides white with blossom. The fruits have only a thin fleshy layer covering the large, pitted stone containing the familiar edible seed. *Status:* probably native to south-western and central Asia; anciently cultivated in southern Europe as a fruit tree and sometimes naturalized. *Similar trees:* Cherry Plum has white flowers and smooth, fleshy fruits, for which it is widely grown. A variety with pink flowers and red leaves (cv. 'Pissardii') is a common street tree.

Cherry Plum (*Prunus cerasifera*)

most white

some dark-leaved

juicy fruit

	ALMOND
Type	deciduous tree
Height	8m
Habitat	orchards, parks, hillsides
Flowering	February–April
Fruiting	May–June

TRUNK AND CROWN

Trunk	straight, slender
Bark	black, cracking into small squares
Crown	rounded; branches angled upwards, later spreading, tangled in wild trees, straight in cultivated trees
Twigs	smooth, spiny in wild trees

LEAVES

Buds	brown, scales fringed with hairs
Leaves	alternate, 4–13cm, narrowly oval-oblong, long-pointed, edges with small, blunt teeth, smooth; stalk 2cm, glandular
Stipules	narrow, papery, falling early

FLOWERS AND FRUIT

Flowers	♀, paired, appearing before the leaves, pink fading to white, flower-tube bell-shaped
Petals	5, 15–25mm, broadly oval and widest above middle, tapered at base; sepals 5, 7–8mm, woolly, reddish
Stamens	15–25, yellow
Stigmas	1, slender, long
Ovaries	1, hairy
Fruit	leathery, 3.5–6cm, egg-shaped, flattened, velvety, ripening grey-green
Seeds	1, in a large, pitted stone, which is ridged around the edge

Blackthorn *Prunus spinosa*

White flowers of Blackthorn contrast starkly with its blackish, thorny shoots, brightening the hedgerows before its leaves appear. Typically a shrub spreading by suckers to form dense thickets, it can reach tree size. Small blue-black fruits (sloes) have a whitish, waxy covering and are very sour. *Status:* native; widespread in Europe except the extreme north. *Similar trees:* Wild Plum, part of a variable species which includes cultivated plums, damsons and greengages, has a brown bark and larger fruit. Native mainly to southern Italy and the Balkans, *P. cocomilia* differs in the non-spiny twigs, hairless leaves and yellow fruit.

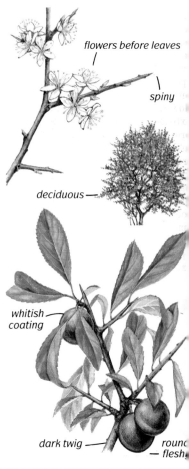

flowers before leaves

spiny

deciduous

whitish coating

dark twig

round — flesh

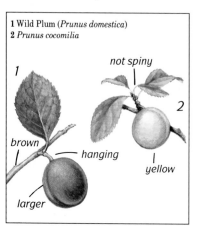

1 Wild Plum (*Prunus domestica*)
2 *Prunus cocomilia*

not spiny

1

2

brown

hanging

yellow

larger

	BLACKTHORN
Type	deciduous shrub or tree
Height	usually up to 4m
Habitat	scrub, light woodland, hedgerows; most soils
Flowering	March–April
Fruiting	September–October

	TRUNK AND CROWN
Trunk	often several, suckering
Bark	blackish, rough
Crown	irregular, dense; branching frequently and widely
Twigs	spiny, initially shortly hairy, dull blackish or dark brown

	LEAVES
Buds	egg-shaped, hairy
Leaves	on alternate sides of stem, 2–4.5cm, narrowly to broadly oval, broadest above middle, tip blunt or pointed, edge with fine rounded or pointed teeth, base wedge-shaped, hairless above, shortly hairy on veins below, dull green; stalk 2–10mm
Stipules	present

	FLOWERS AND FRUIT
Flowers	☿, before leaves, 10–15mm, single or some paired; stalk *c*5mm, hairless
Petals	5, 5–8mm, broadest towards tip, blunt, white; sepals 5
Stamens	*c*20
Stigmas	single; anthers reddish
Ovaries	1
Fruit	1, berry-like, 10–15mm, globular, bluish black with whitish waxy covering, sour
Seeds	single, in globular, smooth or slightly rough, 'stone', 7.5–10mm

Long branches of this attractive tree are smothered with white flowers just before the toothed leaves appear, and later weighed down with fruit. Edible sweet cherries are derived from this species. The double white cv. 'Plena' is one of the last ornamental cherries to flower. *Status:* native except in the extreme north and east; planted for ornament and fruit. *Similar trees:* usually shrubs, two other cherries reach tree size. Dwarf Cherry has spreading, glossy leaves and a broader, bell-shaped base to the flower. Saint Lucie Cherry has smaller, very glossy, minutely toothed leaves and branched heads of small, bitter, black fruits.

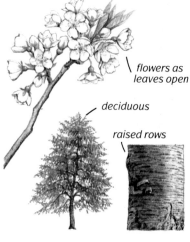

flowers as leaves open

deciduous

raised rows

1 Dwarf Cherry (*Prunus cerasus*)
2 Saint Lucie Cherry (*Prunus mahaleb*)

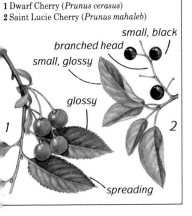

small, black

branched head

small, glossy

glossy

1

2

spreading

toothed

drooping

usually ripens red

	WILD CHERRY		
Type	deciduous tree		
Height	10–30m		
Habitat	woods, hedges, especially on lime-rich, clay soils		
Flowering	April–May		
Fruiting	July		

TRUNK AND CROWN

Trunk	single, well-defined
Bark	reddish brown with horizontal peeling strips, bands of lenticels and blackish fissures
Crown	conical, becoming rounded with almost horizontal branches
Twigs	pale reddish brown, hairless

LEAVES

Buds	pointed, glossy reddish brown
Leaves	on alternate sides of stem, drooping, 8–15cm, oval, broader above, tip slender, with rounded, forward-pointing, blunt teeth and tapered base, dull green, smooth above, paler, slightly hairy below, turning yellow or red in autumn; stalk 2–5cm, glands near top

FLOWERS AND FRUIT

Flowers	☿, before leaves; in stalkless clusters of 2–6; each flower 25–35mm, white, base swollen, narrowed above; stalk 2–5cm
Petals	5, 9–15mm; sepals 5
Stamens	c20
Stigma	1
Ovaries	1
Fruit	berry-like, in bunches, 9–12mm, globular, glossy dark red, yellow or blackish
Seeds	1, in globular, smooth, 'stone'

Bird Cherry *Prunus padus*

An attractive tree, easily recognized amongst native deciduous cherries by its long spikes of fragrant white flowers in late spring. The small, glossy black fruit has a bittersweet or astringent taste, but is edible to birds. *Status:* native to much of Europe; planted for ornament in parks, gardens and streets. *Similar trees:* two introduced North American species have smaller flowers. Rum Cherry has glossy, dark green leaves with wavy, toothed edges, the teeth curving forwards. Choke Cherry has dull leaves with fewer veins and very sharp, spreading teeth, and bears dark red fruits.

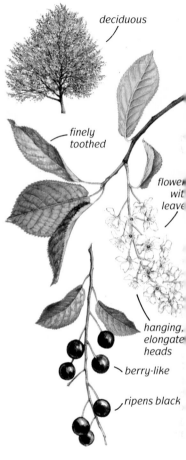

deciduous

finely toothed

flowe wit leave

hanging, elongate heads

berry-like

ripens black

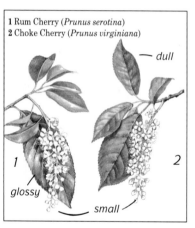

1 Rum Cherry (*Prunus serotina*)
2 Choke Cherry (*Prunus virginiana*)

dull

glossy

small

1

2

	BIRD CHERRY		
Type	deciduous tree or shrub		
Height	3–17m		
Habitat	common on lime-rich soils, often in woods or by water		
Flowering	May		
Fruiting	July–August		

TRUNK AND CROWN

Trunk	distinct, upright
Bark	dark greyish brown, smooth, peeling in horizontal strips
Crown	conical, becoming rounded; branches angled upwards, or lower branches level
Twigs	brown or grey, becoming hairless

LEAVES

Buds	egg-shaped, glossy brown
Leaves	5–10cm, oval or oblong with slender tip, edge finely toothed, base rounded, dull green above, paler and sometimes hairy below, turning yellow or red in autumn; stalk 1–2cm, grooved, red-brown

FLOWERS AND FRUIT

Flowers	♀, strongly scented, 15–40 in drooping cluster 7–15cm long on leafy shoot, each flower 14–20mm, white
Petals	5, 6–9mm, irregularly toothed; sepals 5, short, blunt
Stamens	numerous
Stigmas	1
Ovaries	1
Fruit	berry-like in long heads, each 6–8mm, almost globular, glossy black, bitter
Seeds	1, in globular, grooved 'stone'

evergreen

often several stems

upright spikes

ripens black

berry-like

ick, ossy

few teeth

glossy evergreen tree or shrub that as originally confined to the Balkans ut is now widespread elsewhere. It roduces long, upright clusters of owers but its main use is as a foliage lant. *Status:* native to eastern parts of he Balkan Peninsula; introduced to outhern and western regions as an rnamental and widely naturalized. *imilar trees:* Portugal Laurel has dark ed leaf-stalks, which are much longer han the leaves, and flower-heads that ontain up to 100 flowers. It is native to pain, Portugal and southern France nd also planted for ornament.

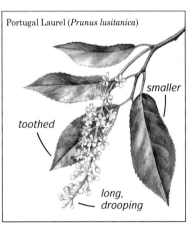

Portugal Laurel (*Prunus lusitanica*)

smaller

toothed

long, drooping

	CHERRY LAUREL	
Type	evergreen tree or shrub	
Height	up to 8m	
Habitat	woodlands	
Flowering	April	
Fruiting	September	

TRUNK AND CROWN

Trunk	slender	
Bark	dark grey-brown, roughened by many lenticels	
Crown	irregularly domed, spreading	
Twigs	pale green, smooth	

LEAVES

Buds	4–7mm, bright green, egg-shaped, pointed	
Leaves	alternate, 10–20cm, oblong to narrowly oval, shortly pointed, base rounded or wedge-shaped, edges sometimes with a few tiny teeth, rather rigid and leathery, dark glossy green above, yellowish green below; stalk green, 1.2cm, with 1–several glands near blade	
Stipules	narrow, papery	

FLOWERS AND FRUIT

Flowers	♂, *c*30 in long, upright spikes, as long as leaves, creamy-white, flower-tube funnel- to bell-shaped	
Petals	5, 4mm, oval to circular, widely separated; sepals 5, short	
Stamens	15–20, yellow	
Stigmas	1, style protrudes well beyond flower	
Ovaries	1	
Fruit	berry-like, *c*1–2cm, globular, ripening purplish black	
Seeds	1, in a smooth, globular 'stone'	

Japanese Cherry *Prunus serrulata*

Horizontal or wide-spreading branches give this tree a characteristically low-domed shape. It is widely planted, especially in streets and avenues, which it brightens in spring with prolific displays of blossom. There are many hybrids and cultivars, with a range of leaf and petal colours, and single or double flowers. *Status:* origin obscure but probably native to China; widespread throughout Europe as an ornamental tree. *Similar trees:* two common ornamental Japanese species are Sargent's Cherry, which has deep pink flowers, and Yoshino Cherry, a hybrid with glossy leaves.

deciduous
often broad
often doub
many grafted
white or pink

1 Sargent's Cherry (*Prunus sargentii*)
2 Yoshino Cherry (*Prunus × yedoensis*)

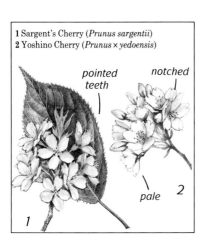

pointed teeth
notched
long tip
pale
2
1
bristle-tipped
fine teeth

JAPANESE CHERRY		with spreading, hair-like points; stalk 2–4cm, with 1–4 reddish glands near blade
Type	deciduous tree	
Height	up to 15m	
Habitat	streets, parks and gardens	**Stipules** narrow, papery
Flowering	April–May	
Fruiting	June	**FLOWERS AND FRUIT**
		Flowers ♂, 2–4, in clusters appearing before leaves, white or pink, flower-tube narrowly bell-shaped
TRUNK AND CROWN		
Trunk	short, abruptly branching to form crown	
Bark	purplish-brown, with bands of lenticels	**Petals** 5, 15–40mm, oval, notched at tip; sepals 5, long, narrow
		Stamens c25–30
Crown	spreading; branches horizontal or angled upwards	**Stigmas** 1, style long and slender
		Ovaries 1
Twigs	smooth	**Fruit** berry-like, 7mm, globular, ripening purplish red, seldom produced
LEAVES		
Buds	large, dark brown	**Seeds** 1, in globular stone
Leaves	alternate, 8–20cm, broadly oval and widest above middle, tip tapering abruptly, teeth sharp	

[Sp]ring Cherry normally flowers in the [ea]rly months of the year, but the [cu]ltivar 'Autumnalis', the Autumn [Ch]erry, flowers from October to April. [Va]rious other cultivars, including [w]eeping and double-flowered forms, are [al]so planted as ornamentals, but it is [th]e Autumn Cherry which is most often [se]en. *Status:* native to Japan; [wi]despread as a street tree and garden [or]namental. *Similar trees:* Tibetan [Ch]erry has glossy red-brown, peeling [ba]rk, white flowers and bright red [fru]its. It is a common tree in parks.

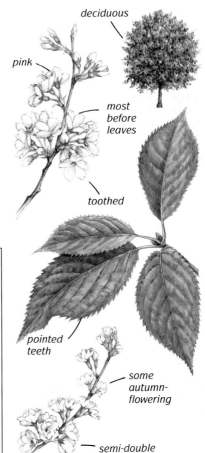

deciduous

pink

most before leaves

toothed

pointed teeth

some autumn-flowering

semi-double

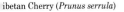

[T]ibetan Cherry (*Prunus serrula*)

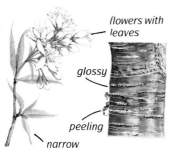

flowers with leaves

glossy

peeling

narrow

	SPRING CHERRY		
Type	deciduous tree		beneath; stalk 7–12mm, downy, crimson
Height	up to 20m	**Stipules**	narrow, papery
Habitat	parks, gardens, streets		
Flowering	March–April		**FLOWERS AND FRUIT**
Fruiting	June	**Flowers**	⚥, 2–5 on short stalks, in clusters appearing before leaves, very pale or rose pink, flower-tube urn-shaped
	TRUNK AND CROWN		
Trunk	thick, straight	**Petals**	5, 8–12mm, oval, widest above middle, notched at tips; sepals 5, 3mm, triangular
Bark	grey-brown		
Crown	dense, rounded; branches slender		
Twigs	crimson, downy	**Stamens**	c20
		Stigmas	1, style slender, longer than stamens, hairy towards base
	LEAVES		
Buds	3–5mm, egg-shaped, dark	**Ovaries**	1
Leaves	alternate, c6cm, oval to oblong, drawn out to a long point, base wedge-shaped, sharply toothed, smooth above, downy on veins	**Fruit**	berry-like, 7–9mm, globose or ellipsoid, ripening purplish black
		Seeds	1, in globular stone

Carob *Ceratonia siliqua*

Leathery-leaved and surviving well in dry conditions, Carob is a characteristic tree of the Mediterranean landscape. The flowers are unusual among members of the pea family, completely lacking petals. A native tree, Carob is also widely cultivated for its pods. Found on the tree at most times of year, these are large and contain seeds and a sugary pulp. They are a rich source of food, used mainly for animal feeds. *Status* native to the Mediterranean region; naturalized in some countries; widely grown as a fodder crop. *Similar trees:* none.

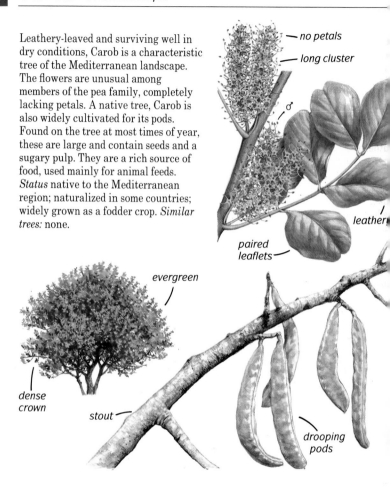

no petals

long cluster

♂

leather

paired leaflets

evergreen

dense crown

stout

drooping pods

	CAROB		
Type	evergreen tree	**Stipules**	tiny, soon falling
Height	up to 10m		**FLOWERS AND FRUIT**
Habitat	dry soils	**Flowers**	♂ and ♀ on same tree or on
Flowering	August–October		different trees, many, in short
Fruiting	September onwards		spikes in angles of leaves, green
		Petals	0; sepals 5, tiny, soon falling
	TRUNK AND CROWN	**Stamens**	5, radiating from a central disc
Trunk	short, often branched from base	**Stigmas**	1, very shortly lobed, style thick, green
Bark	grey, rough		
Crown	dense, low dome	**Ovaries**	1, flask-shaped
Twigs	stout, minutely downy	**Fruit**	pod, 10–20cm, drooping, flattened, ripening violet-brown
	LEAVES	**Seeds**	many, not released
Buds	small, golden-hairy		
Leaves	alternate, 2–5 pairs of leaflets, each 3–5cm, narrowly oval to almost circular, tips notched, smooth, leathery, dark and shiny above, paler below; stalk brown or green		

Gleditsia triacanthos # Honey Locust

tall tree formidably armed with
...sters of spines on the trunk and main
...anches. On smaller branches and
...igs, the spines are usually grouped in
...rees. There are spineless varieties,
...nerally preferred for planting as
...reet trees. *Status:* native to the
...ississippi basin; introduced to
...uthern and central Europe and
...metimes naturalized. *Similar trees:*
...berian Pea-tree is a native of
...orthern Asia often planted for
...nament, and naturalized in France. It
...s leaves with 8–12 leaflets and
...usters of yellow flowers.

paired
leaflets

greenish
white

clustered

deciduous

twisted
pod

spines

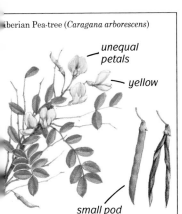

...iberian Pea-tree (*Caragana arborescens*)

unequal
petals

yellow

small pod

	HONEY LOCUST		
Type	deciduous tree		leaflets are themselves divided into 8–14 segments, each 8–20mm, leaf tip ending with a spine; stalk short
Height	up to 45m		
Habitat	mainly parks and streets, also rivers and woods		
		Stipules	minute
Flowering	June		**FLOWERS AND FRUIT**
Fruiting	July–September	**Flowers**	�male, ♀ or ☿, many, in clusters in angles of leaves, each *c*3mm, greenish white
	TRUNK AND CROWN		
Trunk	long, with large clusters of spines	**Petals**	3–5, oval, equal; sepals 3–5, joined below
Bark	brown, vertically fissured	**Stamens**	6–10
Crown	tall and spreading	**Stigmas**	1, lobed, style short and thick
Twigs	smooth, ribbed	**Ovaries**	1, narrow, upright
	LEAVES	**Fruit**	pod, 30–45cm long, 2–3cm wide, flattened, curved and often twisted
Buds	1–2mm, pyramidal, reddish		
Leaves	alternate, 10–20cm, either once divided, when leaves have 7–18 pairs of leaflets, each 20–35mm, or twice divided, when	**Seeds**	numerous, not released

Judas Tree *Cercis siliquastrum*

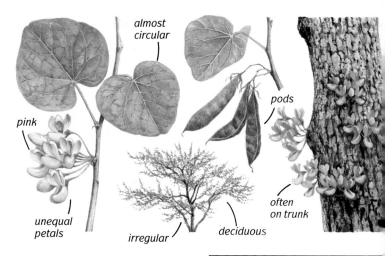

almost circular

pods

pink

often on trunk

unequal petals

irregular

deciduous

An unusual tree that bears its bright pink flowers directly on the trunk and main branches as well as on the twigs. Almost circular leaves with characteristic radiating veins follow the flowers. Attractive reddish purple pods are formed later in the year. *Status:* native throughout Mediterranean regions; often planted and sometimes naturalized in other areas. *Similar trees:* Coral Tree is a Brazilian species forming a small, thick-trunked tree or shrub and grown in mild areas for its scarlet flowers.

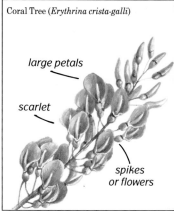

Coral Tree (*Erythrina crista-galli*)

large petals

scarlet

spikes or flowers

	JUDAS TREE	
Type	deciduous tree or shrub	
Height	up to 10m	
Habitat	mainly on dry, rocky soils	
Flowering	April–May	
Fruiting	July	
	TRUNK AND CROWN	
Trunk	slender, often several	
Bark	dark, blackish, cracked	
Crown	rounded, branches angled upwards, spreading	
Twigs	reddish brown, warty	
	LEAVES	
Buds	5–8mm, reddish brown or crimson, egg-shaped, pointed	
Leaves	alternate, 7–12cm, almost circular, rounded or notched at tips, base heart-shaped, smooth, bluish green when	young, becoming dark green above, veins radiating; stalk shorter than blade
Stipules	small, soon falling	
	FLOWERS AND FRUIT	
Flowers	♀, in loose clusters, before or with leaves, on twigs, trunk and branches, pink, 1.5–2cm	
Petals	5, unequal, lower pair joined, side pair overlapping, upper erect; sepals 5, equal, joined below to form a tube	
Stamens	10, free	
Stigmas	1, style curved	
Ovaries	1, narrow	
Fruit	pod, 6–10cm, flattened, with a very narrow wing on one side, smooth, ripening reddish purple, eventually brown	
Seeds	many, released when pod splits	

densely foliaged tree with pink,
ush-like flowers borne on the upper
anches. Individual flowers are small,
t have very long, showy stamens and
e crowded into dense heads. *Status:*
tive to Asia; widely planted as an
namental and street tree in southern
rope, and as an annual in northern
rope. *Similar trees:* Plume Albizia,
m south-western Australia, is also
anted in Mediterranean regions. It
s densely hairy twigs and cylindrical
ads of yellow flowers.

long stamens

pink

small leaflets

divided twice

deciduous

lume Albizia (*Albizia lophantha*)

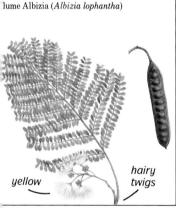

yellow

hairy twigs

flattened pods

	PINK SIRIS	oval, curved, green above, edges and underside shortly hairy; stalk with cup-shaped gland on upper side
Type	deciduous tree	
Height	up to 13m	
Habitat	woods, stream sides	
Flowering	July–August	**Stipules** absent
Fruiting	October	
		FLOWERS AND FRUIT
	TRUNK AND CROWN	**Flowers** ♂, ♀ and sometimes ♂, in branched clusters, each branch with 20 flowers in a dense tuft
Trunk	slender	
Bark	smooth	
Crown	dense, slightly flattened dome; branches spreading	**Petals** 5, joined into a narrow tube, 7–9mm, pink; sepals forming a 5-lobed tube, 3mm
Twigs	brown with many pale, warty lenticels	
		Stamens many, 3.5–4cm, pink, extending well beyond petals
	LEAVES	**Stigmas** 1
Buds	short, black, hairy	**Ovaries** 1
Leaves	alternate, 20–30cm, divided into 10–25 paired segments, each segment with 35–50 paired leaflets, each 1–1.5cm, narrowly	**Fruit** pod, 8–15cm, flat with tapering tip, slightly pinched in between seeds, ripening brown
		Seeds 10–15, orbicular

Silver Wattle *Acacia dealbata*

A pale, silvery green tree, with finely divided, feathery leaves. It is the mimosa of floristry. The pretty, globular flower-heads are very numerous and can turn the whole crown yellow. *Status:* native to south-eastern Australia and Tasmania; planted on a large scale in southern Europe as a timber tree and soil stabilizer; now widely naturalized and spreading. *Similar trees:* Green Wattle has bright green deciduous leaves with spiny stipules. Native to the Caribbean, it is grown in south-western Europe for ornament and for the perfume industry.

globular heads

yellow stamens

fine leaflets

divic twice

silvery green

evergre

flattened pod

smooth, greenish

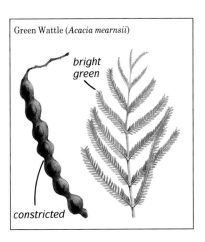

Green Wattle (*Acacia mearnsii*)

bright green

constricted

	SILVER WATTLE	
Type	evergreen tree	
Height	up to 30m	
Habitat	hillsides, forests and plantations	
Flowering	January–March	
Fruiting	May	
	TRUNK AND CROWN	
Trunk	slender	
Bark	smooth, greyish green, becoming black	
Crown	irregular, rather open	
Twigs	densely hairy, hairs short, silvery white	
	LEAVES	
Buds	minute	
Leaves	alternate, divided into 8–20 pairs of segments, each segment with 30–50 pairs of leaflets, each 3–5mm, very	narrow, densely white-hairy when young; stalk with cup-shaped glands wherever segments branch off
Stipules	absent	
	FLOWERS AND FRUIT	
Flowers	♀, in branched, spreading clusters of globular heads, each head 5–6mm, containing 30–40 bright yellow flowers, stalks of flower-heads with dense hairs	
Petals	5, equal, short; sepals 5, hairy	
Stamens	many, protruding well beyond petals, yellow	
Stigmas	1, style very long, slender	
Ovaries	1	
Fruit	pod, 4–10cm, flattened, of equal width for most of its length, ripening waxy brown	
Seeds	many, released when pod splits	

slender tree with drooping foliage
nd distinctly blue-green leaves. The
right yellow flower-heads are
relatively large among *Acacia* species
found in Europe. *Status:* native to
estern Australia; widely planted in
any Mediterranean countries as a soil
abilizer and ornamental. *Similar trees:*
wamp Wattle and Blackwood, both
ative to southern Australia, are also
lanted and naturalized in southern
urope. Swamp Wattle has seeds with
carlet stalks. Blackwood has leaves
ith two to six veins, and twisted pods.

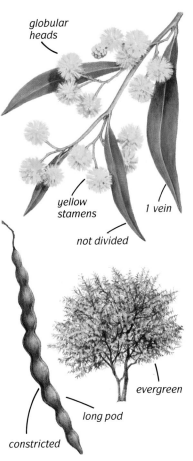

globular heads

yellow stamens

1 vein

not divided

evergreen

long pod

constricted

1 Blackwood (*Acacia melanoxylon*)
2 Swamp Wattle (*Acacia retinodes*)

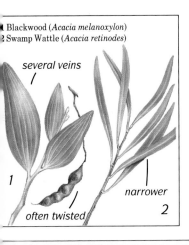

several veins

1

often twisted

narrower

2

	GOLDEN WREATH		
Type	evergreen tree or shrub		bluish green, with a single pale and conspicuous vein; stalkless
Height	up to 10m	**Stipules**	absent
Habitat	mainly in dry, coastal areas		
Flowering	March–May		**FLOWERS AND FRUIT**
Fruiting	July	**Flowers**	♂, in drooping clusters of 2–8 globular heads, each head 1–1.5cm in diameter and containing 25–70 bright yellow flowers
	TRUNK AND CROWN		
Trunk	often forked from base and suckering		
Bark	smooth, grey, becoming grey-brown and cracked	**Petals**	5, 1.5mm, equal; sepals 5
		Stamens	many, yellow
Crown	broad, irregular	**Stigmas**	1; style long, slender
Twigs	smooth, ribbed, drooping, bluish green	**Ovaries**	1
		Fruit	pod, 6–12cm, narrow, flattened, pinched in between each seed, ripening brown
	LEAVES		
Buds	tiny, egg-shaped to rounded	**Seeds**	many, attached by short, whitish stalk encircling seed, released when pod splits
Leaves	alternate, variable, usually 6–20cm, spear-shaped, straight or curved, drooping, dull or shiny,		

Common Laburnum *Laburnum anagyroides*

An erect tree with arching branches and cascades of flowers hanging from the twigs. Split pods hang on the tree for some time after the seeds are shed. All parts are poisonous, especially the seeds. *Status:* native to mountainous areas of southern and central Europe; widely planted for ornament; naturalized elsewhere. *Similar trees:* Scotch Laburnum, native to the same areas as Common Laburnum, is a shrub or small tree with glossy leaves and longer flower clusters. Voss's Laburnum is a hybrid between the above two species, which has largely replaced Common Laburnum as an ornamental in many areas.

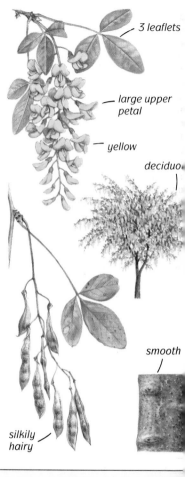

3 leaflets

large upper petal

yellow

deciduo|

smooth

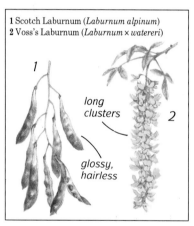

1 Scotch Laburnum (*Laburnum alpinum*)
2 Voss's Laburnum (*Laburnum × watereri*)

long clusters

1

2

glossy, hairless

silkily hairy

	COMMON LABURNUM
Type	deciduous tree or shrub
Height	up to 7m
Habitat	mountain woods and scrub
Flowering	May–June
Fruiting	July–September

TRUNK AND CROWN

Trunk	slender
Bark	smooth, greenish to brown
Crown	irregular, open; branches angled upwards or arching
Twigs	grey-green, downy with long, silky, close-pressed hairs

LEAVES

Buds	5–6mm, egg-shaped, with white, silky hairs
Leaves	alternate, 3 leaflets, each 3–8cm, elliptical or widest above middle, blunt but with a tiny, sharp tip, grey-green, young leaves hairy below; stalk 2–6cm
Stipules	absent

FLOWERS AND FRUIT

Flowers	♀, many, in long, drooping clusters from angles of leaves and tips of shoots, each 2cm, golden yellow
Petals	5, unequal, lower pair joined, side pair overlapping, upper erect; sepals joined into a 2-lipped tube, with short teeth
Stamens	10, fused together into a tube
Stigmas	1, style curved upwards
Ovaries	1, narrow, curved, silky-hairy
Fruit	pod, 4–6cm, hairy, ripening smooth, dull brown, persisting on tree after splitting
Seeds	numerous, black, round, released after pod splits

uckering readily, False-acacia may
oduce many young stems. Mature
ees develop ridged and furrowed bark.
has attractive yellowish green leaves
nd fragrant white flowers, which are
metimes confined to the upper
ranches. *Status:* a woodland species
ative to eastern and central North
merica; widespread as an ornamental;
naturalized in southern and western
urope. *Similar trees:* pink flowered and
ickily hairy Clammy Locust is also
anted for ornament. Pagoda-tree is a
ountain species from Asia. It is tall,
ith twisted branches; the white
owers appear only on old trees.

paired
leaflets

unequal
petals

deciduous

white

Clammy Locust (*Robinia viscosa*)
Pagoda-tree (*Sophora japonica*)

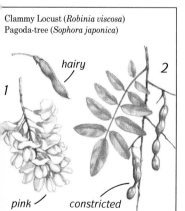

hairy

1

2

pink

constricted

ridged
or deeply
furrowed

smooth

	FALSE-ACACIA		
Type	deciduous tree		hairy below; leaves and leaflets stalked
Height	up to 25m	**Stipules**	woody and spiny; tiny stipules at base of each leaflet
Habitat	streets, parks, woods		
Flowering	June		**FLOWERS AND FRUIT**
Fruiting	September – October	**Flowers**	☿, many, in long, drooping clusters of 10–20cm, white with yellow spot, fragrant
	TRUNK AND CROWN		
Trunk	short, often suckering	**Petals**	5, unequal, lower pair joined, side pair overlapping, upper erect; sepals joined into a tube with 2 shallow lips
Bark	smooth, dark brown, becoming grey with spiralled ridges		
Crown	broad, open; branches twisted		
Twigs	green with dark reddish lines	**Stamens**	10, 9 joined in a tube, 1 free
	LEAVES	**Stigmas**	1, style curved, hairy at tip
Buds	sunk in base of leaf-stalk, flanked by 2 spines	**Ovaries**	1, long, narrow, hairy
		Fruit	pod, 5–10cm, smooth, ripening dull brown, often slow to release seeds
Leaves	alternate, 15–20cm, 7–21 leaflets, mostly paired leaflet at tip, each 2.5–4.5cm, oval or elliptic, yellowish green, sparsely		
		Seeds	4–8, brown with black streaks, kidney-shaped

131

Sweet Orange *Citrus sinensis*

A small evergreen tree bearing delightfully scented flowers and familiar, juicy fruits. Oranges take up to a year or more to ripen; there may be one or even two crops of fruit still on the tree when it flowers. Various cultivars with different ripening times ensure oranges are available more or less all year round. *Status:* native to China and eastern Asia; a common orchard tree in Mediterranean regions. *Similar trees:* several relatives, each with distinctive fruits, are commonly cultivated. Lemon has leaves with a spine at the base of the stalk. Grapefruit has large, broadly winged leaves as well as large fruits.

winged stalk

glos[sy]

very fragr[ant]

white

evergre[en]

not toothed

juicy, globular

oran[ge]

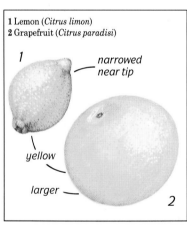

1 Lemon (*Citrus limon*)
2 Grapefruit (*Citrus paradisi*)

1

narrowed near tip

yellow

larger

2

	SWEET ORANGE
Type	evergreen tree
Height	up to 10m
Habitat	orchard tree, often near sea
Flowering	mainly May, also other times of year
Fruiting	up to 1 year or more after flowering

TRUNK AND CROWN

Trunk	short, slender
Bark	blackish brown
Crown	rounded, bushy
Twigs	angled, spiny when young, becoming cylindrical, unarmed

LEAVES

Buds	very small, domed, green
Leaves	alternate, 5–8cm oval, pointed, base rounded, glossy, smooth and leathery but thin, dotted with shiny oil glands; stalk with a narrow, leafy wing
Stipules	absent

FLOWERS AND FRUIT

Flowers	☿, single or few in short, loose spikes in leaf angles, pure white, fragrant
Petals	5, narrowly oval; sepals 4–5, short, pointed, joined below
Stamens	20–60, grouped in bundles
Stigmas	1, club-shaped on thick style
Ovaries	1, green, 10–13-chambered
Fruit	berry-like, with nearly smooth, leathery rind enclosing sweet juicy pulp, ripening orange
Seeds	6–many, creamy, pointed, not released

...trong- and unpleasant-smelling when ...rushed, the leaves of this tree are ...ivided into three spreading leaflets. ...he bark and young fruits are similarly ...romatic. The ripe, straw-coloured fruit ...as a broad, papery wing. *Status:* native ...o eastern North America; planted for ...rnament and naturalized in central ...urope. *Similar trees:* Amur Cork-tree, ...om China, has leaves with 5–11 ...aflets and black, berry-like fruits. It is ...rown in parks and gardens.

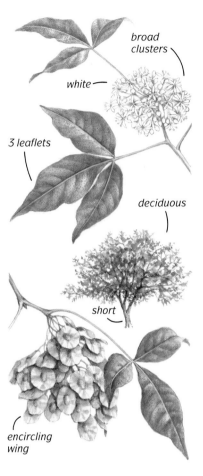

broad clusters

white

3 leaflets

deciduous

short

encircling wing

Amur Cork-tree (*Phellodendron amurense*)

ripens blackish

berry-like   5–11 leaflets

HOP-TREE	
Type	deciduous tree or shrub
Height	up to 8m
Habitat	mainly in parks
Flowering	June–July
Fruiting	July–October
TRUNK AND CROWN	
Trunk	short, often branching
Bark	brown, strong-smelling
Crown	rounded
Twigs	smooth, dark, shiny brown
LEAVES	
Buds	small, very hairy, hidden by base of leaf stalk
Leaves	alternate, 3 leaflets, each 6–12cm, oval, tapered at both ends, edge unbroken or with faint teeth, smooth, shiny; stalkless

Stipules	absent
FLOWERS AND FRUIT	
Flowers	♂, ♀ and ⚥, mixed in clusters at tips of shoots, greenish white
Petals	4–5, 4mm, narrowly oval, blunt, hairy on inner surface; sepals 4–5, c1.5mm, pointed, hairy
Stamens	4, woolly below, rudimentary in ♀ flowers
Stigmas	1, 2-lobed on short, thick style
Ovaries	1, 2-chambered, rudimentary in ♂ flowers
Fruit	nut-like, with a circular, notched, straw-coloured wing 1.5–2.5cm across and net-veined
Seeds	1, not released

Tree-of-Heaven *Ailanthus altissima*

A stately tree with young leaves emerging bright red before turning green. Unfortunately, the foliage is rank-smelling. The fruits hang in large bunches, each fruit with a twisted, propeller-like wing. In Europe, the tree reproduces most easily by means of suckers. *Status:* native to China; very common as a street and park tree, and naturalized in much of Europe except for the far north. *Similar trees:* a second Chinese species, Downy Tree-of-Heaven, is more rarely grown. The leaves have a bright red stalk, and darker leaflets that are hairy below, with unbroken edges.

greenish

paired leaflets

strong-smelling

deciduous

reddish

smooth

whitish lines

elongated wing

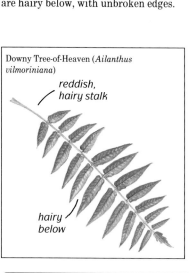

Downy Tree-of-Heaven (*Ailanthus vilmoriniana*)

reddish, hairy stalk

hairy below

	TREE-OF-HEAVEN		25 paired leaflets, each 7–12cm, narrowly oval, pointed, smooth but for fringe of hairs, with 2–4 teeth towards base; stalked
Type	deciduous tree		
Height	20–30m		
Habitat	light, dry and unstable soils		
Flowering	May–July		
Fruiting	August–September	**Stipules**	absent
	TRUNK AND CROWN		**FLOWERS AND FRUIT**
Trunk	straight, often suckering	**Flowers**	usually ♂ and ♀, on different trees, sometimes ⚥, many in branched clusters 10–20cm long, each 7–8mm, greenish white, strong-smelling
Bark	grey, often with silvery lines smooth, becoming scaly		
Crown	irregular; branches stout, angled upwards		
Twigs	thick, smooth, brown, with large leaf-scars and lenticels	**Petals**	5, pointed; sepals 5, green
		Stamens	10 in ♂ flowers, 2–3 in ♀ flowers
	LEAVES	**Stigmas**	2–5, joined
Buds	2mm, scarlet, egg-shaped	**Ovaries**	1, 5–6-chambered
Leaves	alternate, 45–60cm, deep red when emerging, later glossy green, unpleasant-smelling; 13–	**Fruit**	nut-like, with narrow, twisted, papery wing 3–4cm long, reddish, ripening straw-coloured
		Seeds	1, not released

A slender, open tree with delicately coloured and scented flowers. United stamens form an upright tube that is darker than the spreading petals. Bead-like fruits remain on the tree for a long time after the leaves have fallen. *Status:* a mountain species native to eastern Asia; naturalized in the Balkan Peninsula; widely planted in southern Europe for ornament and shade. *Similar trees:* Chinese Cedar has shaggy bark and drooping white flowers. Native to eastern Asia, it is grown for its fragrant timber.

purplish

branched heads

doubly divided

many leaflets

deciduous

furrowed

Chinese Cedar (*Cedrela sinensis*)

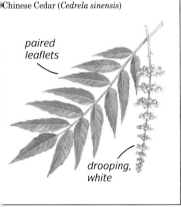

paired leaflets

drooping, white

globular

yellow

	PERSIAN LILAC
Type	deciduous tree or shrub
Height	up to 15m
Habitat	dry mountain areas, planted elsewhere
Flowering	June
Fruiting	July–October

TRUNK AND CROWN

Trunk	short, often slender
Bark	greyish brown, furrowed
Crown	open and spreading
Twigs	sparsely hairy with star-shaped hairs, becoming smooth

LEAVES

Buds	small, globular, densely white-hairy
Leaves	alternate, up to 90cm, divided into segments, each segment divided into leaflets, each 2.5– 5cm, narrowly oval, pointed, base wedge-shaped, sharply-toothed, glossy green; stalked
Stipules	absent

FLOWERS AND FRUIT

Flowers	♀, many, in branched, open clusters 10–20cm long, in leaf angles, lilac, fragrant
Petals	5, 18mm, narrow, spreading or curved back; sepals 5, green, short, joined below
Stamens	10, joined into an erect tube
Stigmas	1, club-shaped with a thick style, hidden in stamen tube
Ovaries	1, 5–8-chambered
Fruit	6–18mm, globular, ripening creamy-yellow
Seeds	1, not released

Stag's-horn Sumach *Rhus typhina*

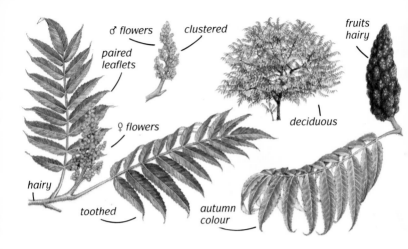

♂ flowers · *clustered* · *paired leaflets* · *fruits hairy* · *♀ flowers* · *deciduous* · *hairy* · *toothed* · *autumn colour*

Velvet-hairy twigs, and leaves with drooping leaflets immediately distinguish this small, suckering tree. It produces bright autumn colours and female plants have dark crimson fruiting heads. *Status:* native to eastern North America; widespread as an ornamental and naturalized in parts of northern and central Europe. *Similar trees:* Sumach is a semi-evergreen shrub or small tree with narrowly winged, hairy leaflets and purplish fruits. It occurs in rocky places in southern Europe. Varnish-tree, from China, is sometimes planted. It has loose, branched fruiting heads.

1 Sumach (*Rhus coriaria*)
2 Varnish-tree (*Rhus verniciflua*)

long cluster · *winged stalk*

	STAG'S-HORN SUMACH	
Type	deciduous tree or shrub	
Height	10m	
Habitat	thickets	
Flowering	May–July	
Fruiting	September–October	
	TRUNK AND CROWN	
Trunk	slender, often several and suckering	
Bark	brown, with yellow warts	
Crown	flattened, open dome; branches forking regularly	
Twigs	curved, velvety when young	
	LEAVES	
Buds	minute, lacking scales	
Leaves	alternate, oval in outline, broadest at the middle, drooping, 11–29 stalkless leaflets, paired with one at the tip, each 5–12cm, very narrowly oval, pointed, coarsely toothed, softly hairy, rich orange and red in autumn; stalk hairy	
Stipules	absent	
	FLOWERS AND FRUIT	
Flowers	♀, more usually ♂ and ♀ on different trees in branched clusters 10–20cm; ♂ greenish, clusters open; ♀ dull red, clusters downy, spike-like	
Petals	5, narrow, spreading; sepals 5, short, hairy	
Stamens	5 in ♂ and ♀ flowers	
Stigmas	3, on a single short style	
Ovaries	1, in ♀ and ♂ flowers	
Fruit	nut-like, *c*4mm, covered with crimson hairs, remaining on tree through winter	
Seeds	1, not released	

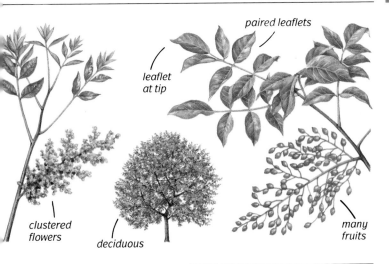

paired leaflets

leaflet
at tip

clustered
flowers

deciduous

many
fruits

1 Pistachio (*Pistacia vera*)
2 Mastic Tree (*Pistacia lentiscus*)

few
leaflets

spine

1

edible
fruit

2

common tree in dry, chalky
rubland. It has leathery leaves with
-6 pairs of leaflets and a single leaflet
the tip. Dull flowers are followed by
ight, coral red young fruits. *Status:*
ative to Mediterranean regions and
uth-western Asia. *Similar trees:* an
sian species cultivated in
lediterranean regions for its edible
uts, Pistachio has leaves with hairy
alks and usually only 3 leaflets.
lastic Tree, a native of dry parts of the
lediterranean, is usually an evergreen
hrub; the leaves have 4 leaflets and end
a short spine.

	TURPENTINE TREE		
Type	deciduous tree or shrub		each 2–8.5cm, oval, tipped with a small spine, leathery, smooth and shiny, dark green; stalks smooth, round in cross-section
Height	up to 10m		
Habitat	scrub, light woodland, on dry chalky slopes	**Stipules**	absent
Flowering	March–April		**FLOWERS AND FRUIT**
Fruiting	September–October	**Flowers**	♂ and ♀ on different trees, many in long-branched clusters, greenish brown, appearing with the leaves
	TRUNK AND CROWN		
Trunk	short, slightly sinuous, forking		
Bark	grey, finely cracked into oblong plates	**Petals**	absent
		Stamens	3–5 in ♂ flowers
Crown	open, irregular; branches few, twisted	**Stigmas**	3, on a single style
		Ovaries	1 in ♀ flowers
Twigs	reddish, becoming brown, stout, sticky with resin	**Fruit**	nut-like, 5–7mm, egg-shaped, tipped with slender point, coral-red, ripening brown
	LEAVES		
Buds	3–9mm, dark-red, egg-shaped	**Seeds**	1, not released
Leaves	alternate, 3–9, stalked leaflets,		

Pepper Tree *Schinus molle*

An evergreen tree with a crown of weeping foliage. The leaves are aromatic, smelling distinctly of pepper. It is most attractive in autumn, when the long clusters of pink fruits appear. Only flourishing in warm climates, it is widely planted in Mediterranean regions. *Status:* native to Central and South America, grown as an ornamental in southern Europe and naturalized in places. *Similar trees:* a less frequent South American species, Brazilian Pepper, has erect branches, broader leaflets and bright red fruits.

narrow leaflets

long cluster

evergreen

pink, berry-like

Brazilian Pepper (*Schinus terebinthifolia*)

winged

red

	PEPPER TREE	
Type	evergreen tree	
Height	12m	
Habitat	warm, dry areas	
Flowering	June–August	
Fruiting	July–December	

TRUNK AND CROWN

Trunk	stout, straight, cylindrical
Bark	grey-brown
Crown	tall, domed; branches slender
Twigs	bluish, drooping

LEAVES

Buds	scaly, tiny
Leaves	alternate, tipped with a leaflet or with a short spine, 7–13 pairs of leaflets, each 2–6cm, very narrow, spine-tipped, often toothed, hairy, becoming smooth, aromatic; stalk flattened
Stipules	absent

FLOWERS AND FRUIT

Flowers	♀, or ♂ and ♀ on different trees, many in loose, hanging clusters 25cm long, creamy-white
Petals	5, *c*2mm, oval, widest above middle, blunt; sepals 5
Stamens	10 in ♂ and ♀ flowers
Stigmas	3, on a single style
Ovaries	1, in ♀ and ♂ flowers
Fruit	berry-like, 6–7mm, globular, ripening shiny pink, remaining on tree throughout winter
Seeds	1, not released

Koelreuteria paniculata Golden-rain-tree

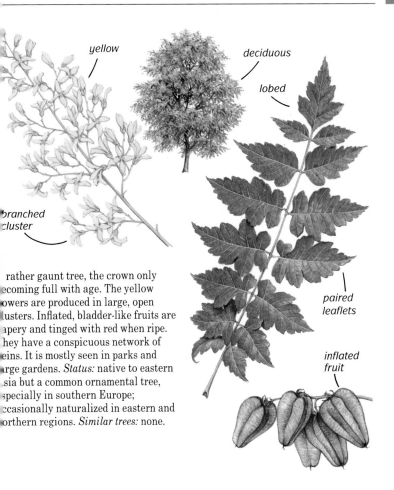

yellow

deciduous

lobed

branched cluster

paired leaflets

inflated fruit

... rather gaunt tree, the crown only ...ecoming full with age. The yellow ...owers are produced in large, open ...usters. Inflated, bladder-like fruits are ...apery and tinged with red when ripe. ...hey have a conspicuous network of ...eins. It is mostly seen in parks and ...rge gardens. *Status:* native to eastern ...sia but a common ornamental tree, ...specially in southern Europe; ...ccasionally naturalized in eastern and ...orthern regions. *Similar trees:* none.

	GOLDEN-RAIN-TREE
Type	deciduous tree
Height	9–18m
Habitat	parks and gardens, occasionally waste ground on rich soils
Flowering	July–August
Fruiting	September–October

TRUNK AND CROWN

Trunk	thick, sinuous
Bark	brown, showing orange in deep cracks
Crown	sparse when young, becoming full with age; branches angled upwards, twisted
Twigs	downy, becoming smooth

LEAVES

Buds	squat with curved tip
Leaves	alternate, 15–40cm; 9–15 paired leaflets each 3–8cm, coarsely toothed, the lowest themselves sometimes divided into leaflets, smooth, dark green above, pale below; stalked
Stipules	absent

FLOWERS AND FRUIT

Flowers	☿, but often functionally either ♂ or ♀, in branched clusters up to 40cm at tips of shoots, 1cm across, yellow
Petals	4, narrow, pointed; 4 sepals short, hairy
Stamens	8, often less, hairy
Stigmas	1, style longer than stamens
Ovaries	1, 3-sided, 3-chambered, hairy
Fruit	pod-like, 5.5cm, conical and papery, red-tinged and veined, splitting into 3 when ripe
Seeds	3, black, released

Horse-chestnut *Aesculus hippocastanum*

A massive, spreading tree with large leaves divided like the fingers of a hand. Showy, upright clusters of flowers are visible from some distance away. Shiny seeds, called conkers, are enclosed in a thick, prickly case. Winter twigs have distinctive horseshoe-shaped leaf scars and very large, sticky buds. *Status:* originally a mountain species native to the Balkan Peninsula; widely planted in much of Europe for timber, ornament and shade; often naturalized. *Similar trees:* the widely planted Red Horse-chestnut is a hybrid between Horse-chestnut and an American species. It has red flowers and non-spiny fruits.

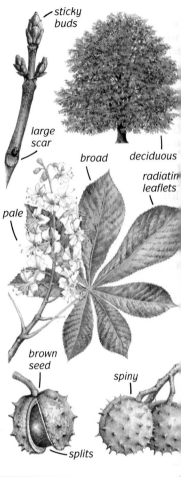

sticky buds

large scar

broad

deciduous

radiating leaflets

pale

brown seed

spiny

splits

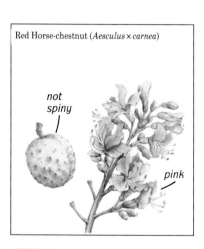

Red Horse-chestnut (*Aesculus × carnea*)

not spiny

pink

	HORSE-CHESTNUT
Type	deciduous tree
Height	up to 25m
Habitat	thickets, hedges, woodland
Flowering	May–June
Fruiting	September

	TRUNK AND CROWN
Trunk	stout, broad-based, fluted
Bark	dark red- or grey-brown, scaly
Crown	huge, spreading dome; branches arching, tips upturned
Twigs	red-brown with pale lenticels; leaf-scars horseshoe-shaped

	LEAVES
Buds	up to 3.5cm, shiny brown, sticky
Leaves	paired on stem; 5–7 radiating, stalkless leaflets, the largest up to 25cm, widest above middle, pointed, tapering at base, toothed, woolly below, becoming smooth; long-stalked
Stipules	absent

	FLOWERS AND FRUIT
Flowers	♀ or ♂, in showy, erect, pyramidal spikes of 15–30cm at tips of shoots
Petals	5, or 4, *c*10mm, frilly, unequal, the lowest largest, white with yellow to pink spot at base; sepals 5, unequal, short, joined in a tube
Stamens	6–7, protruding, down-curved
Stigmas	1, on a long, curved style
Ovaries	1, 3-chambered
Fruit	spiny, 6cm, globular, ripening brown and splitting into 3
Seeds	1, sometimes 2–3, smooth, dark glossy brown with a round, pale scar, released when fruit splits

Very similar to Horse-chestnut, this Indian species differs in having stalked leaflets and fruits lacking prominent spines. The smaller spikes of flowers are white or pink, spotted with red and yellow. Winter buds are green, not brown like those of its more common relative. *Status:* native to the Himalayas; planted in parks and gardens for ornament. *Similar trees:* Yellow Buckeye, from south-eastern North America, has narrow yellow or sometimes pink flowers; it is frequently planted in parks.

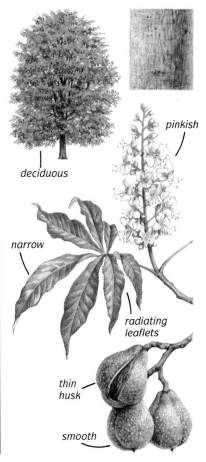

pinkish

deciduous

narrow

radiating leaflets

thin husk

smooth

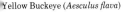

Yellow Buckeye (*Aesculus flava*)

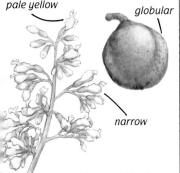

pale yellow

globular

narrow

	INDIAN HORSE-CHESTNUT		
Type	deciduous tree		narrowly oval, widest above middle, base tapered at both ends, finely toothed
Height	19–30m		
Habitat	moist soils	**Stipules**	absent
Flowering	June		
Fruiting	October		**FLOWERS AND FRUIT**
		Flowers	♀, in erect, pyramidal spikes of usually 10–15cm
	TRUNK AND CROWN		
Trunk	stout, straight, rather short	**Petals**	5 or 4, white or pink, slightly unequal, the lowest largest, the upper spotted with red or yellow; 5 sepals small, joined in a tube
Bark	greenish to reddish grey, smooth, cracking into rectangular plates		
Crown	tall, rounded; spreading branches arching upwards		
Twigs	grey-brown, with prominent horseshoe-shaped leaf scars	**Stamens**	5–8, long and protruding
		Stigmas	1, on a long, protruding style
		Ovaries	1, 3-chambered
	LEAVES	**Fruit**	pear-shaped, ripening greenish brown with thin, rough-skinned husk splitting into 3 when ripe
Buds	c10mm, green, shiny, very sticky		
Leaves	paired on stems; 5–9, but usually 7, radiating, short-stalked leaflets up to 8cm,		
		Seeds	2–3, wrinkled, glossy brown, released when fruit splits

Sycamore *Acer pseudoplatanus*

Originally confined to mountain regions, Sycamore has been introduced to many parts of Europe and is now widely naturalized. The winged seeds help it to spread easily and rapidly. It makes a large, spreading tree, often wider than it is tall. *Status:* native to mountains of central and southern Europe, and western Asia; naturalized as far north as Sweden. *Similar trees:* with a similar distribution but reaching even further north, Norway Maple differs in its horizontally winged fruits. Italian Maple is also a mountain tree; its fruits have almost parallel-wings.

broad lobes

coarse teeth

branched clusters

paired

domed

cracks into plates

deciduous

angled apart

winged fruits

1 Norway Maple (*Acer platanoides*)
2 Italian Maple (*Acer opalus*)

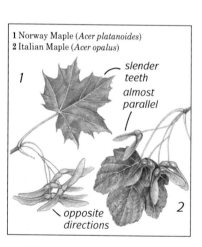

slender teeth

almost parallel

1

2

opposite directions

SYCAMORE

Type	deciduous tree
Height	up to 35m
Habitat	woods, hedges, mountainous areas; often planted
Flowering	April–May
Fruiting	June–September

TRUNK AND CROWN

Trunk	stout, often developing buttresses
Bark	smooth, grey, becoming pinkish brown, fissured and cracking into small irregular plates
Crown	domed, spreading, dense; lower branches often stout
Twigs	short, grey-green, smooth

LEAVES

Buds	0.8–1cm, oval, reddish green
Leaves	opposite, 10–15cm, with 5 deep and broad spreading lobes, each pointed and coarsely toothed, dark green above, pale blue-green beneath; stalk up to 20cm, usually reddish
Stipules	absent

FLOWERS AND FRUIT

Flowers	♂ and ♀ in separate clusters, many in branched, hanging clusters 6–12 cm long, with the leaves, greenish yellow, each *c*6mm
Petals	5; sepals 5
Stamens	8 in ♂; sterile in ♀
Stigmas	2, on short style
Ovaries	1, 2-chambered, hairy
Fruit	paired, smooth, each with a grey-brown wing *c*2.5cm long; diverging at right-angles
Seeds	1 per fruit, not released

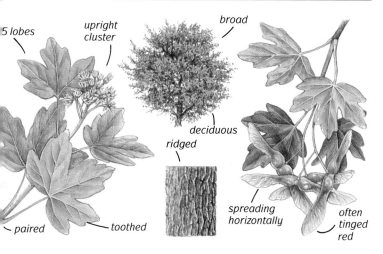

5 lobes

upright cluster

broad

deciduous

ridged

spreading horizontally

often tinged red

paired

toothed

A small, colourful tree with young leaves that are pink in spring and turn deep yellow in autumn. It is most common in northern Europe, where it often grows in hedges. The twigs become winged with thick, corky flanges, and the leaves have either 3 or 5 lobes. *Status:* native more or less throughout Europe and western Asia; planted for autumn colour. *Similar species:* two species from southern and central Europe are distinguished by their parallel-winged fruits. Montpellier Maple has leaves with toothless lobes. The rarer Tartar Maple has undivided leaves and striped bark.

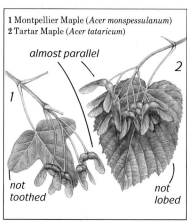

1 Montpellier Maple (*Acer monspessulanum*)
2 Tartar Maple (*Acer tataricum*)

almost parallel

2

1

not toothed

not lobed

FIELD MAPLE

Type	deciduous tree or shrub
Height	up to 26m
Habitat	hedgerows, open woods, usually on chalk or limestone soils
Flowering	April–June
Fruiting	May–September
Trunk	sinuous, usually distinct

TRUNK AND CROWN

Bark	grey or light brown, finely ridged and fissured
Crown	broadly domed; branches angled upwards at tips
Twigs	dark brown and finely hairy, becoming paler and ribbed

LEAVES

Buds	3mm, red-brown, hairy at tip
Leaves	opposite, 4–7cm, thick, deeply divided into 3 or 5 rounded lobes, opening pinkish, later dull green above, downy below, turning yellow in autumn; stalk c5cm
Stipules	absent

FLOWERS AND FRUIT

Flowers	♂ and ♀, few in separate, upright, branched clusters, appearing with the leaves, each c6mm, yellow-green; stalkless
Stamens	8 in ♂; sterile in ♀
Stigmas	2, on single, short style
Ovaries	1, 2-chambered
Fruit	paired, each with a pale green wing, often tinged with crimson and hairy, spreading horizontally
Seeds	1 per fruit, not released

Box-elder *Acer negundo*

A fast-growing North American tree that is readily distinguished from other maples by its leaves, which are mostly divided into 5 leaflets. The flowers open before the leaves, the crimson anthers of male trees being particularly noticeable. The fruits mature early and persist on the tree for a long time. The cultivar 'Variegatum' is planted for its yellow and green variegated leaves. *Status:* native to eastern North America; planted for ornament and shelter; naturalized mainly in central regions. *Similar trees:* the decorative Paper-bark Maple, from China, has reddish bark, which peels in broad, papery strips.

hanging clusters

red ♂

greenish ♀

deciduous

paired

3 or 5 leaflets

angled apart

Paper-bark Maple (*Acer griseum*)

papery strips

3 leaflets

	BOX-ELDER	**Stipules**	absent
Type	deciduous tree		**FLOWERS AND FRUIT**
Height	up to 20m	**Flowers**	♂ and ♀ on different trees, appearing before leaves
Habitat	parks and gardens, street tree		
Flowering	March–April	♂	in short, hanging clusters of 12–16, red
Fruiting	June–September		
		♀	6–12 in loose hanging clusters 5cm long, greenish
	TRUNK AND CROWN		
Trunk	short, often sprouting numerous burrs	**Petals**	absent; sepals 5
		Stamens	4–6 in ♂, red
Bark	smooth, grey, becoming darker and shallowly fissured	**Stigmas**	2, spreading, styles very short
		Ovaries	1, 2-chambered
Crown	irregularly domed, spreading	**Fruit**	paired, *c*2cm, smooth, each with a brown wing and diverging at a narrow angle
Twigs	green, straight, smooth		
	LEAVES	**Seeds**	1 per fruit, not released
Buds	small, with 2 silky white scales		
Leaves	opposite, with 2 or 4 paired leaflets and a leaflet at tip, each oval, long-pointed, shallowly toothed; stalk 6–8cm		

lued in North America as a source of
ple syrup, which is made from the
p, this tree is planted in Europe
inly for ornament. The leaves are
very beneath and attractive in
mmer, before turning pale yellow or
l later. *Status:* North American,
tive from Quebec to Florida; widely
ltivated. *Similar trees:* a more
portant source of maple syrup, and
e brightest autumn-coloured species,
Sugar Maple. Red Maple has dense
d flower clusters, red fruits and red
tumn leaves. Both are North
nerican trees that are commonly
nted in Europe.

deciduous

small
clusters

deep
lobes

paired

sharp
teeth

silvery
below

narrow
angle

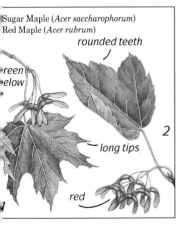

Sugar Maple (*Acer saccharophorum*)
Red Maple (*Acer rubrum*)

rounded teeth

reen
elow

2

long tips

red

	SILVER MAPLE		
Type	deciduous tree		occasionally brilliant red in autumn; stalk 8–13cm, pink
Height	up to 36m	**Stipules**	absent
Habitat	roadsides, parks, gardens		
lowering	March		**FLOWERS AND FRUIT**
Fruiting	May–June	**Flowers**	♂ and ♀ in separate clusters of 4–5, appearing before the leaves, greenish or red
	TRUNK AND CROWN	♂	short-stalked
Trunk	short, stout, often with burrs	♀	long-stalked
Bark	smooth, grey-brown, later flaking and becoming shaggy	**Petals**	absent; sepals 5
Crown	tall, spreading above; branches numerous, slender, arching	**Stamens**	3–7 in ♂s
		Stigmas	2, on short style
Twigs	brown or purplish	**Ovaries**	1, 2-chambered
	LEAVES	**Fruit**	paired, 1 often fails to develop, 5–6 cm, stalked, with elliptical, twisted wing diverging at a narrow angle
Buds	*c*1cm, oval, angular, red		
Leaves	opposite, 9–16 cm, deeply 5-lobed, lobes deeply and irregularly toothed, silvery-hairy beneath, pale yellow or	**Seeds**	1 per fruit, not released

Père David's Maple   *Acer davidii*

One of a group of decorative trees known as 'snake-bark' maples. The young olive-green bark is patterned with a network of white lines, resembling the skin of a reptile. The lines fade with age and the bark turns uniform dark brown. Several cultivars, all differing somewhat in overall shape, are planted. *Status:* native to China; cultivated for ornament. *Similar trees:* native to Japan, Snake-bark Maple has downy grey twigs and leaves with three triangular lobes. Hers's Maple, from China, has marbled bark and long spikes of flowers.

drooping cluster

deciduo

scarcely lobed

strip bark

paired

usua red

fruits spread wide

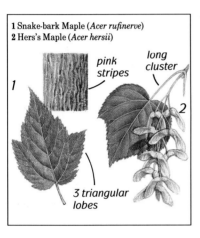

1 Snake-bark Maple (*Acer rufinerve*)
2 Hers's Maple (*Acer hersii*)

1

pink stripes

long cluster

2

3 triangular lobes

PÈRE DAVID'S MAPLE

Type	deciduous tree
Height	up to 16m
Habitat	parks and gardens
Flowering	May
Fruiting	July–August

TRUNK AND CROWN

Trunk	short, stout
Bark	smooth, greenish, with network of white stripes when young, becoming brown and fissured
Crown	narrow; branches angled upwards
Twigs	smooth, purple or red when young, white striped

LEAVES

Buds	*c*1cm, narrowly conical, dark red with paler markings
Leaves	opposite, up to 15 × 10 cm, broadly oval, heart-shaped at the base, with a short slender tip, edges finely toothed, shiny green above, whitish green beneath; stalk 6cm, red
Stipules	absent

FLOWERS AND FRUIT

Flowers	♂ and ♀ in separate clusters, many in arching clusters 7–10 cm long, appearing with leaves, greenish yellow
Petals	absent; sepals 5
Stamens	4–10 in ♂
Stigmas	2, spreading
Ovaries	1, 2-chambered
Fruit	paired, each with a wing 2.5–3.7cm long, spreading nearly horizontally
Seeds	1 per fruit, not released

Various maples are cultivated for ornament and this species is particularly attractive, with many different forms. In the typical tree the leaves have narrow, pointed lobes and turn red or purple in autumn. In some cultivars they are finely divided and deep purple throughout the year. Others have bright red winter shoots. *Status:* native to China, Japan and Korea, and a common ornamental, especially in small gardens. *Similar trees:* Downy Japanese-maple, another ornamental species, has leaves with 7–11 short lobes. It too has fine-leaved cultivars.

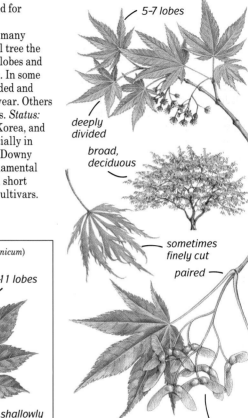

5-7 lobes

deeply divided

broad, deciduous

sometimes finely cut

paired

spreading apart

Downy Japanese-maple (*Acer japonicum*)

7–11 lobes

shallowly divided

SMOOTH JAPANESE-MAPLE

Type	deciduous tree or shrub
Height	up to 16m
Habitat	gardens and parks
Flowering	April–May
Fruiting	June–September

TRUNK AND CROWN

Trunk	usually very short, sinuously twisted and soon dividing
Bark	smooth and rich brown striped with pale yellow, becoming grey
Crown	domed and spreading
Twigs	slender, smooth, reddish above, green beneath

LEAVES

Buds	oval, 2–3mm, often red-tinged
Leaves	opposite, 7–9cm, deeply divided into 5–7 spreading, oval, pointed and sharply toothed lobes, bright green, turning yellow, red or crimson in autumn; stalks 3–5cm
Stipules	absent

FLOWERS AND FRUIT

Flowers	♀, in upright clusters of 12–15; each 6–8mm across, dark purple; stalks slender, *c*4cm long
Petals	absent; sepals 5
Stamens	4–10
Stigmas	2 on short style
Ovaries	1, 2-chambered
Fruit	paired, each with a pale green wing tinged with red, *c*1cm long and diverging at a wide angle
Seeds	1 per fruit, not released

Holly *Ilex aquifolium*

A stiff and prickly-leaved evergreen tree, often a shrub. When growing in deep shady woods it is often sterile. In more open sites it bears white flowers and, on female trees, bright red berries. *Status:* native to western and southern Europe and western Asia. *Similar trees:* Highclere Holly is a hybrid that is resistant to air pollution. It has broader, flatter leaves bearing short, forward-pointing spines. It is often planted in towns. Canary Holly, native to the Azores, Canaries and Madeira, has flat leaves with few, if any, fine spines and pale pink flowers.

wavy edge

white

evergreen

large spines

smooth, silvery

often variegated

red berries

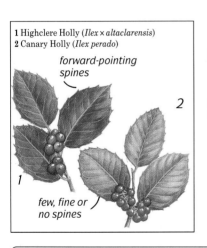

1 Highclere Holly (*Ilex × altaclarensis*)
2 Canary Holly (*Ilex perado*)

forward-pointing spines

2

1

few, fine or no spines

	HOLLY		oblong, 5–12cm, edges wavy and spiny, leathery and waxy, dark, shiny green above, pale and matt below; stalk 1cm, thick and grooved
Type	evergreen tree or shrub		
Height	2–25m		
Habitat	woods, scrub, on moist soils		
Flowering	May–August		
Fruiting	September–March	**Stipules**	very small and inconspicuous
	TRUNK AND CROWN		**FLOWERS AND FRUIT**
Trunk	straight, cylindrical	**Flowers**	♂ and ♀ on different trees, in clusters in angles of leaves on old wood, white
Bark	silvery grey, smooth, warty or fissured when old		
Crown	narrow, conical to cylindrical; young branches curved upwards	**Petals**	4, c4mm, joined at base; sepals 4, joined
		Stamens	4 in ♂ flowers, rudimentary in ♀ flowers
Twigs	slightly hairy and bright green when young, becoming smooth and darker	**Stigmas**	1 in ♀
		Ovaries	1, green, barrel-shaped, rudimentary in ♂ flowers
	LEAVES		
Buds	2–3mm, egg-shaped	**Fruit**	berry-like, 8–10mm, globular, ripening scarlet, on ♀ trees only
Leaves	alternate, oval to roughly	**Seeds**	several, not released

A slender tree, often with several trunks, and small, inconspicuous flowers. In contrast the 4-lobed fruits are very obvious, ripening deep pink and splitting to reveal the fleshy, orange covering of the seeds. *Status:* native to all but the extreme north and south of Europe; several cultivars are used as ornamentals. *Similar trees:* a second European species, Broad-leaved Spindle, has flowers with 5 broad, pink petals. Japanese Spindle, from eastern Asia, has thick, blunt leaves and broad, yellowish petals. Several cultivars planted for their foliage are naturalized in southern Europe.

1 Broad-leaved Spindle (*Euonymus latifolius*)
2 Japanese Spindle (*Euonymus japonicus*)

4 petals

deciduous

finely toothed

often several trunks

smooth

pink fruit

4-lobed

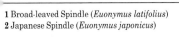
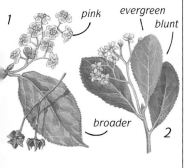

1

pink

evergreen

blunt

broader

2

	SPINDLE	
Type	deciduous tree or shrub	
Height	2–6m	
Habitat	woodland and scrub on chalky soils	
Flowering	May–June	
Fruiting	September–October	
	TRUNK AND CROWN	
Trunk	slender, often several	
Bark	fawn to grey-green, smooth, with fine vertical lines	
Crown	bushy; numerous branches arching upwards	
Twigs	green, 4-angled	
	LEAVES	
Buds	5–6mm, greenish brown, slightly curved	
Leaves	paired on stem, up to 10cm, narrowly oval to elliptical, pointed, base wedge-shaped, edges finely toothed, red in autumn; short-stalked	
Stipules	absent	
	FLOWERS AND FRUIT	
Flowers	☿, in clusters of 3–8 in angles of leaves, 8–10mm across, yellow with a green central disc	
Petals	4, narrow, widely separated; sepals 4, 1–2mm, green	
Stamens	4, alternating with petals	
Stigmas	1, style short, straight	
Ovaries	1, bright green	
Fruit	10–15mm across, 4-lobed, pink and fleshy, splitting to release seeds	
Seeds	4, each with a fleshy, bright orange covering	

Box *Buxus sempervirens*

A neat, dense evergreen, often no more than a shrub. Slow-growing and small-leaved, it forms a dense bush when clipped. Tiny flowers form inconspicuous clusters. Fruits are tipped with distinctive, spreading and woody styles. The many cultivars are popular hedging and topiary plants. *Status:* native and scattered through parts of western Europe with chalky soils. *Similar trees:* the larger-leaved Balearic Box is a stiff tree with pinkish bark, confined to parts of Spain, the Balearic Islands and Sardinia.

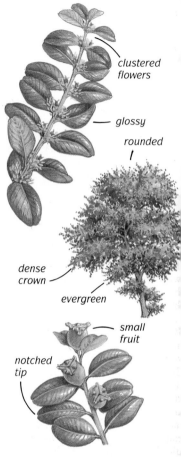

clustered flowers

glossy

rounded

dense crown

evergreen

small fruit

notched tip

Balearic Box (*Buxus balearica*)

larger leaves

	BOX		
Type	evergreen tree or shrub		above, pale below; stalk short
Height	2–5m, rarely as much as 11m	**Stipules**	absent
Habitat	calcareous soils		
Flowering	April		**FLOWERS AND FRUIT**
Fruiting	September	**Flowers**	♂ and ♀, in clusters 5mm across in angles of leaves, each cluster with one stalked ♀ and several stalkless ♂ flowers
	TRUNK AND CROWN		
Trunk	cylindrical, often leaning	**Petals**	absent; ♂ flowers with 4 small sepals; ♀ flowers with only a whorl of small bracts
Bark	brown, ageing grey, finely fissured		
Crown	dense, rounded	**Stamens**	4 in ♂ flowers
Twigs	4-angled, white-woolly, becoming smooth	**Stigmas**	3 in ♀ flowers, each 2-lobed on a thick, spreading style
	LEAVES	**Ovaries**	1, 3-chambered, blue-green
Buds	5–7mm, narrow, bright green	**Fruit**	nut-like, *c*7mm, oblong to egg-shaped, tipped with the horn-like styles, ripening brown, splitting into 3 parts
Leaves	paired on stem, 15–30mm, oval, oblong or elliptical, tip notched, edges slightly turned under, thick and leathery, glossy green		
		Seeds	6, 5–6mm, glossy black, released when fruit splits

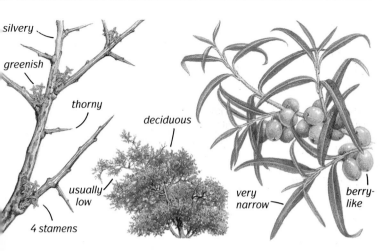

silvery

greenish

thorny

deciduous

usually low

4 stamens

very narrow

berry-like

..., small, silvery, thorny tree. All parts
[o]f the plant, particularly the leaves and
[t]wigs, are covered with intricately
[s]haped but minute silver scales.
[G]rowing in coastal sites, it is often only
[a] shrub in more exposed habitats.
[S]tatus: native to much of Europe,
[m]ainly coastal regions of the north-
[w]est, but also occurring inland; widely
[p]lanted on sand dunes and often
[n]aturalized. *Similar trees:* Oleaster,
[fr]om western Asia, and the North
[A]merican Silver Berry are widely
[n]aturalized ornamentals. Both have
[fr]agrant flowers *c*1cm long. Oleaster has
[j]uicy berries; Silver Berry, dry berries.

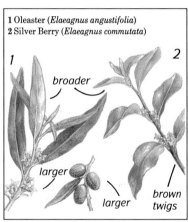

1 Oleaster (*Elaeagnus angustifolia*)
2 Silver Berry (*Elaeagnus commutata*)

1

2

broader

larger

larger

brown twigs

	SEA-BUCKTHORN		
Type	deciduous tree or shrub		
Height	up to 11m but often shorter		
Habitat	dunes and sea-shores		
Flowering	March–April		
Fruiting	September–November		
	TRUNK AND CROWN		
Trunk	much-branched near the base, suckering		
Bark	pale-brown, ridged		
Crown	open, rounded		
Twigs	thorny, covered with minute silvery scales		
	LEAVES		
Buds	3mm, squat with thick scales		
Leaves	alternate or spiralled on stem, 1–6cm, very narrow, pointed, silvery green; stalks very short		

Stipules	absent
	FLOWERS AND FRUIT
Flowers	♂ and ♀ on different trees, in short spikes appearing before leaves on previous year's growth; ♂ 4mm, stalkless, ♀ 1.5mm, stalked, greenish with rusty scales
Petals	absent; sepals 2, joined, short in ♂ flowers, long in ♀
Stamens	4 in ♂ flowers
Stigmas	1, thread-like on a long cylindrical style
Ovaries	1, sunk into base of ♀ flowers
Fruit	berry-like, 6–8mm, almost globular, ripening orange
Seeds	1, not released

Common Jujube *Ziziphus jujuba*

A small tree or tangled shrub, armed with very sharp, curved and straight spines. The long, slender twigs are markedly zigzag. Sweet and juicy, the fruits are edible. *Status:* native to Asia; widely grown in southern Europe for the edible fruits and often naturalized. *Similar trees: Z. lotus* is a shrub with deep yellow fruits, found in dry parts of Spain, Sicily and Greece. Christ's Thorn is a very spiny and tangled tree or shrub of Mediterranean regions. The distinctive, woody and winged fruit resembles a broad-brimmed hat.

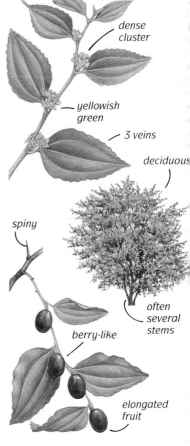

dense cluster

yellowish green

3 veins

deciduous

spiny

berry-like

elongated fruit

often several stems

1 *Ziziphus lotus*
2 Christ's Thorn (*Paliurus spina-christi*)

1

2

yellow

globular

winged fruit

	COMMON JUJUBE		
Type	deciduous tree or shrub		with tiny, gland-tipped teeth; stalk short
Height	up to 8m	**Stipules**	transformed into sharp, brown spines, 1 long and straight, 1 short and curved
Habitat	hedgerows near houses, orchards		
Flowering	April–May		**FLOWERS AND FRUIT**
Fruiting	September	**Flowers**	♀, in small, dense, stalked clusters in angles of leaves, yellowish green
	TRUNK AND CROWN		
Trunk	slender, sinuous, often several	**Petals**	5, 1.5mm, hooded, tapering at base; sepals 5, 2mm
Bark	dark grey-brown		
Crown	dense, rounded	**Stamens**	5, alternating with, and often concealed by, petals
Twigs	zigzag, smooth, green, non-flowering twigs often spiny		
		Stigmas	2, minute, styles joined at base
	LEAVES	**Ovaries**	1, sunk into 5-lobed disc in base of flower
Buds	pointed, hairy		
Leaves	alternate, 2–5.5cm, oval, blunt, with 3 conspicuous veins, bright, shiny green above, downy on veins below, edges	**Fruit**	berry-like, 1.5–3cm, egg-shaped, ripening red to black, sweet-tasting
		Seeds	1, 6–7mm, stony, not released

regularly branched tree, its new twigs always growing out at right angles. The shoots are of two kinds, long and short; only short shoots bear flowers and fruits. *Status:* native to much of Europe but confined to chalky soils and absent from the Mediterranean region. *Similar trees:* Mediterranean Buckthorn is an evergreen shrub lacking spines, with yellow sepals. Alder Buckthorn has leaves with unbroken edges, ♂ flowers with 5 sepals and fruits ripening from yellow, through red to black. It grows in wet woods through most of Europe.

finely, toothed

4 petals

paired leaves

deciduous

paired buds

berry-like, black

short side shoots

spiny

1 Mediterranean Buckthorn (*Rhamnus alaternus*); **2** Alder Buckthorn (*Frangula alnus*)

evergreen

leaves not paired

1

2

red, then black

few teeth

no teeth

	BUCKTHORN		**Leaves**	paired on twigs, crowded on short side shoots, 3–7cm, oval or elliptical, blunt or even notched at tip, edges finely toothed, 2–4 pairs of curving veins; stalk short
Type	deciduous tree or shrub			
Height	4–6m			
Habitat	hedges and woodland on chalky soils			
Flowering	May–June		**Stipules**	soft, soon falling
Fruiting	September–October			
				FLOWERS AND FRUIT
	TRUNK AND CROWN		**Flowers**	♂ and ♀ on different trees, in clusters on short side shoots, 4mm across, greenish white, fragrant
Trunk	short, often several or forking near the ground			
Bark	black, flaking to reveal orange patches		**Petals**	4, rarely 5, triangular; sepals 4, very small
Crown	regular; branches spreading at right angles to trunk		**Stamens**	4, rudimentary in ♀ flowers
			Stigmas	4 in ♀ flowers, on single style
Twigs	smooth or hairy, grey, some ending in spines, many short side shoots		**Ovaries**	1 in ♀ flowers, globose
			Fruit	berry-like, 6–8mm, globose but slightly flattened, ripening black
	LEAVES		**Seeds**	2–4, stony, yellow
Buds	4mm, brown, pointed			

Tamarisk *Tamarix gallica*

Resistant to the drying effects of salt winds, this feathery tree or shrub is often seen near coasts, and thrives on sand-dunes. The pink flower-spikes normally appear in summer but may occur up to December in mild areas. *Status:* native to western Europe as far north as France; often planted and naturalized elsewhere. *Similar trees:* two other species widespread in western Europe can be distinguished by their flowers. African Tamarisk has larger, white flowers with petals 2–3mm long. It grows mainly in salt-marshes and along rivers. Canarian Tamarisk has pinkish petals, only 1.5mm or less, and is found on coastal sands.

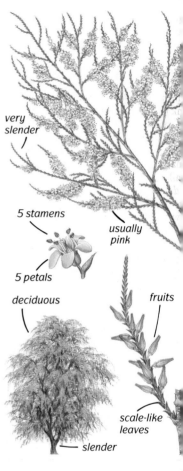

very slender

5 stamens

usually pink

5 petals

deciduous

fruits

scale-like leaves

slender

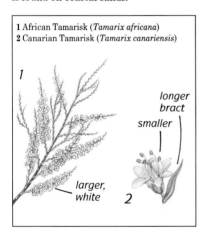

1 African Tamarisk (*Tamarix africana*)
2 Canarian Tamarisk (*Tamarix canariensis*)

1

longer bract

smaller

larger, white

2

	TAMARISK		
Type	deciduous shrub or small tree	Stipules	stalkless
Height	up to 10m		absent
Habitat	riversides, coastal areas, marshes	**FLOWERS AND FRUIT**	
Flowering	April–September	Flowers	☿, in spike-like clusters to 3cm long on young shoots, each c2mm, pink or white
Fruiting	May–October		
	TRUNK AND CROWN	Petals	5, 1.5–2mm, elliptical; sepals 5, 0.75–1.25mm
Trunk	usually curved or twisted, slender	Stamens	5
Bark	dull brown to dark purple, rough and fibrous	Stigmas	3–4, styles very short
		Ovaries	1, bottle-shaped
Crown	much-branched with long slender branches	Fruit	hard brown capsule, splitting to release seeds
Twigs	willowy, very slender, reddish	Seeds	numerous, oval, brown, each with a long tuft of hairs
	LEAVES		
Buds	minute, green		
Leaves	alternate, c2mm, scale-like and clasping the stem, blue-green;		

Tamarix parviflora **Small-flowered Tamarisk**

predominantly eastern
[M]editerranean species that is more
[of]ten seen as a shrub than a tree. The
[ve]ry slender twigs and tiny, scale-like,
[cl]asping leaves give a delicate, wispy
[eff]ect. The flower spikes are also very
[sli]m, being less than 5mm wide. The
[pi]nk or white petals usually number 4,
[bu]t sometimes there are 5. *Status:*
[na]tive to the Balkan Peninsula and
[A]egean region; planted elsewhere for
[or]nament. *Similar trees:* two very
[si]milar species are *T. tetrandra* and
[T.] dalmatica, also from south-eastern
[Eu]rope. Both have longer, broader
[flo]wer spikes and larger petals.
[T.] tetrandra has black bark.

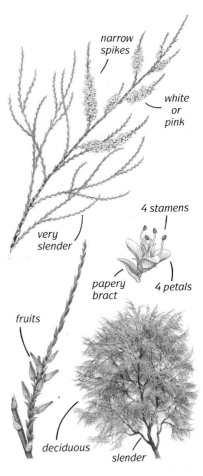

narrow
spikes

white
or
pink

very
slender

4 stamens

papery
bract

4 petals

fruits

deciduous

slender

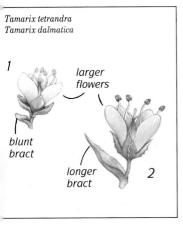

Tamarix tetrandra
Tamarix dalmatica

1

larger
flowers

blunt
bract

longer
bract

2

	SMALL-FLOWERED TAMARISK	Stipules	absent
Type	deciduous shrub or small tree		**FLOWERS AND FRUIT**
Height	2–3m	**Flowers**	♂, in dense, spike-like clusters
Habitat	hedges and river banks		3–5mm wide, white or pink
Flowering	March–June	**Petals**	4, less than 2mm, upright,
Fruiting	April–June		persistent; sepals 2–2.5mm,
			minutely toothed
	TRUNK AND CROWN	**Stamens**	4
Trunk	slender, often several or	**Stigmas**	3, styles very short
	branching low-down	**Ovaries**	1, bottle-shaped
Bark	brown to purple	**Fruit**	hard capsule, splitting to
Crown	low, rounded		release seeds
Twigs	very slender, drooping, red-	**Seeds**	numerous, each with a long tuft
	brown, black in winter		of hairs
	LEAVES		
Buds	minute, egg-shaped		
Leaves	alternate, 3–5mm, scale-like		
	and half clasping stem with tips		
	spreading, sharply pointed,		
	edges papery-edged; stalkless		

Large-leaved Lime *Tilia platyphyllos*

This is the first of the limes to begin flowering. A tall tree, it has upwardly angled branches and large leaves. The fragrant flowers hang in clusters beneath a narrow, wing-like bract, attracting large numbers of bees. *Status:* native from central Europe to Russia and western Asia; introduced elsewhere and often planted. *Similar trees:* Common Lime, a hybrid between Large- and Small-leaved Limes, is widely planted. In many areas it is more common than the parent species. The leaves have tufts of white hairs beneath and drooping yellowish flowers.

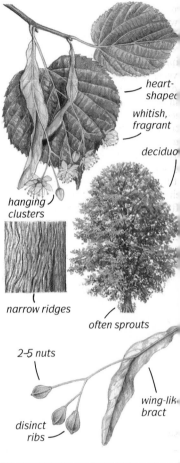

heart-shaped

whitish, fragrant

deciduous

hanging clusters

narrow ridges

often sprouts

2–5 nuts

disinct ribs

wing-like bract

Common Lime (*Tilia* × *vulgaris*)

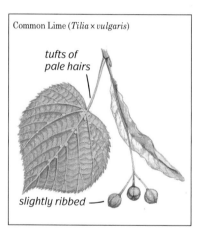

tufts of pale hairs

slightly ribbed

	LARGE-LEAVED LIME	
Type	deciduous tree	
Height	up to 40m	
Habitat	woods, often on limestone	
Flowering	June–July	
Fruiting	July–October	

	TRUNK AND CROWN
Trunk	occasionally with outgrowths of bushy stems from base
Bark	smooth, dark grey, developing narrow cracks and ridges
Crown	tall and narrowly domed; branches angled upwards
Twigs	dark reddish green, softly hairy

	LEAVES
Buds	oval, dark red
Leaves	alternate, up to 12cm, heart-shaped, sharply pointed, sharply toothed, dark green,

hairy above, paler, more densely hairy below; stalk 1.5–5cm, hairy

Stipules	small, acting as bud scales, falling early

FLOWERS AND FRUIT

Flowers	♀, yellowish white, fragrant, in clusters of 2–5 hanging beneath a whitish green, wing-like bract 5–12 cm
Petals	5, 5–8mm, spreading; sepals 5
Stamens	numerous
Stigmas	1, 5-lobed
Ovaries	1, 5-chambered
Fruit	cluster of hard, globular nuts, each 8–10mm, 3- to 5-ribbed, densely hairy; whole cluster and bract shed together
Seeds	1, not released

owing on lime-rich soils, this tree has wnward-arching branches and heart-aped leaves. It is often planted as a eet tree but aphids attack the leaves, pping half-digested sap onto the vements below, leaving them sticky d unpleasant. Fungi also attack and figure the leaves. Other, resistant, es are now preferred. Bees are racted by the nectar-rich flowers.
ıtus: native to most of Europe and *r*thern Asia; frequently planted.
nilar trees: Caucasian Lime is a tural hybrid from the Crimea. It has h yellow flowers and leaves with 'ts of reddish brown hairs in the vein gles beneath.

aucasian Lime (*Tilia × euchlora*)

glossy, dark above

larger

slightly ribbed ——

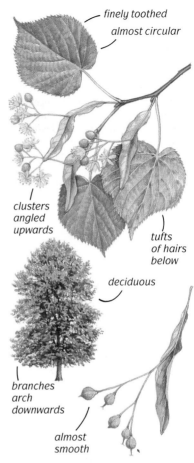

finely toothed
almost circular

clusters angled upwards

tufts of hairs below

deciduous

branches arch downwards

almost smooth

SMALL-LEAVED LIME			
Type	deciduous tree		shining green above, paler beneath, smooth except for reddish brown tuft of hair in vein angles; stalk 1.5–4cm
Height	up to 32m		
Habitat	woods, often on limestone		
Flowering	June–July	**Stipules**	small, scale-like, soon falling
Fruiting	July–September		

TRUNK AND CROWN		**FLOWERS AND FRUIT**	
Trunk	burred	**Flowers**	♂, greenish yellow, fragrant, in clusters of 4–15 held above leaf-like bract up to 8cm long
Bark	smooth, grey, becoming dark, fissured, cracked into plates		
Crown	irregularly domed; branches downwardly arching	**Petals**	5, 7–8mm, narrowly oval; sepals 5–6, 3mm, elliptical
Twigs	smooth, reddish above, greenish brown beneath	**Stamens**	c40
		Stigmas	1, 5-lobed
LEAVES		**Ovaries**	1, 5-chambered
Buds	dark red, smooth and shiny	**Fruit**	cluster of hard, globular nuts, each c6mm, smooth or shallow ribbed; whole cluster and bract shed together
Leaves	alternate, 3–9cm, almost circular, finely pointed, notched at base, sharply toothed, dark		
		Seeds	1, not released

Silver-lime *Tila tomentosa*

A handsome tree with contrasting leaf surfaces, green above and silver below. Upwardly angled branches give a full, rounded crown. It is resistant to drought and frequently used as a street tree. The ground around these trees is often littered with drowsy and dying bees, drugged by the narcotic nectar from the flowers. *Status:* native from Hungary and the Balkans to western Asia; planted elsewhere for ornament. *Similar trees:* of unknown origin, and sometimes regarded as merely an odd form of Silver-lime, Weeping Silver-lime has branches that are angled upwards before drooping conspicuously towards the tips.

unequal teeth

white-woolly below

hanging clusters

deciduous

large bract

warty, downy

Weeping Silver-lime (*Tilia petiolaris*)

weeping twigs

long stalk

usually sterile

	SILVER-LIME		
Type	deciduous tree		green above, white-woolly beneath, the hairs star-shaped; stalk c5cm
Height	up to 30m		
Habitat	woods; often planted	**Stipules**	small, acting as bud scales, falling early
Flowering	July–August		
Fruiting	July–September		
			FLOWERS AND FRUIT
	TRUNK AND CROWN	**Flowers**	♀, dull white or pale yellow, fragrant, in clusters of 6–10 hanging beneath a yellowish green, leaf-like bract
Trunk	stout, well-defined		
Bark	dark grey-green or grey, networked with shallow ridges		
Crown	broadly domed, compact; branches upwardly angled	**Petals**	5, 5–8mm; sepals 5
		Stamens	numerous
Twigs	whitish hairy when young, becoming green, smooth	**Stigmas**	1, 5-lobed
		Ovaries	1, 5-chambered
	LEAVES	**Fruit**	cluster of nuts, each 6–12 mm long, 5-sided, warty and downy; cluster and bract shed together
Buds	6–8mm, oval, green-brown		
Leaves	alternate, 8–10cm, heart-shaped, finely pointed, lop-sided at base, sharply toothed, dark	**Seeds**	1, not released

Davidia involucrata **Handkerchief-tree**

spectacular tree when in full bloom, becoming completely covered with conspicuous, white flower-heads. The tree's real flowers are small and grouped into a globular, purplish head. This is enveloped by two large, triangular, handkerchief-like bracts – hence the common name. When the bracts unfold, they give the impression of a single large flower with white petals and a purple centre. Though the flower-heads are similar in structure to those of the dogwoods, Handkerchief-tree is usually placed within its own family. The most commonly planted form is var. *vilmoriniana*, which is distinguished by narrow, smooth and shiny leaves. *Status:* native to China; cultivated as an ornamental in parks and gardens. *Similar trees:* none.

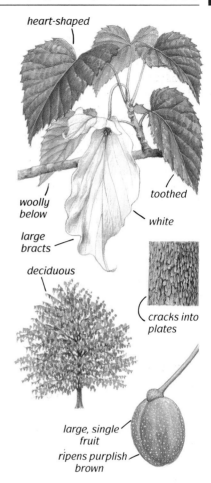

heart-shaped

woolly below

large bracts

toothed

white

deciduous

cracks into plates

large, single fruit

ripens purplish brown

HANDKERCHIEF-TREE			
Type	deciduous tree		
Height	up to 18m		
Habitat	parks and gardens		
Flowering	May		
Fruiting	October		

TRUNK AND CROWN

Trunk	straight, well-defined
Bark	grey-brown to purplish, cracking
Crown	tall, domed; branches wide-spreading
Twigs	brown, with lines of warty lenticels

LEAVES

Buds	9mm, dark, shiny red, pointed
Leaves	alternate, 3.5cm, broadly oval, pointed, base heart-shaped, edges sharply toothed, dull green above, white-woolly below, fragrant when unfolding; stalkless
Stipules	absent

FLOWERS AND FRUIT

Flowers	♂ and ♀ in separate clusters, or ♀; flower cluster *c*2cm across, purplish, flanked by 2 very large, showy white bracts
Perianth	0 in ♂ flowers, many in ♀ and ♀ flowers
Stamens	usually 5–6
Stigmas	1, lobed, style curved
Ovaries	1, 6–10-chambered, sunk into base of flower
Fruit	single, berry-like, 4cm, egg-shaped, ridged, ripening purplish brown
Seeds	6–10, not released

Black-gum *Nyssa sylvatica*

Growing in swampy areas, Black-gum forms a very tall tree, up to 100m, where it is native in eastern North America. In Europe, however, it is generally much smaller, reaching only 30m at the most. Producing inconspicuous flowers and rather dull fruits, it is planted for its brilliant autumn leaf colours, which are dominated by bright reds and orange. Black-gum only thrives in mild areas, so is little planted in northern regions. However, it is quite common from southern England southwards. *Status:* native to the swamps of eastern North America; grown in Europe mainly for ornament. *Similar trees:* relatives of the Black-gum are only rarely cultivated, in private gardens.

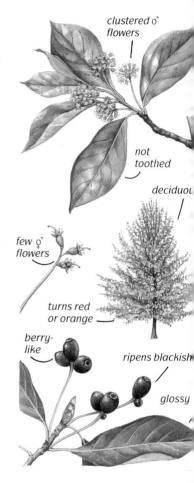

clustered ♂ flowers

not toothed

deciduo[us]

few ♀ flowers

turns red or orange

berry-like

ripens blackish

glossy

	BLACK-GUM		
Type	deciduous tree		bright orange and red in autumn; stalkless
Height	up to 30m	**Stipules**	absent
Habitat	parks and gardens; wet soils		
Flowering	June		**FLOWERS AND FRUIT**
Fruiting	October	**Flowers**	♂ and ♀ on different trees; ♂ in rounded clusters 1cm across; ♀ single or paired
	TRUNK AND CROWN		
Trunk	tapering	**Petals**	5, free in ♂, in ♀ joined into a bell-shaped tube; sepals 5, tiny, tooth-like
Bark	grey or brown, deeply ridged and fissured		
Crown	cylindrical, flat-topped	**Stamens**	8, longer than petals in ♂ flowers
Twigs	grey-brown, smooth		
		Stigmas	1 in ♀ flowers, on a long, curved style
	LEAVES		
Buds	small, red-brown, downy tips	**Ovaries**	1 in ♀ flowers, sunk into base of flower
Leaves	alternate, 4.5cm, oval, widest above middle, tapered at both ends, edge unbroken, slightly leathery, glossy green above, pale and matt below, turning	**Fruit**	berry-like, 12mm, oval, widest above middle, ripening blue-black
		Seeds	1, stony

Cornus mas **Cornelian Cherry**

very attractive tree in late winter, ~~wh~~en bright yellow flowers appear. Dull ~~gr~~een leaves which follow have strongly ~~ma~~rked veins. The succulent fruits are ~~oft~~en used in conserves. *Status:* native ~~in~~ central and south-eastern Europe; ~~wi~~dely cultivated and naturalized ~~els~~ewhere. *Similar trees:* Dogwood is a ~~co~~mmon summer-flowering shrub with ~~cl~~usters of small white flowers and ~~bl~~ack berries. Nuttall's Dogwood is a ~~wi~~dely planted American species. The ~~tig~~ht flower clusters are surrounded by ~~4–~~7 large pink or white bracts, the ~~wh~~ole assembly resembling a single, ~~lar~~ge, flower.

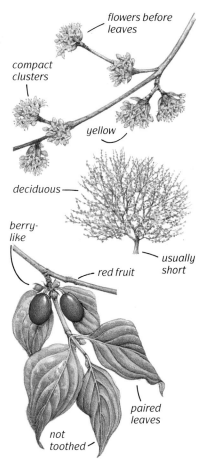

flowers before leaves

compact clusters

yellow

deciduous

berry-like

red fruit

usually short

paired leaves

not toothed

Nuttall's Dogwood (*Cornus nuttallii*)
Dogwood (*Cornus sanguinea*)

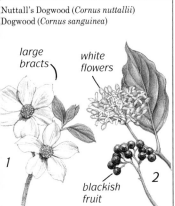

large bracts

white flowers

1

blackish fruit

2

	CORNELIAN CHERRY
Type	deciduous tree or shrub
Height	up to 8m
Habitat	scrub, thickets and woodland, especially on chalk
Flowering	February–March
Fruiting	August–September

TRUNK AND CROWN

Trunk	short, often several
Bark	grey-brown, scaly
Crown	open; branches spreading or downswept
Twigs	greenish yellow, minutely downy

LEAVES

Buds	7mm, paired, pointed, yellowish, lacking scales but with short, close-pressed hairs
Leaves	paired on stem, 4–10cm, elliptical to oval, drawn out to a pointed tip, base rounded, downy, dull green, 3–5 pairs of conspicuous curved veins; stalk 6mm
Stipules	absent

FLOWERS AND FRUIT

Flowers	☿, yellow, before leaves in paired, thick-stalked clusters of 10–25, 4 yellowish bracts at base of cluster soon falling
Petals	4, 2–2.5mm, hooded; sepals very small
Stamens	4, alternating with petals
Stigmas	1–several, in base of flower-tube
Ovaries	1, sunk in base of flower
Fruit	berry-like, 12–20mm, roughly cylindrical, drooping, ripening bright red
Seeds	1, stony, not released

Orange-bark Myrtle *Myrtus apiculata*

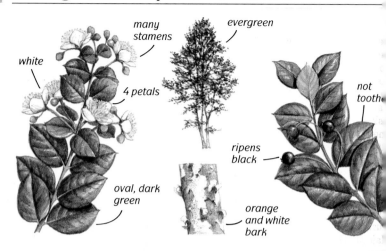

many stamens

evergreen

white

4 petals

not tooth

ripens black

oval, dark green

orange and white bark

Seldom more than a large shrub outside its South American home, this spicily aromatic plant has gland-dotted leaves, which release their scent when crushed. Attractive, cinnamon-coloured bark peels away from the base of the trunk, revealing the grey or creamy inner bark. *Status:* native to Chile; planted for ornament. *Similar trees:* Myrtle, from southern Europe, is very similar but always shrubby, and lacks colourful bark. Crape Myrtle, a deciduous shrub or small tree from China is grown in gardens and streets. Clusters of red, pink or white flowers, each up to 4cm across, have crinkled petals.

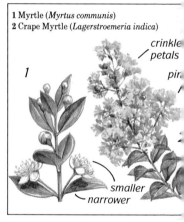

1 Myrtle (*Myrtus communis*)
2 Crape Myrtle (*Lagerstroemeria indica*)

crinkle petals

pin

1

smaller narrower

	ORANGE-BARK MAPLE			and sharply pointed, dark green
Type	evergreen tree or shrub			above, paler beneath and
Height	up to 13m			minutely hairy; almost stalkless
Habitat	parks, gardens		**Stipules**	absent
Flowering	August–October			
Fruiting	October–November			**FLOWERS AND FRUIT**
			Flowers	☿, 2cm across, white; stalks
	TRUNK AND CROWN			*c*1.5cm, pink
Trunk	slender, often several		**Petals**	4, round, *c*1.3cm; sepals 4,
Bark	orange to cinnamon, peeling to			bowl-shaped, persisting on fruit
	leave areas of white; old trees		**Stamens**	many, arranged in several rings
	with broad, tapering white		**Stigmas**	1, style long, straight
	streaks		**Ovaries**	1
Crown	loosely conical		**Fruit**	berry, initially red, ripening to
Twigs	dark pink above, green to pale			black
	brown beneath, hairy		**Seeds**	3–6, not released
	LEAVES			
Buds	minute, globular, deep red,			
	shiny			
Leaves	opposite, 2.5 × 1.5cm, oval, finely			

arge plantations of this gum are
ncreasingly seen in hot European
ountries. It is one of the largest and
astest-growing trees, a source of
mber, paper pulp and eucalyptus oil.
ark is shed annually and can be a fire-
sk. Paired juvenile leaves are short
nd very blue, but adult leaves are
lternate, long and dull green. *Status:*
ative to Tasmania and south-eastern
ustralia; planted on a massive scale in
e Mediterranean region. *Similar trees:*
ommon in gardens, Cider Gum has
lmost circular juvenile leaves and
usters of stalked flowers. The rarer
laiden's Gum has clusters of stalkless
owers.

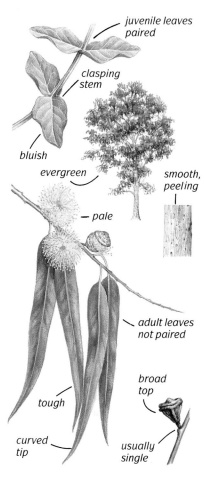

juvenile leaves
paired

clasping
stem

bluish

evergreen

smooth,
peeling

pale

adult leaves
not paired

broad
top

tough

curved
tip

usually
single

. Maiden's Gum (*Eucalyptus maidenii*)
: Cider Gum (*Eucalyptus gunnii*)

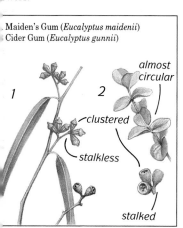

almost
circular

1

2

clustered

stalkless

stalked

	TASMANIAN BLUE-GUM		
Type	evergreen tree		sickle-shaped, drawn out into a long slender tip, hanging downwards, dark green; shortly stalked
Height	up to 40m		
Habitat	streets, plantations		
Flowering	September–December		
Fruiting	January–March	**Stipules**	absent
	TRUNK AND CROWN		**FLOWERS AND FRUIT**
Trunk	tall, straight, cylindrical	**Flower buds**	up to 30 × 20 mm, covered by a pale bluish, hemispherical, rough and waxy cap
Bark	smooth, grey-brown, peeling away in long strips		
Crown	narrowly conical, very dense	**Flowers**	♀, single or clusters of 2–3; each c4cm, whitish; almost stalkless
Twigs	greenish brown, smooth		
	LEAVES	**Stamens**	numerous
Buds	minute, concealed	**Stigmas**	1, style short and straight
Leaves	juvenile leaves opposite, to 16 × 9cm, oval, heart-shaped base clasps stem, blue-green, stalkless; adult leaves alternate, up to 30 × 4cm, narrowly oval to	**Ovaries**	1, 2–8-chambered
		Fruit	woody capsule, 10–25 × 15–25mm, top-shaped, strongly ribbed, with waxy white bloom
		Seeds	numerous, hard, wedge-shaped, black

Red Mahogany *Eucalyptus resinifer*

One of the 'stringybark' group of gums, the rough, reddish bark of this large tree is very fibrous. The narrow adult leaves are similar to the juvenile leaves, but darker in colour. The flowers have a pointed, orange lid. Red Mahogany favours sandy soils in sheltered places and is grown mainly for timber. *Status:* native to Queensland and New South Wales; planted from Portugal to Italy, mainly in coastal areas. *Similar trees:* Swamp Mahogany has pink-lidded fruits and prefers wet ground. It has larger fruits with a rim raised above the short teeth.

— pale

orange, beaked cap

evergreen

rough, fibrous

strin bark

juvenile leaves often paired projecti tee

Swamp Mahogany (*Eucalyptus robustus*)

broad juvenile leaves

rim

almost stalkless

narrow

clusters of 5–10

stalked

	RED MAHOGANY		
Type	evergreen tree	**Stipules**	glossy green above; stalked absent
Height	up to 40m		
Habitat	plantations		**FLOWERS AND FRUIT**
Flowering	September–February	**Flower**	up to 17mm, with an orange,
Fruiting	December–March	**buds**	conical or beak-like cap
		Flowers	♀, in clusters of 5–10, white;
	TRUNK AND CROWN		stalks of clusters up to 2cm,
Trunk	tall, straight, cylindrical		flattened
Bark	reddish, fibrous, rough	**Stamens**	numerous
Crown	small, narrowly domed and open	**Stigmas**	1; style short
		Ovaries	1, 2–8-chambered
Twigs	green, smooth	**Fruit**	woody capsule, 5–18 x 5–18mm, hemispherical, stalked, opening by 3–4 teeth
	LEAVES	**Seeds**	numerous
Buds	minute, concealed		
Leaves	juvenile leaves opposite, to 6 × 2cm, lance-shaped, pale green, stalked; adult leaves alternate, up to 16 × 3cm, lance-shaped to narrowly oval, dark,		

A large, pallid tree with thin outer bark, which shreds and hangs from the trunk and branches in long ribbons, revealing the white inner bark. Both juvenile and adult leaves are pale green. Red flowers have rounded, woody ds. Ribbon Gum provides timber but is mainly used for shade and shelter in owns. *Status:* native to southern and eastern Australia and Tasmania; planted in Spain, Portugal and Italy. *imilar trees:* Snow Gum has peeling rey outer bark over white inner bark, nd leaves which age from orange-rown to grey-green. It grows at high ltitudes in the wild and is planted as a old-tolerant ornamental.

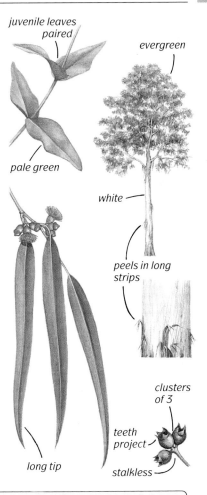

juvenile leaves paired

evergreen

pale green

white

peels in long strips

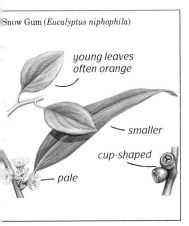

Snow Gum (*Eucalyptus niphophila*)

young leaves often orange

smaller

cup-shaped

pale

clusters of 3

teeth project

stalkless

long tip

	RIBBON GUM		
Type	evergreen tree		
Height	up to 50m		
Habitat	plantations		
Flowering	December–June		
Fruiting	January–July		

TRUNK AND CROWN

Trunk	tapering from base		
Bark	smooth, white, falling away in long ribbon-like strips		
Crown	drooping branches festooned with ribbons of bark		
Twigs	greenish brown, smooth		

LEAVES

Buds	minute, concealed		
Leaves	variable, pale green, juvenile leaves opposite, up to 10 × 3cm, oval, stalkless, surrounding the stem at their base; adult leaves		

alternate, up to 18 × 2cm, narrowly oval, drawn out into a long slender tip; stalked

Stipules	absent

FLOWERS AND FRUIT

Flower buds	7mm, covered by a scarlet, hemispherical to conical cap
Flowers	♀, in shortly stalked clusters of 3, 1.5cm across
Stamens	numerous
Stigmas	1; style short
Ovaries	1, 2–8-chambered
Fruit	woody capsule, 5–8 × 7–9mm, more or less spherical, slightly tapering to the base, opening by 3–4 valves; stalkless
Seeds	numerous

Red Gum *Eucalyptus camaldulensis*

Cultivated for its timber, this tree is widely planted on a world scale. Large and spreading, it shows considerable natural variation. The white bark is mottled with pink and grey and is shed in plates. It has red flowers with conical, woody lids, and fruit with projecting teeth. *Status:* native to much of Australia; planted in the Mediterranean region, especially Spain. *Similar trees:* Lemon-scented Spotted Gum, from Queensland, is a slender tree with strongly lemon-scented leaves. The flowers have domed lids and the fruits have inward-pointing teeth. It is grown as an ornamental in Spain, Portugal and Italy.

red

conical cap

juvenile leaves bluish

dull green

projecting teeth

evergreen

smooth

falls in plates

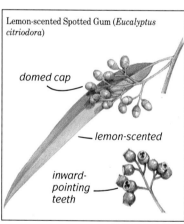

Lemon-scented Spotted Gum (*Eucalyptus citriodora*)

domed cap

lemon-scented

inward-pointing teeth

	RED GUM		
Type	evergreen tree		green; shortly stalked
Height	up to 20m	**Stipules**	absent
Habitat	plantations		**FLOWERS AND FRUIT**
Flowering	December–February	**Flower buds**	up to 10 × 5mm, cap brownish, conical or beak-like
Fruiting	May	**Flowers**	♀, in clusters of 5–10, white; stalk of cluster up to 2.5cm, slender
	TRUNK AND CROWN		
Trunk	short, stout, soon forking		
Bark	smooth, white, pink and grey, falling away on plates	**Stamens**	numerous
Crown	open; irregularly branched	**Stigmas**	1; style short
Twigs	green, strongly ribbed	**Ovaries**	1, 2–8-chambered
	LEAVES	**Fruit**	woody capsule, 7–8 × 5–6mm, hemispherical with a broad raised rim, opening by 4 teeth
Buds	minute, concealed	**Seeds**	numerous
Leaves	young leaves opposite, up to 9 × 4cm, oval, bluish green; adult leaves alternate, up to 25 × 2cm, narrowly oval, drawn out into a long slender tip, dull		

triking scarlet flowers tip the shoots of
his small tree. White-flowered forms of
omegranate also occur but are much
arer. Both petals and sepals are
ariable in number; the petals are
oticeably crumpled until fully
xpanded. The branches are sometimes
narmed, but more usually bear spines.
omegranate's large, globular fruit has
leathery, rather hard rind and a
ubular crown formed by the persistent
epals; the pulp contains numerous
eeds. Although at first acid-tasting, the
uit usually becomes sweet. *Status:*
troduced from western Asia in
ncient times for its fruit; cultivated
nd widely naturalized in Mediterranean
egions. *Similar trees:* none.

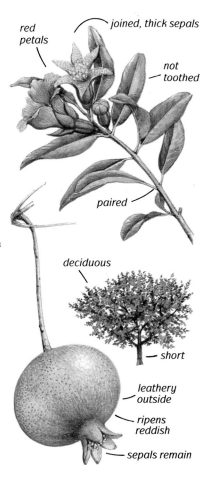

red
petals

joined, thick sepals

not
toothed

paired

deciduous

short

leathery
outside

ripens
reddish

sepals remain

POMEGRANATE		
Type	deciduous tree	
Height	up to 8m	
Habitat	scrub, field margins, orchards	
Flowering	June–October	
Fruiting	July onwards	
TRUNK AND CROWN		
Trunk	slender, branching from near ground	
Bark	pale brown, finely grooved	
Crown	irregular; branches slender, angled upwards	
Twigs	4-angled, smooth, often spiny	
LEAVES		
Buds	small, pyramidal, tinged red	
Leaves	paired on stem, 2–8cm, oblong to narrowly oval and widest above middle, smooth and shiny; stalk very short	

Stipules	absent
FLOWERS AND FRUIT	
Flowers	☿, single or paired at tips of shoots, 2.5–4cm across, red, occasionally white
Petals	5–7, crumpled before opening fully; sepals 5–7 hooded, leathery, red, joined into a long tube, persisting on fruit
Stamens	numerous, in whorls in throat of flower
Stigmas	1, globular on a long style
Ovaries	1, sunk into base of flower
Fruit	berry-like, 5–8cm, globular, leathery skin surrounding translucent purple or yellowish pulp, ripening reddish or yellow
Seeds	numerous, embedded in pulp, not released

Date-plum *Diospyros lotus*

Persimmons, the group to which this tree belongs, produce edible fruit, but that of Date-plum is small, only c1.5cm across, and rather insipid. It may be either yellow or blue-black when ripe. The tree is cultivated in the south as a fruit tree but in the north only as an ornamental. *Status:* native to Asia; cultivated and sometimes naturalized in Europe. *Similar trees:* Common Persimmon, from eastern and central North America, has tart fruit. Chinese Persimmon, from Asia, has much larger fruit, up to 7.5cm, which is very sour until overripe.

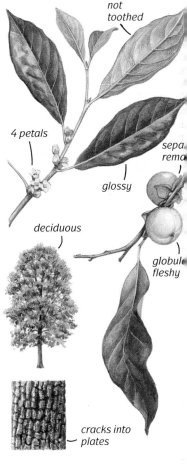

not toothed

4 petals

sepa rema

glossy

deciduous

globul fleshy

cracks into plates

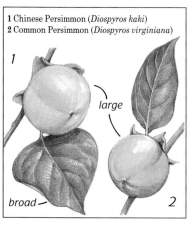

1 Chinese Persimmon (*Diospyros kaki*)
2 Common Persimmon (*Diospyros virginiana*)

1

large

broad

2

	DATE-PLUM		
Type	deciduous tree		smooth; stalk hairy
Height	up to 14m	**Stipules**	absent
Habitat	gardens, parks, orchards		
Flowering	July		**FLOWERS AND FRUIT**
Fruiting	July–October	**Flowers**	♂ and ♀ on different trees, stalkless, reddish or greenish white, petals forming an urn-shaped tube with 4 fringed, curved-back lobes, sepals forming a 4-lobed cup
	TRUNK AND CROWN		
Trunk	well-defined		
Bark	grey, tinged pink, cracking into small plates		
Crown	tall and narrowly domed	♂	in clusters of 2–3, each c5mm
Twigs	downy when young	♀	single, each 8–10mm
		Stamens	4 in ♂; reduced and sterile in ♀
	LEAVES	**Stigmas**	4 in ♀
Buds	4–5mm, sharp-pointed	**Ovaries**	1, several chambers
Leaves	alternate, elliptical to oblong with wavy edges, base rounded, somewhat leathery, dark green above, bluish below, hairy on both sides but becoming almost	**Fruit**	1.5cm, globular, fleshy and ripening yellow or nearly black with a glistening bloom
		Seeds	3–4, large, not released

A small tree in which all the parts, including the drooping white flowers and grey fruits, are covered with star-shaped hairs. It is one of the very few plants native to the climatically similar Mediterranean region and California. Storax yields an aromatic gum, also called storax, collected from cuts made in the trunk and branches, and used for incense. *Status:* native from Italy eastwards; naturalized in parts of France. *Similar trees:* Snowbell-tree, from the Far East, reaches 11m and flowers prolifically. Snowdrop-tree is a North American species with flowers opening mostly before the leaves, and 4-winged fruits up to 5cm long.

1 Snowbell-tree (*Styrax japonica*)
2 Snowdrop-tree (*Halesia monticola*)

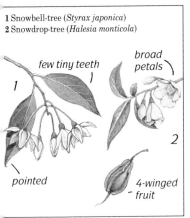

few tiny teeth

broad petals

1

2

pointed

4-winged fruit

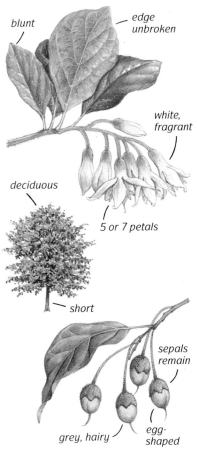

blunt

edge unbroken

white, fragrant

deciduous

5 or 7 petals

short

sepals remain

grey, hairy

egg-shaped

STORAX		**FLOWERS AND FRUIT**	
Type	deciduous shrub or small tree	**Flowers**	♀, in short, drooping clusters of 3–6, each 2cm long, bell-shaped, white, fragrant
Height	2–7m		
Habitat	thickets, woods, stream-sides		
Flowering	April–May	**Petals**	5 or 7, overlapping at the edges above, joined into a short tube at the base; sepals joined for most of their length, cup-shaped, hairy
Fruiting	July–September		
TRUNK AND CROWN			
Trunk	short, slender		
Bark	brown, shredding slightly	**Stamens**	10, fused to base of the petal-tube
Crown	irrgularly branched		
Twigs	white-woolly	**Stigmas**	1, style long, slender
LEAVES		**Ovaries**	1, 3-chambered
Buds	small, ellipsoid, white-woolly	**Fruit**	egg-shaped, dry, leathery, grey and densely hairy, cupped by persistent white-woolly sepals
Leaves	alternate, 3–7cm, oval, blunt-tipped, base rounded, edge unbroken, green above, white-hairy, especially beneath; stalked		
		Seeds	1 or 2, large, hard
Stipules	absent		

Manna Ash *Fraxinus ornus*

Unlike most European ashes, this species has scented flowers with petals, forming large showy heads after the leaves appear. In winter it can be distinguished by its very smooth bark and pale brown buds. It is a commercial source of manna, not the biblical food but an edible sugary gum, which seeps from cuts in the trunk and dries into flakes on contact with air. *Status:* native to central Europe and the Mediterranean region; planted for ornament. *Similar trees:* two North American species are planted, mainly for timber. Red Ash has sharp-toothed leaves, hairy below. White Ash has bluntly toothed, smooth leaves.

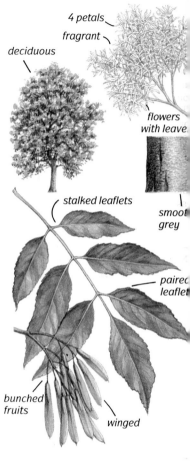

deciduous

4 petals

fragrant

flowers with leave

stalked leaflets

smoot grey

pairec leaflet

winged

bunched fruits

1 Red Ash (*Fraxinus pennsylvanica*)
2 White Ash (*Fraxinus americana*)

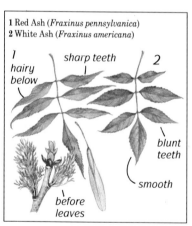

1
hairy below

sharp teeth

2

blunt teeth

smooth

before leaves

MANNA ASH

Type	deciduous tree
Height	up to 24m, often smaller
Habitat	open woods, thickets, rocky places; often planted
Flowering	April–June
Fruiting	May–September

TRUNK AND CROWN

Trunk	cylindrical
Bark	smooth, dark grey, or black
Crown	hemispherical, fairly dense
Twigs	grey to yellowish, smooth

LEAVES

Buds	pyramidal, blunt, grey or brown
Leaves	opposite, up to 30cm, with 4–8 paired, stalked leaflets and a leaflet at the tip, each 3–10cm long, oblong-oval, abruptly and sharply pointed, shallowly toothed, unequal at base, pale and hairy on the veins beneath; stalks up to 1.5cm
Stipules	absent

FLOWERS AND FRUIT

Flowers	⚥, many in pyramidal clusters to 20cm long, white, fragrant
Petals	4, 5–6mm, narrow, strap-shaped; sepals 4, joined near base
Stamens	2, on long stalks
Stigmas	2
Ovaries	1, 2-chambered
Fruit	hanging in dense bunches, 1.5–2.5cm, on wiry stalks 3–10mm long, with slender wing 1.5–2.5cm, sometimes notched at tip, green becoming brown
Seeds	1 per fruit, not released

Fraxinus excelsior Ash

A common tree, readily distinguished by its divided leaves in pairs on the stem and by its distinctive, winged fruits. In winter it is recognized by the prominent, paired, black buds. Growing mainly on lime-rich soils, it is sometimes planted for its tough timber. The cultivar 'Pendula' is a weeping form, often grafted onto the trunk of the common form and grown as an ornamental. *Status:* native throughout Europe, western Asia and North Africa. *Similar trees:* Narrow-leaved Ash is similar but has very narrow leaflets. It has a more southern distribution.

black bud — no petals — before leaves — leaflets stalkless — paired leaflets — toothed — winged — becomes fissured — deciduous

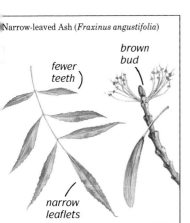

Narrow-leaved Ash (*Fraxinus angustifolia*)

fewer teeth — brown bud — narrow leaflets

	ASH	
Type	deciduous tree	oblong-oval, with long slender tip, shallowly toothed, dark green above, hairy at the base and on the midrib beneath; stalked
Height	up to 40m	
Habitat	hedgerows, open woods, roadsides, often on limestone	
Flowering	April–May	**Stipules** absent
Fruiting	July–November	
	TRUNK AND CROWN	**FLOWERS AND FRUIT**
Trunk	suckering; many pollarded	**Flowers** ♀, or ♂ and ♀ in separate rounded clusters before leaves, purplish, dark red, then yellow
Bark	smooth, grey, becoming rough and shallowly fissured	
Crown	domed; branches well-spaced	**Petals** absent; sepals absent
Twigs	flattened at nodes, greenish grey, smooth	**Stamens** 2
		Stigmas 2
	LEAVES	**Ovaries** 1, 2-chambered
Buds	pyramidal, hard, black	**Fruit** 2.5–5cm, with twisted wing notched and spiny at tip, green ripening dull brown, in hanging clusters
Leaves	opposite, up to 35cm, with usually 6–12 paired leaflets and a leaflet at tip, each 3–12cm,	
		Seeds 1 per fruit, not released

Olive *Olea europaea*

Long-lived, this evergreen tree has a distinctive silvery grey bark. Old trees have gnarled trunks pitted with holes. Ripe fruits are black; green olives are simply unripe fruits. Widely cultivated since classical times, olives crop heavily and are the basis for the important olive and olive-oil industries. Wild Olives (var. *sylvestris*) are bushy, spiny trees of dry woodlands, with smaller leaves and fruits. *Status:* native throughout the Mediterranean region. *Similar trees:* Phillyrea is a dense, rounded tree with shallowly toothed leaves and round, purplish black fruits. It grows in evergreen woods and is planted for ornament.

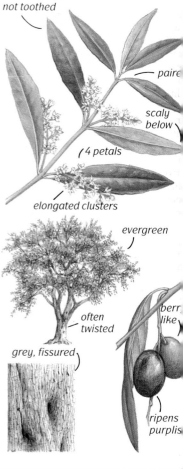

not toothed

paire

scaly below

4 petals

elongated clusters

evergreen

berr like

often twisted

grey, fissured

ripens purplis

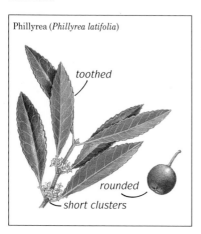

Phillyrea (*Phillyrea latifolia*)

toothed

rounded

short clusters

	OLIVE		
Type	evergreen tree or shrub		
Height	up to 15m		
Habitat	dry rocky places, woods and scrub; planted in large groves	**Stipules**	smooth above, greyish or brownish white and hairy beneath; almost stalkless
Flowering	May–June		absent
Fruiting	September–November		**FLOWERS AND FRUIT**
	TRUNK AND CROWN	**Flowers**	mostly ♀, many in branched or unbranched clusters from angles of leaves, each *c*1cm across, yellowish white
Trunk	thick, becoming gnarled and twisted, developing holes	**Petals**	4, joined for most of their length, spreading at the top; sepals 4, short, joined
Bark	silvery grey, shallowly fissured		
Crown	broad; irregularly, branching	**Stamens**	2
Twigs	slender, greyish, covered with small, scurfy scales	**Stigmas**	1, style short
		Ovaries	1, 2-chambered
	LEAVES	**Fruit**	berry-like, 1–3.5cm, oval, somewhat fleshy with a tough outer skin, green ripening blackish purple
Buds	very small, greyish		
Leaves	opposite, 2–10cm, lance-shaped, with a sharp tip, leathery, dark grey-green and	**Seeds**	1, stony, brown

Highly glossed leaves and clusters of fragrant white flowers produced late in the year, when few other trees are flowering, make this an attractive ornamental tree. It is often seen in towns and cities. *Status:* native to China; planted for ornament, mainly in southern Europe. *Similar trees:* Wild Privet is a native species that is widespread on chalky soils. Always a shrub, it is semi-evergreen, sometimes losing its leaves late in the year. Garden Privet is the commonly seen hedge plant. Also semi-evergreen, it tolerates poor soil but sheds leaves in polluted air and cold weather. It originates in Japan.

1 Wild Privet (*Ligustrum vulgare*)
2 Garden Privet (*Ligustrum ovalifolium*)

4 petals
branched head
fragrant
glossy
paired leaflets
pointed
rounded
small berries
evergreen
short

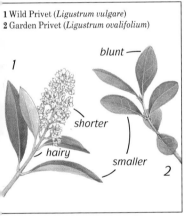

1
blunt
shorter
hairy
smaller
2

	GLOSSY PRIVET		
Type	evergreen tree		reddish when young, later very glossy dark green above, pale and matt below; stalked
Height	up to 15m		
Habitat	gardens, especially as a hedge, streets, parks	**Stipules**	absent
Flowering	August–September		**FLOWERS AND FRUIT**
Fruiting	October–November, often not produced	**Flowers**	♀, many in branched, conical clusters 12–20cm long, at shoot-tip; each white, fragrant
	TRUNK AND CROWN	**Petals**	4, joined in a long tube with spreading lobes; sepals 4, forming bell-shaped, short-toothed tube
Trunk	short, often several		
Bark	grey with brown streaks, smooth or finely cracked		
Crown	domed	**Stamens**	2, attached to petal-tube
Twigs	grey with white lenticels	**Stigmas**	1, style short
		Ovaries	1, 2-chambered
	LEAVES	**Fruit**	rather egg-shaped berry, *c*1cm long, ripening black with conspicuous white bloom
Buds	globular to egg-shaped, tiny		
Leaves	opposite, 8–12cm, oval, tip drawn out to a long point, edge unbroken, thick and leathery,	**Seeds**	1, not released

Strawberry-tree *Arbutus unedo*

Taking a full year to mature, the fruits on this tree ripen as the next year's flowers open. The fruits barely resemble strawberries, being round and covered with soft pimples; they are edible though insipid. Attractive bell-shaped flowers hang in large clusters. *Status:* native to Mediterranean region and Atlantic Europe north to Ireland; planted for ornament. *Similar trees:* Eastern Strawberry-tree, from the Aegean region, has orange-red bark, and flowers in spring. Fruits are nearly smooth. This and Strawberry-tree are the parents of Hybrid Strawberry-tree, which has bright bark, and flowers in spring or autumn.

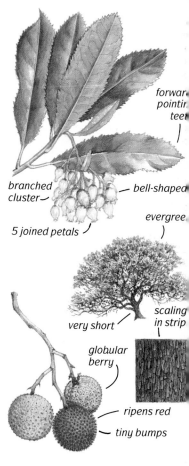

forward pointing teeth

branched cluster

bell-shaped

5 joined petals

evergreen

very short

scaling in strips

globular berry

ripens red

tiny bumps

1 Eastern Strawberry-tree (*Arbutus andrachne*)
2 Hybrid Strawberry-tree (*Arbutus × andrachnoides*)

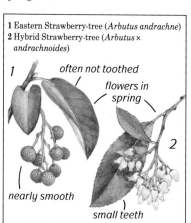

1

often not toothed

flowers in spring

2

nearly smooth

small teeth

	STRAWBERRY-TREE	
Type	evergreen tree or shrub	
Height	tree up to 10m, or shrub	
Habitat	dry rocky slopes, bushy places	
Flowering	October – November	
Fruiting	October of following year	

TRUNK AND CROWN

Trunk	very short, soon forking
Bark	dull reddish brown, rough, scaling away in thin strips
Crown	dense, rounded; branches numerous and ascending
Twigs	red above and hairy when young, green beneath

LEAVES

Buds	1–2mm, conical, purplish red
Leaves	alternate, 4–10 × 1.5–5cm, oblong-oval, leathery, with forward-pointing teeth towards tip, dark glossy green above, paler beneath; stalks 5–10mm, pinkish red, hairy
Stipules	absent

FLOWERS AND FRUIT

Flowers	♀, many in drooping, branched clusters 4–5cm long, pinkish white, each urn-shaped, 0.5–1cm
Petals	5, joined for most of length, tips bent back; sepals 5, *c*1.5mm, forming circular lobes
Stamens	10
Stigmas	1
Ovaries	1, 5-chambered
Fruit	fleshy, globular berry, 1.5–2cm across, covered with pimples, yellow, ripening to orange and finally bright red
Seeds	numerous, tiny, pear-shaped, brown, not released

An attractive, rounded tree with very smooth, dark green leaves and pale green twigs. It is usually a small tree but is very variable in size and may form only a shrub. The flowers have petals spotted with purple and bearing a beard of curled, white hairs on the inner face. Used mainly to provide shelter, it is sometimes planted as an ornamental tree in streets and squares. *Status:* native to eastern Australia and New Caledonia; planted in Spain, Portugal and the Balearic Islands. *Similar trees: M. tetrandrum* is a shrub that has toothed leaves; it is planted along the coasts of Portugal.

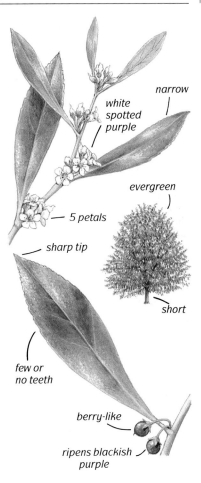

white spotted purple

narrow

evergreen

5 petals

sharp tip

short

few or no teeth

berry-like

ripens blackish purple

Myoporum tetrandrum

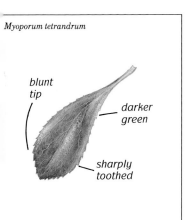

blunt tip

darker green

sharply toothed

	BOOBIALLA		FLOWERS AND FRUIT
Type	evergreen tree or shrub	**Flowers**	♂, usually in dense clusters in angles of leaves, each 10–12mm across, white, spotted with purple and with curly white hairs on inner surface, fragrant; stalks up to 12mm
Height	up to 8m		
Habitat	planted for shelter		
Flowering	January–April		
Fruiting	March–June		
	TRUNK AND CROWN	**Petals**	5, joined at the base into a short tube, spreading above; sepals 2–3mm, joined at the base for about half their length
Trunk	short, rather sinuous		
Bark	brownish grey, finely fissured		
Crown	rounded or domed	**Stamens**	4
Twigs	greenish, smooth	**Stigmas**	1, style slender with short bristles
	LEAVES	**Ovaries**	1
Buds	dark, very small	**Fruit**	berry-like but only slightly fleshy, 7–9mm, oval, ripening blackish purple
Leaves	alternate, 4.5–10cm, narrowly oval, pointed, base sharply tapered, bright green and glossy above, dotted with pale, shiny glands; stalk 5–10mm		
Stipules	absent	**Seeds**	1, stony

Foxglove-tree *Paulownia tomentosa*

The branches of this deciduous tree are clothed with very large leaves. They are heart-shaped with unbroken edges but in young trees may have up to 3 short, tapering lobes on each side. The tubular flowers, violet to bluish on the outside and flushed yellow within, form large and very showy heads before the leaves appear. *Status:* native to China; common as an ornamental and, in southern Europe, a street tree. *Similar trees:* Jacaranda, an especially attractive ornamental tree from Argentina, has leaves twice-divided into small leaflets, and clusters of drooping, blue, trumpet-like flowers.

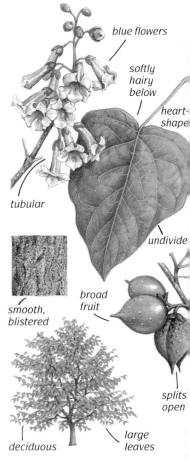

blue flowers

softly hairy below

heart-shape

tubular

undivide

smooth, blistered

broad fruit

splits open

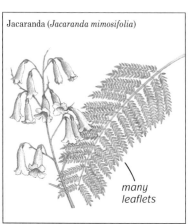

Jacaranda (*Jacaranda mimosifolia*)

many leaflets

deciduous

large leaves

	FOXGLOVE-TREE	
Type	deciduous tree	
Height	up to 15m	
Habitat	roadsides, parks and gardens	
Flowering	April–May	
Fruiting	July	

TRUNK AND CROWN

Trunk	slightly sinuous
Bark	greyish, smooth, marked with orange blisters
Crown	domed; branches stout, spreading
Twigs	pale pink-brown

LEAVES

Buds	minute, purplish, hairy
Leaves	opposite, to 30cm long, oval to heart-shaped with 3 to 5 lobes, tip long and slender, pale green above, softly hairy below; stalk 10–15cm, pink-yellow, densely hairy
Stipules	absent

FLOWERS AND FRUIT

Flowers	♂, in large upright clusters 20–30 cm long, opening before the leaves, each 5–6 cm long, violet-blue, yellow within
Petals	bell-shaped tube with 5 spreading lobes; sepals 5, joined below
Stamens	4, inside petal-tube
Stigmas	2-lobed, style long
Ovaries	1, 2-chambered
Fruit	3–5cm long, oval, beaked, green, ripening brown and splitting to release seeds, sticky; stalk 1.5cm, stout, hairy
Seeds	numerous, winged, released when fruit splits

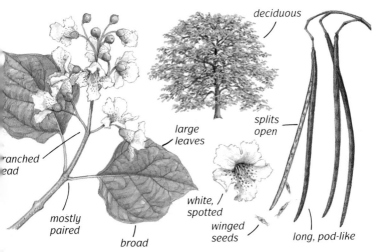

deciduous

splits open

large leaves

branched head

mostly paired

white, spotted

broad

winged seeds

long, pod-like

onspicuous in winter, when the very ng, slender pods hang in numbers om the bare branches, this showy tree a common sight in parks and gardens. he leaves are light, matt green and eart-shaped. The large flowers have reading, frilled lobes and are borne in ranched, conical heads. *Status:* native south-eastern North America; widely anted in all but northern parts of urope. *Similar trees:* Yellow Catalpa, om China, has roughly 5-sided leaves nd smaller, yellow flowers. Hybrid atalpa has 5-sided leaves, up to 60cm, nd large heads of white flowers. Both re planted for ornament.

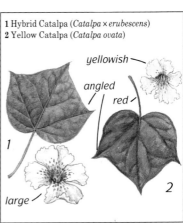

1 Hybrid Catalpa (*Catalpa* × *erubescens*)
2 Yellow Catalpa (*Catalpa ovata*)

yellowish

angled

red

1

large

2

INDIAN BEAN-TREE

Type	deciduous tree
Height	up to 15m, occasionally taller
Habitat	streets, parks and gardens
Flowering	June–August
Fruiting	July–October but persisting on tree all winter

TRUNK AND CROWN

Trunk	short, stout
Bark	dull pink- or grey-brown, fissured or scaling
Crown	domed; branches wide-arching
Twigs	stout, grey-brown, smooth, with prominent oval leaf scars

LEAVES

Buds	minute, orange-brown
Leaves	opposite or in 3s, up to 25 × 22cm, heart-shaped with slender tip, pale green, smooth above, hairy beneath; stalk 10–18cm
Stipules	absent

FLOWERS AND FRUIT

Flowers	♂, in branched, pyramidal heads, each to 5cm across, bell-shaped, white, spotted with yellow and purple, fragrant
Petals	5, unequal, upper 2 smaller, crinkly-edged, joined for most of their length; sepals 5, joined
Stamens	2, curved
Stigmas	2-lobed, style long, slender
Ovaries	1, 2-chambered
Fruit	pod-like, slender, 15–40cm, hanging, dark brown,
Seeds	many, 2.5cm, white, flat, with a tuft of long hairs at each end and papery wing, released in spring

Elder   *Sambucus nigra*

Large, plate-like heads of white flowers
decorate this common tree in summer.
They are followed by heavy clusters of
berries, which droop as the fruit ripens.
The flowers have a sweet, slightly
cloying scent, in contrast to the leaves,
which smell unpleasant when bruised.
Both flowers and fruit are used to make
wines; the fruit is also used in pies and
preserves, and Elder is often planted
near houses for this reason. *Status:*
native throughout Europe, western
Asia, North Africa; often cultivated in
southern Europe. *Similar trees:* Red-
berried Elder, also native to Europe, is
a shrub to only 4m, with egg-shaped
clusters of flowers and scarlet fruit.

5 petals

broad
head

toothed

paired
leaflets

paired

deeply
grooved

deciduous

often several

berry-like

broad
head

ripening
black

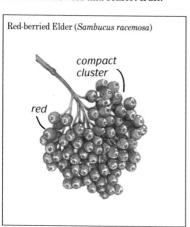

Red-berried Elder (*Sambucus racemosa*)

compact
cluster

red

	ELDER		Leaves	paired on stem; 2–4 pairs of
Type	deciduous tree, often shrubby			leaflets, leaflet at tip, 3–12cm,
Height	up to 10m			oval to elliptical, pointed,
Habitat	damp woods, hedgerows, on			sharply toothed, sparsely hairy
	rich, disturbed soils			below, dull green; stalkless
Flowering	June–July		**Stipules**	very small or absent
Fruiting	August–September			

TRUNK AND CROWN

Trunk often crooked, vigorous straight
shoots grow from base

Bark deeply grooved, brownish grey,
becoming thick and corky

Crown irregularly rounded; branches
arching downwards

Twigs thick, fawn, warty, filled with
white pith

LEAVES

Buds lacking scales, tight-furled
young leaves purplish

FLOWERS AND FRUIT

Flowers ♀, many in large, circular,
branched heads, each 5mm,
white, rarely pink

Petals 5, equal, spreading; sepals 5,
small joined into a tube

Stamens 5, yellowish white

Stigmas 3–5, very short

Ovaries 1

Fruit berry-like, globular, 6–8mm,
ripening black

Seeds 3, leathery, not released

Viburnum opulus **Guelder Rose**

Distinctive flower-heads readily identify this attractive small tree. The small, fertile inner flowers are surrounded by much larger, showy, but sterile blossoms. *Status:* native to most of Europe except for much of the Mediterranean region. *Similar trees:* from similar areas, Wayfaring-tree has oval, lobeless leaves white-felted below, lacks sterile flowers and has fruit eventually ripening black. It favours chalky soils. Laurustinus is a winter-flowering evergreen with glossy, oval leaves, equal-sized, pink-tinged flowers and metallic blue fruit. Native to southern Europe, it is often planted as an ornamental elsewhere.

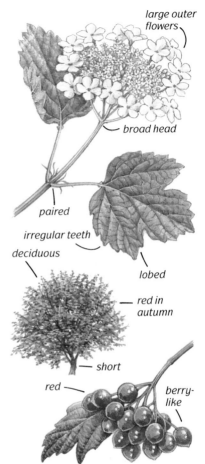

large outer flowers

broad head

paired

irregular teeth

deciduous

lobed

red in autumn

short

red

berry-like

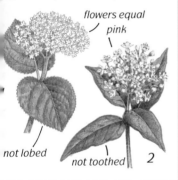

1 Wayfaring-tree (*Viburnum lantana*)
2 Laurustinus (*Viburnum tinus*)

flowers equal

pink

not lobed

not toothed 2

	GUELDER ROSE		
Type	deciduous tree or shrub		
Height	1–4m		
Habitat	damp woods, hedges, riversides		
Flowering	May–June		
Fruiting	September–October		

TRUNK AND CROWN

Trunk	short, slender
Bark	greyish brown
Crown	spreading; branches few
Twigs	angled, smooth

LEAVES

Buds	5mm, green, edges purple
Leaves	paired on stem, 5–8cm, with 3–5 radiating, pointed, irregularly toothed lobes, sparsely hairy below, becoming smooth, dull red in autumn; stalk 1–2.5cm

Stipules	very narrow, thread-like

FLOWERS AND FRUIT

Flowers	☿, many in broad, circular clusters, stalk of flower-head 1–4cm; funnel- or bell-shaped, inner flowers 6mm, fertile; outer flowers 15–20mm, sterile, both types white
Petals	5, equal; sepals 5, very small
Stamens	5, as long as petals
Stigmas	3, short
Ovaries	1
Fruit	berry-like, c8mm, almost globular, ripening red, drooping and persisting on stems after leaves fall
Seeds	1, stony, not released

179

Cabbage Palm *Cordyline australis*

This palm-like tree often has several trunks, which fork after flowering. The 2m-long flower-head emerges from the centre of the crown. A hardy tree, often planted as an unusual ornamental. *Status:* native to New Zealand; often planted in mild, coastal areas of western and central Europe. *Similar trees:* two related species, both native to south-eastern North America, are commonly planted in parks and gardens. Spanish Bayonet is a much-branched tree up to 10m. Adam's Needle has a very short, thick, unbranched trunk topped with a single, dense rosette of leaves. Both species have large, white flowers, tinged with purple.

6 petals

branched head

sword-shaped

leaves at tip

branched

berry

ripens bluish white

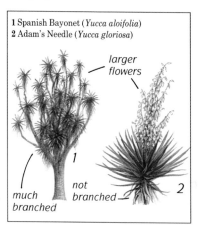

1 Spanish Bayonet (*Yucca aloifolia*)
2 Adam's Needle (*Yucca gloriosa*)

larger flowers

much branched

not branched

1

2

	CABBAGE PALM		FLOWERS AND FRUIT	
Type	evergreen tree	**Flowers**	♂, many in very large, upright, branched head from centre of crown, each c10mm, creamy-white, fragrant	
Height	up to 13m			
Habitat	dry soils in mild coastal areas			
Flowering	June–July			
Fruiting	September–October	**Perianth**	3 inner and 3 outer segments, all petal-like, joined at base	
	TRUNK AND CROWN	**Stamens**	6	
Trunk	cylindrical, often forked after flowering, suckering from base	**Stigmas**	1, slender	
		Ovaries	1	
Bark	pale grey-brown	**Fruit**	berry, 6mm, globose, ripening bluish white	
Crown	dense tuft of leaves	**Seeds**	several, black, not released	
	LEAVES			
Buds	1, large, hidden by leaves			
Leaves	in a single, domed cluster at tip of trunk, mostly upright but lowermost drooping, 30–90cm, sword-shaped, veins all parallel, dark green; stalkless			

Dracaena draco Dragon Tree

very slow-growing tree capable of attaining a great age – one specimen, destroyed in a hurricane in 1867, was said to be over 6000 years old. The tree forms a very thick trunk and short, stubby branches with a dense, umbrella-shaped crown of spiky leaves. It can survive in areas of low rainfall; moisture condensing on the leaves runs down the trunk to the roots. The Dragon Tree is very rare in the wild, but often planted for ornament. A bright red resin obtained from this tree, and known as dragon's blood, has been used medicinally since the Middle Ages. *Status:* native to the Canary Islands and Madeira; commonly planted in Mediterranean areas in streets, gardens and parks. *Similar trees:* none.

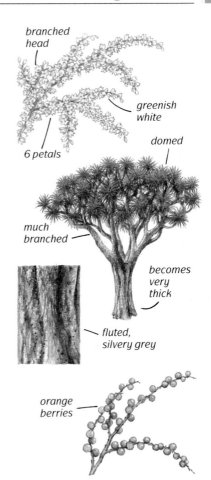

branched head

greenish white

6 petals

domed

much branched

becomes very thick

fluted, silvery grey

orange berries

	DRAGON TREE		FLOWERS AND FRUIT	
Type	evergreen tree	**Flowers**	♀, in spreading, much-branched heads from centre of leaf tufts, greenish white	
Height	2–6m			
Habitat	dry, rocky slopes often near the sea; street tree	**Perianth**	3 inner and 3 outer segments, all petal-like and united towards base	
Flowering	August–September			
Fruiting	February–April			
		Stamens	6	
	TRUNK AND CROWN	**Stigmas**	1, style slender	
Trunk	massive, cylindrical, becoming fluted	**Ovaries**	1	
		Fruit	berry, c1.5cm, globular, ripening deep orange	
Bark	silvery			
Crown	broad, shallow-domed; branches thick, short, regularly forked	**Seeds**	1, not released	
	LEAVES			
Buds	1, large, hidden by leaves			
Leaves	in dense tufts at tips of branches, 30–50cm, sword-shaped, bluish green; stalkless			

181

European Fan-palm *Chamaerops humilis*

Usually forming clumps of several well-developed trunks, this Fan-palm may have only one trunk. Wild trees often produce no trunk at all, the crown of leaves growing directly from the ground. A thick covering of fibres from old leaves protects the stem from fire damage. It is the only common native European palm. *Status:* native to coastal areas of the Mediterranean region; often planted for ornament. *Similar trees:* Australian Fan-palm is native to eastern Australia. It is a tall tree with golden-green leaf-segments, which droop at the tips, and is often planted as a street tree.

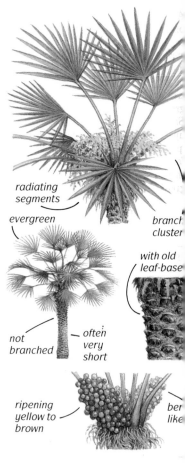

radiating segments

evergreen

branch cluster

with old leaf-base

not branched

often very short

ripening yellow to brown

berry like

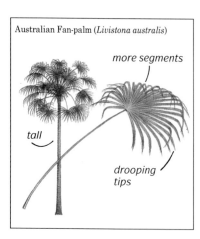

Australian Fan-palm (*Livistona australis*)

more segments

tall

drooping tips

	EUROPEAN FAN-PALM		
Type	evergreen tree, often bushy		green, greyish or bluish; stalk very long and spiny
Height	rarely more than 2m		
Habitat	sandy soils near the sea		**FLOWERS AND FRUIT**
Flowering	March–June	**Flowers**	♂ and ♀ on separate trees, many crowded in large branched spikes initially sheathed by 2 large bracts and hidden among leaves, yellow
Fruiting	September–October		
	TRUNK AND CROWN		
Trunk	short, thick, sometimes absent, covered with white or grey fibres and bases of old leaves	**Perianth**	6, inner 3 spreading
		Stamens	6; in ♂ flowers bases joined into fleshy disc; in ♀ flowers sterile, forming cup-shaped base
Bark	grey, concealed by fibres		
Crown	single, large tuft of leaves	**Stigmas**	3, styles short
	LEAVES	**Ovaries**	1, 3-chambered
Buds	1, large, hidden by leaves	**Fruit**	berry-like, 4.5cm, globular to oblong, ripening yellow or brown
Leaves	up to 1m across, stiff, fan-shaped blade deeply divided into spreading segments; segments many, sword-shaped,		
		Seeds	3, grooved on one side, not released

A frost-resistant, compact tree and the only palm widely grown in northern regions. Very stiff leaves form a spreading crown. As they die, they hang downwards, together with the old leaf bases, hiding the upper part of the trunk. *Status:* native to China; widely grown, mainly as a street and park tree. *Similar trees:* Petticoat Palm has the upper part of the trunk hidden by a 'petticoat' of numerous dead leaves. The fan-shaped leaves have many long threads attached to the segments, giving a frayed appearance.

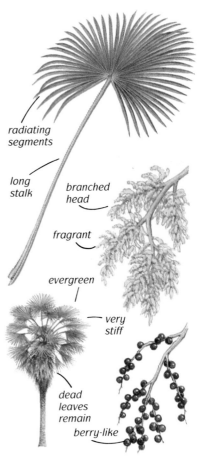

radiating segments

long stalk

branched head

fragrant

evergreen

very stiff

dead leaves remain

berry-like

Petticoat Palm (*Washingtonia filifera*)

long threads on leaves

more dead leaves

	CHINESE WINDMILL-PALM		
Type	evergreen tree		100cm, toothed, with long, brown fibres at base
Height	up to 14m		
Habitat	gardens, streets, sea-fronts		**FLOWERS AND FRUIT**
Flowering	March–June	**Flowers**	♀, many in large, much-branched spike 70–80cm long sheathed by large bract when young, bright yellow, fragrant
Fruiting	September–October		
	TRUNK AND CROWN		
Trunk	slender, straight, at least upper part covered with old, shaggy, brown leaf-bases	**Perianth**	6, inner 3 large, touching near tips
		Stamens	6, small and sterile in ♀
Bark	brown, with irregular rings	**Stigmas**	1, tiny, style short
Crown	spreading, open tuft of leaves	**Ovaries**	3, only 2 developing; all small and sterile in ♂
	LEAVES	**Fruit**	berry-like, *c*2cm, 3-lobed, ripening purplish black with bluish white bloom
Buds	1, large, hidden by leaves		
Leaves	stiff blades up to 1m, divided almost to base into radiating segments; segments many, narrow, pleated, bluish above, dark green below; stalk 50–	**Seeds**	1, grooved

Chilean Wine-palm *Jubaea chilensis*

A very slow-growing tree, producing a dense crown and the thickest trunk of any palm. The leaden-grey bark is distinctive. Native to Chile, where it is cut for its sugary sap, it grows well in mild climates and is a common ornamental palm, especially in southern France. *Status:* native to central Chile; widely grown in Mediterranean regions. *Similar trees:* two other South American palms are also grown as street trees in the Mediterranean region. Queen Palm is a slender tree with a distinctly ringed trunk and leaves 5m long. Royal Palm has a smooth trunk, bulging in the middle, and leaves that are only 3m long.

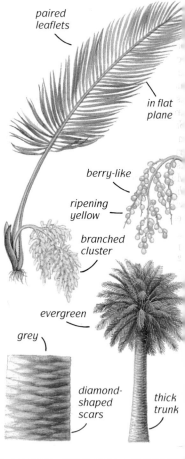

paired leaflets

in flat plane

berry-like

ripening yellow

branched cluster

evergreen

grey

diamond-shaped scars

thick trunk

1 Royal Palm (*Roystonea regia*)
2 Queen Palm (*Arecastrum romanzoffianum*)

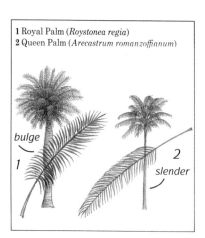

bulge

1

2

slender

	CHILEAN WINE-PALM		FLOWERS AND FRUIT	
Type	evergreen tree	**Flowers**	♂ and ♀ on the same tree, purplish; many upright, dense, branched clusters 1.5m long in angles of lower leaves and initially sheathed by large woody bracts	
Height	up to 30m			
Habitat	parks and streets near coasts			
Flowering	July–September			
Fruiting	November–January			
	TRUNK AND CROWN	**Perianth**	6; in ♂ 3 outer narrow, joined at base, 3 inner longer, thick, pointed; in ♀ 3 outer broad, 3 inner overlapping	
Trunk	straight, up to 2m thick			
Bark	grey, smooth, patterned with diamond-shaped leaf-scars			
Crown	dense tuft of upright to spreading leaves arranged in almost vertical rows	**Stamens**	*c*30; in ♀ sterile, joined in a membranous cup	
	LEAVES	**Stigmas**	3; minute and sterile in ♂	
		Ovaries	3-chambered in ♀	
Buds	1, large, hidden by leaves	**Fruit**	berry-like, in large, drooping clusters, roughly globose to egg-shaped, ripening yellow	
Leaves	feathery, up to 4m; numerous paired leaflets up to 70cm, split at tip; stalkless			
		Seeds	1, with 3 vertical lines alternating with 3 black pores	

Phoenix canariensis Canary Island Date-palm

Large and spreading, this is the most common ornamental palm in Europe. The thick trunk is covered with old leaf-bases. These leave diamond-shaped scars when they fall away. The fruits are rather dry and inedible. *Status:* native to the Canary Islands; common as an ornamental in streets and parks around the Mediterranean region. *Similar trees:* Date-palm is a taller, more slender tree with larger, succulent fruits, and is planted for ornament and as a fruit tree in southern Mediterranean areas. *Phoenix theophrasti* is a very small, slender tree with blackish, fibrous fruits, and is restricted to Crete.

1 Date Palm (*Phoenix dactylifera*)
2 *Phoenix theophrasti*

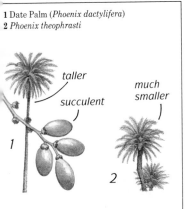

taller

succulent

much smaller

1

2

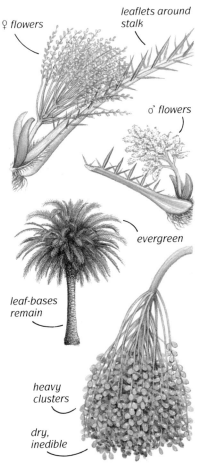

♀ flowers

leaflets around stalk

♂ flowers

evergreen

leaf-bases remain

heavy clusters

dry, inedible

CANARY ISLAND DATE-PALM

Type	evergreen tree
Height	up to 20m
Habitat	dry places; also streets, coastal roads
Flowering	March–May
Fruiting	September–October

TRUNK AND CROWN

Trunk	stout, straight, patterned with old leaf scars
Bark	brown, with old leaf bases
Crown	large, spreading tuft of up to 200 leaves

LEAVES

Buds	1, large, hidden by leaves
Leaves	feathery, 5–6m; 150–200 pairs of leaflets radiating from stalk at different angles, narrow, pointed, folded upwards longitudinally, light green; stalk stout, very spiny

FLOWERS AND FRUIT

Flowers	many in upright, branched clusters up to 2m hanging from angles of lower leaves, ♂ and ♀ on separate trees, creamy yellow
Perianth	6; in ♂ 3 outer fused into a small cup, 3 inner longer, edges touching; in ♀ 3 outer form 3-lobed cup, 3 inner overlapping
Stamens	usually 6, very small in ♀
Stigmas	3, style short, curved
Ovaries	3 in ♀, only 1 developing
Fruit	nut-like, in heavy, hanging clusters, 3cm, egg-shaped, ripening orange
Seeds	1, cylindrical, with a deep longitudinal groove

Index

Abies alba, 20
  cephalonica, 20
  concolor, 22
  grandis, 22
  homolepis, 23
  nordmanniana, 20
  numidica, 23
  pinsapo, 23
    cv. 'Glauca', *23*
  procera, 21
  sibirica, 21
  veitchii, 21
Acacia cyanophylla, 129
  dealbata, 128
  mearnsii, 128
  melanoxylon, 129
  retinodes, 129
Acer campestre, 143
  davidii, 146
  griseum, 144
  hersii, 146
  japonicum, 147
  monspessulanum, 143
  negundo, 144
    cv. 'Variegatum', 144
  opalus, 142
  palmatum, 147
  platanoides, 142
  pseudoplatanus, 142
  rubrum, 145
  rufinerve, 146
  saccharinum, 145
  saccharophorum, 145
  tataricum, 143
Adam's Needle, 180
Aesculus × carnea, 140
  flava, 141
  hippocastanum, 140
  indica, 141
African Tamarisk, 154
Ailanthus altissima, 134
  vilmoriniana, 134
Albizia julibrissin, 127
  lophantha, 127
Albizia, Plume, 127
Aleppo Pine, 34
Algerian Fir, 23
Almond, 117
Almond-leaved Pear, 100
Almond Willow, 54
Alnus cordata, 62
  glutinosa, 62
  incana, 62
  rugosa, 63
  viridis, 63
Amelanchier lamarckii, 110
  ovalis, 110
American Aspen, 59
American Plane, 88
Amur Cork-tree, 133
Antarctic Beech, 69

Apple, Cultivated, 102
Apricot, 116
Araucaria araucana, 19
  heterophylla, 19
Arbutus andrachne, 174
  × *andrachnoides*, 174
  unedo, 174
Arecastrum romanzoffianum, 184
Arolla Pine, 37
Ash, 171
  Manna, 170
  Narrow-leaved, 171
  Red, 170
  White, 170
Aspen, 59
  American, 59
  Big-toothed, 59
Atlas Cedar, 31
Austrian Pine, 33
Autumn Cherry, 123
Avocado, 96
Azarole, 114

Balearic Box, 150
Balm-of-Gilead, 57
Balsam-poplar, Eastern, 57
  Western, 57
Banyan Tree, 85
Bastard Service-tree, 105
Bay, Sweet, 96
Bay Willow, 51
Bayberry, 77
Bean-tree, Indian, 177
Beech, 68
  Antarctic, 69
  Copper, 68
  Oriental, 68
  Roble, 69
  Southern, 69
Berlin Poplar, 60
Betula papyrifera, 64
  pendula, 64
  pubescens, 64
Bhutan Pine, 37
Big-toothed Aspen, 59
Birch, Downy, 64
  Paper-bark, 64
  Silver, 64
Bird Cherry, 120
Bitternut, 92
Black-gum, 160
Black Italian Poplar, 61
Black Mulberry, 83
Black Poplar, 60
Black Walnut, 91
Blackthorn, 118
Blackwood, 129
Blue-gum, Tasmanian, 163
Blue Spruce, 28
Boobialla, 175
Box, 150
  Balearic, 150
Box-elder, 144
Brazilian Pepper, 138
Brewer's Weeping-spruce, 29

Broad-leaved Cockspur
  Hawthorn, 115
Broad-leaved Spindle, 149
Broad-leaved Whitebeam, 105
Broussonetia papyrifera, 84
Buckeye, Yellow, 141
Buckthorn, 153
  Alder, 153
  Mediterranean, 153
  Sea-, 151
Buxus balearica, 150
  sempervirens, 150

Cabbage-palm, 180
Calabrian Pine, 34
California Nutmeg, 41
Campbell's Magnolia, 94
Canarian Tamarisk, 154
Canary Holly, 148
Canary Island Date-palm, 185
Canary Island Pine, 35
Caragana arborescens, 125
Carob, 124
Carpinus betulus, 66
  orientalis, 66
Carya cordiformis, 92
  glabra, 92
  ovata, 92
Castenea sativa, 76
Casuarina equisetifolia, 89
  stricta, 89
Catalpa bignonioides, 177
  × *erubescens*, 177
Catalpa, Hybrid, 177
Catalpa ovata, 177
Catalpa, Yellow, 177
Caucasian Elm, 81
Caucasian Fir, 20
Caucasian Lime, 157
Caucasian Wing-nut, 90
Cedar, Atlas, 31
  Chinese, 135
  Pencil, 47
Cedar-of-Lebanon, 31
Cedrela sinensis, 135
Cedrus atlantica, 31
  deodara, 31
  libani, 31
Celtis australis, 82
  occidentalis, 82
  tournefortii, 82
Ceratonia siliqua, 124
Cercis siliquastrum, 126
Chaenomeles japonica, 98
  speciosa, 98
Chamaecyparis lawsoniana, 42
  nootkatensis, 43
  obtusa, 42
  pisifera, 42
Chamaerops humilis, 182
Cherry, Autumn, 123
  Bird, 120
  Choke, 120
  Cornelian, 161
  Dwarf, 119
  Japanese, 122
  Rum, 120

Index

Saint Lucie, 119
Sargent's, 122
Spring, 123
Tibetan, 123
Wild, 119
Yoshino, 122
Cherry Laurel, 121
Cherry Plum, 117
Chestnut, Golden, 76
Sweet, 76
Chilean Wine-palm, 184
Chinese Cedar, 135
Chinese Elm, 79
Chinese Fir, 39
Chinese Juniper, 47
Chinese Persimmon, 168
Chinese Tulip-tree, 95
Chinese Weeping-willow, 56
Chinese White-cedar, 45
Chinese Windmill-palm, 183
Chinese Wing-nut, 90
Choke Cherry, 120
Christ's Thorn, 152
Chrysolepis chrysophylla, 76
Cider Gum, 163
Citrus limon, 132
paradisi, 132
sinensis, 132
Clammy Locust, 131
Coast Redwood, 39
Cockspur Hawthorn, 115
Broad-leaved, 115
Hybrid, 115
Colorado Spruce, 28
Colorado White-fir, 22
Common Jujube, 152
Common Lime, 156
Common Pear, 99
Common Persimmon, 168
Common Silver-fir, 20
Common Whitebeam, 106
Copper Beech, 68
Coral Tree, 126
Cordyline australis, 180
Cork Oak, 70
Cork-tree, Amur, 133
Cornelian Cherry, 161
Cornus mas, 161
nuttallii, 161
sanguinea, 161
Corsican Pine, 33
Corylus avellana, 65
colurna, 65
maxima, 65
Cotoneaster bullatus, 111
frigidus, 111
× *watereri*, 111
Cottonwood, 61
Crab Apple, 102
Japanese, 103
Purple, 103
Siberian, 103
Crack Willow, 51
Crape Myrtle, 162
Crataegus azarolus, 114
calycina, 112
crus-galli, 115

laciniata, 114
laevigata, 112
× *lavallei*, 115
monogyna, 112
nigra, 113
pentagyna, 113
× *prunifolia*, 115
Cricket-bat Willow, 50
Cryptomeria japonica, 38
Cultivated Apple, 102
Cunninghamia lanceolata, 39
× *Cupressocyparis leylandii*, 43
Cupressus glabra, 44
lusitanica, 44
macrocarpa, 43
sempervirens, 44
Cydonia oblonga, 98
Cypress, Hinoki, 42
Italian, 44
Lawson, 42
Leyland, 43
Mexican, 44
Monterey, 43
Nootka, 43
Sawara, 42
Smooth, 44
Swamp, 40

Dahurian Larch, 30
Dark-leaved Willow, 55
Date-palm, 185
Canary Island, 185
Date-plum, 168
Davidia involucrata, 159
var. *vilmoriniana*, 159
Dawn Redwood, 40
Deodar, 31
Diospyros kaki, 168
lotus, 168
virginiana, 168
Dogwood, 161
Nuttall's, 161
Douglas-fir, 24
Large-coned, 24
Downy Birch, 64
Downy Japanese-maple, 147
Downy Oak, 74
Downy Tree-of-Heaven, 134
Dracaena draco, 181
Dragon-tree, 181
Drooping She-oak, 89
Dutch Elm, 80
Dwarf Cherry, 119
Dwarf Fan-palm, 182
Dwarf Mountain-pine, 32
Dwarf Quince, 98

Eastern Balsam-poplar, 57
Eastern Hemlock-spruce, 25
Eastern Hop-hornbeam, 67
Eastern Hornbeam, 66
Eastern Strawberry-tree, 174
Elaeagnus angustifolia, 151
commutata, 151
Elder, 178
Red-berried, 178

Elm, Caucasian, 81
Chinese, 79
Dutch, 80
English, 78
Grey-leaved, 79
Huntingdon, 80
Small-leaved, 79
Wych, 80
Engelmann Spruce, 28
English Elm, 78
Eriobotrya japonica, 108
Erythrina crista-galli, 126
Eucalyptus camaldulensis, 166
citriodora, 166
globulus, 163
gunnii, 163
maidenii, 163
niphophila, 165
resinifer, 164
robustus, 164
viminalis, 165
Euonymus europaeus, 149
japonicus, 149
latifolius, 149
European Larch, 30
European White-elm, 78
Evergreen Magnolia, 94
Evergreen Oak, 70

Fagus orientalis, 68
sylvatica, 68
cv. 'Purpurea', 68
False-acacia, 131
Fan-palm, Australian, 182
European, 182
Faya, 77
Ficus benghalensis, 85
carica, 85
elastica, 85
Field Maple, 143
Fig, 85
Filbert, 65
Fir, Algerian, 23
Caucasian, 20
Chinese, 39
Douglas-, 24
Grand, 22
Grecian, 20
Hedgehog, 23
Large-coned Douglas-, 24
Nikko, 23
Noble, 21
Siberian, 21
Spanish, 23
Five-seeded Hawthorn, 113
Flowering Quince, 98
Foxglove-tree, 176
Frangula alnus, 153
Fraxinus americana, 170
angustifolia, 171
excelsior, 171
cv. 'Pendula', 171
ornus, 170
pennsylvanica, 170

Garden Privet, 173
Ginkgo biloba, 18

Index

Gleditsia triacanthos, 125
Glossy Privet, 173
Goat Willow, 52
Golden Chestnut, 76
Golden-rain-tree, 139
Golden Weeping-willow, 56
Golden Willow, 50
Golden Wreath, 129
Grand Fir, 22
Grapefruit, 132
Grecian Fir, 20
Greek Juniper, 49
Greek Whitebeam, 106
Green Alder, 63
Green Wattle, 128
Grey Alder, 62
Grey-leaved Elm, 79
Grey Poplar, 58
Grey Willow, 52
Guelder-rose, 179
Gum, Cider, 163
  Lemon-scented Spotted, 166
  Maiden's, 163
  Red, 166
  Ribbon, 165
  Snow, 165
  Tasmanian Blue-, 163

Hackberry, 82
Halesia monticola, 169
Hamamelis mollis, 87
  virginiana, 87
Handkerchief-tree, 159
Hawthorn, Common, 112
  Five-seeded, 113
  Midland, 112
  Oriental, 114
Hazel, 65
  Turkish, 65
Hedgehog Fir, 23
Hemlock-spruce, Eastern, 25
  Mountain, 25
  Western, 25
Hers's Maple, 146
Hickory, Shagbark, 92
Highclere Holly, 148
Himalayan Tree-cotoneaster, 111
Hinoki Cypress, 42
Hippophae rhamnoides, 151
Hoary Willow, 54
Holly, 148
  Canary, 148
  Highclere, 148
  White, 93
Hondo Spruce, 27
Honey-locust, 125
Hop-hornbeam, 67
  Eastern, 67
Hop-tree, 133
Hornbeam, 66
  Eastern, 66
Horse-chestnut, 140
  Indian, 141
  Red, 140
Horsetail She-oak, 89
Hungarian Oak, 73

Hungarian Thorn, 113
Huntingdon Elm, 80
Hupeh Rowan, 104
Hybrid Black Poplar, 61
Hybrid Catalpa, 177
Hybrid Cockspur-thorn, 115
Hybrid Strawberry-tree, 174

Ilex × altaclarensis, 148
  aquifolium, 148
  perado, 148
Indian Bean-tree, 177
Indian Horse-chestnut, 141
Indian Rubber-tree, 85
Ironwood, Persian, 87
Italian Alder, 62
Italian Cypress, 44
Italian Maple, 142

Jacaranda, 176
Jacaranda mimosifolia, 176
Japanese Cherry, 122
Japanese Crab-apple, 103
Japanese Larch, 30
Japanese-maple, Downy, 147
  Smooth, 147
Japanese Red-cedar, 38
Japanese Spindle, 149
Jubaea chilensis, 184
Judas-tree, 126
Juglans nigra, 91
  regia, 91
Jujube, Common, 152
Juneberry, 110
Juniper, 46
  Chinese, 47
  Greek, 49
  Phoenicean, 48
  Prickly, 46
  Spanish, 48
  Stinking, 49
  Syrian, 46
Juniperus chinensis, 47
  communis, 46
  drupacea, 46
  excelsa, 49
  foetidissima, 49
  oxycedrus, 46
  phoenicea, 48
  sabina, 47
  thurifera, 48
  virginiana, 47

Karo, 93
Keaki, 81
Kermes Oak, 70
Koelreuteria paniculata, 139

Laburnum, 130
  Scotch, 130
  Voss's, 130
Laburnum alpinum, 130
  anagyroides, 130
  × *watereri*, 130
Lagerstroemeria indica, 162
Larch, Dahurian, 30
  European, 30

Japanese, 30
Large-coned Douglas-fir, 24
Large-leaved Lime, 156
Larix decidua, 30
  gmelinii, 30
  kaempferi, 30
Laurel, Cherry, 121
  Portugal, 121
Laurus nobilis, 96
Laurustinus, 179
Lawson Cypress, 42
Lemon, 132
Lemon-scented Spotted Gum, 166
Leyland Cypress, 43
Ligustrum lucidum, 173
  ovalifolium, 173
  vulgare, 173
Lilac, Persian, 135
Lime, Caucasian, 157
  Common, 156
  Large-leaved, 156
  Silver-, 158
  Small-leaved, 157
  Weeping Silver-, 158
Liquidambar orientalis, 86
  styraciflua, 86
Liriodendron chinense, 95
  tulipifera, 95
Livistona australis, 182
Locust, Clammy, 131
Lombardy Poplar, 60
London Plane, 88
Loquat, 108
Lotus Tree, 152
Lucombe Oak, 71

Macedonian Oak, 71
Macedonian Pine, 37
Maclura pomifera, 84
Magnolia, 94
Magnolia campbellii, 94
Magnolia, Campbell's, 94
  Evergreen, 94
Magnolia grandiflora, 94
  × *soulangiana*, 94
Mahogany, Red, 164
  Swamp, 164
Maidenhair-tree, 18
Maiden's Gum, 163
Malus baccata, 103
  dasyphylla, 102
  domestica, 102
  × *floribunda*, 103
  × *purpurea*, 103
  sylvestris, 102
Manna Ash, 170
Maple, Downy Japanese-, 147
  Field, 143
  Hers's, 146
  Italian, 142
  Montpellier, 143
  Norway, 142
  Paper-bark, 144
  Père David's, 146
  Red, 145
  Silver, 145

Index

Smooth Japanese-, 147
Snake-bark, 146
Sugar, 145
Tartar, 143
Maritime Pine, 34
Mastic Tree, 137
Mediterranean Buckthorn, 153
Medlar, 109
Melia azedarach, 135
Mespil, Snowy, 110
Mespilus germanica, 109
Metasequoia glyptostroboides, 40
Mexican Cypress, 44
Midland Hawthorn, 112
Mimosa, 128
Monkey-puzzle, 19
Monterey Cypress, 43
Monterey Pine, 36
Montpellier Maple, 143
Morinda, 29
Morus alba, 83
nigra, 83
Mountain Hemlock-spruce, 25
Mountain-pine, 32
Dwarf, 32
Mulberry, Black, 83
Paper, 84
White, 83
Myoporum tenuifolium, 175
tetrandrum, 175
Myrica caroliniensis, 77
faya, 77
Myrtle, 162
Myrtle, Crape, 162
Orange-bark, 162
Myrtus communis, 162
luma, 162

Narrow-leaved Ash, 171
Nettle-tree, Southern, 82
Nikko Fir, 23
Noble Fir, 21
Nootka Cypress, 43
Norfolk Island Pine, 19
Norway Maple, 142
Norway Spruce, 26
Nothofagus antarctica, 69
obliqua, 69
procera, 69
Nutmeg, California, 41
Nuttall's Dogwood, 161
Nyssa sylvatica, 160

Oak, Cork, 70
Downy, 74
Evergreen, 70
Hungarian, 73
Kermes, 70
Lucombe, 71
Macedonian, 71
Pedunculate, 72
Pin, 75
Pyrenean, 74
Red, 75
Scarlet, 75

Sessile, 73
Turkey, 71
Valonia, 71
Olea europaea, 172
var. *sylvestris*, 172
Oleaster, 151
Olive, 172
Wild, 172
Orange-bark Myrtle, 162
Orange, Osage, 84
Sweet, 132
Oriental Beech, 68
Oriental Hawthorn, 114
Oriental Plane, 88
Oriental Spruce, 26
Oriental Sweet-gum, 86
Osage Orange, 84
Osier, 54
Ostraya carpinifolia, 67
virginiana, 67

Pagoda-tree, 131
Paliurus spina-christi, 152
Palm, Australian Fan-, 182
Canary Island Date-, 185
Chilean Wine-, 184
Chinese Windmill-, 183
Date-, 185
European Fan-, 182
Petticoat, 183
Queen, 184
Royal, 184
Paper-bark Birch, 64
Paper-bark Maple, 144
Paper Mulberry, 84
Parrotia persica, 87
Paulownia tomentosa, 176
Peach, 116
Pear, Common, 99
Plymouth, 99
Sage-leaved, 100
Wild, 100
Willow-leaved, 101
Pedunculate Oak, 72
Pencil Cedar, 47
Pepper, Brazilian, 138
Pepper Tree, 138
Père David's Maple, 146
Persea americana, 96
Persian Ironwood, 87
Persian Lilac, 135
Persimmon, Chinese, 168
Common, 168
Petticoat Palm, 183
Phellodendron amurense, 133
Phillyrea, 172
Phillyrea latifolia, 172
Phoenicean Juniper, 48
Phoenix canariensis, 185
dactylifera, 185
theophrasti, 185
Phytolacca, 97
Phytolacca dioica, 97
Picea abies, 26
brewerana, 29
engelmannii, 28
glauca, 28

jezoensis var. *hondoensis*, 27
obovata, 26
omorika, 27
orientalis, 26
polita, 27
pungens, 28
sitchensis, 27
smithiana, 29
Pignut-tree, 92
Pin Oak, 75
Pine, Aleppo, 34
Arolla, 37
Austrian, 33
Bhutan, 37
Bosnian, 33
Calabrian, 34
Canary Island, 35
Corsican, 33
Dwarf Mountain-, 32
Macedonian, 37
Maritime, 36
Monterey, 36
Mountain-, 32
Norfolk Island, 19
Scots, 32
Shore, 36
Stone, 35
Weymouth, 37
Pink Siris, 127
Pinus brutia, 34
canariensis, 35
cembra, 37
contorta, 36
halepensis, 34
leucodermis, 33
mugo, 32
nigra, 33
subsp. *laricio*, 33
subsp. *nigra*, 33
peuce, 37
pinaster, 34
pinea, 35
ponderosa, 36
radiata, 36
strobus, 37
sylvestris, 32
uncinata, 32
wallichiana, 37
Pistachio, 137
Pistacia lentiscus, 137
terebinthus, 137
vera, 137
Pittosporum, 93
Pittosporum crassifolium, 93
tenuifolium, 93
undulatum, 93
Plane, American, 88
London, 88
Oriental, 88
Platanus × *hybrida*, 88
occidentalis, 88
orientalis, 88
Plum, Cherry, 117
Wild, 118
Plume Albizia, 127
Plum-fruited Yew, 41
Plymouth Pear, 99

Index

Podocarpus andinus, 41
Pomegranate, 167
Poplar, Berlin, 60
  Black, 60
  Black Italian, 61
  Eastern Balsam-, 57
  Grey, 58
  Hybrid Black, 61
  Lombardy, 60
  Railway, 61
  Western Balsam-, 57
  White, 58
Populus alba, 58
  balsamifera, 57
  × *berolinensis*, 60
  × *canadensis*, 61
    cv. 'Marilandica', 61
    cv. 'Regenerata', 61
    cv. 'Serotina', 61
  candicans, 57
  × *canescens*, 58
  deltoides, 61
  grandidentata, 59
  laurifolia, 60
  nigra, 60
    cv. 'Italica', 60
  tremula, 59
  tremuloides, 59
  trichocarpa, 57
Portugal Laurel, 121
Prickly Juniper, 46
Privet, Garden, 173
  Glossy, 173
  Wild, 173
Prunus armeniaca, 116
  avium, 119
  cerasifera, 117
    cv. 'Pissardii', 117
  cerasus, 119
  cocomilia, 118
  domestica, 118
  dulcis, 117
  laurocerasus, 121
  lusitanica, 121
  mahaleb, 119
  padus, 120
  persica, 116
  sargentii, 122
  serotina, 120
  serrula, 123
  serrulata, 122
  spinosa, 118
  subhirtella, 123
    cv. 'Autumnalis', 123
  virginiana, 120
  × *yedoensis*, 122
Pseudotsuga macrocarpa, 124
  menziesii, 24
Ptelea trifoliata, 133
Pterocarya fraxinifolia, 90
  stenoptera, 90
Punica granatum, 167
Purple Crab-apple, 103
Purple Willow, 53
Pyrenean Oak, 74
Pyrus amygdaliformis, 100
  bourgeana, 100

communis, 99
  cv. *culta*, 101
  cordata, 99
  elaeagrifolia, 101
  nivalis, 101
  pyraster, 100
  salicifolia, 101
    cv. 'Pendula', 101
  salvifolia, 100

Queen Palm, 184
Quercus borealis var. *maxima*, 75
  cerris, 71
  coccifera, 70
  coccinea, 75
  dalechampii, 73
  frainetto, 73
  × *hispanica*, 71
  ilex, 70
  macrolepis, 71
  palustris, 75
  pedunculiflora, 72
  petraea, 73
  pubescens, 74
  pyrenaica, 74
  robur, 72
  suber, 70
  trojana, 71
  virgiliana, 74
Quince, 98
  Dwarf, 98
  Flowering, 98

Railway Poplar, 61
Raoul, 69
Red Ash, 170
Red-berried Elder, 178
Red-cedar, Japanese, 38
  Western, 45
Red Gum, 166
Red Horse-chestnut, 140
Red Mahogany, 164
Red Maple, 145
Red Oak, 75
Redwood, Coast, 39
  Dawn, 40
Rhamnus alaternus, 153
  catharticus, 153
Rhus coriaria, 136
  typhina, 136
  verniciflua, 136
Ribbon Gum, 165
Robinia pseudacacia, 131
  viscosa, 131
Roble Beech, 69
Rock Whitebeam, 106
Rowan, 104
  Hupeh, 104
Royal Palm, 184
Roystonea regia, 184
Rubber-tree, Indian, 85
Rum Cherry, 120
Rusty Willow, 52

Sage-leaved Pear, 100
Saint Lucie Cherry, 119

Salix acutifolia, 53
  alba, 50
    subsp. *coerulea*, 50
    subsp. *vitellina*, 50
  babylonica, 56
  borealis, 55
  caprea, 52
  cinerea, 52
    subsp. *cinerea*, 52
    subsp. *oleifolia*, 52
  daphnoides, 53
  elaeagnos, 54
  fragilis, 51
  myrsinifolia, 55
  pentandra, 51
  phylicifolia, 55
  purpurea, 53
  × *rubens*, 51
  × *sepulcralis* nv.
    chrysocoma, 56
  triandra, 54
  viminalis, 54
Sambucus nigra, 178
  racemosa, 178
Sargent's Cherry, 122
Savin, 47
Sawara Cypress, 42
Scarlet Oak, 75
Schinus molle, 138
  terebinthifolia, 138
Scotch Laburnum, 138
Scots Pine, 32
Sea-buckthorn, 151
Sequoia sempervirens, 39
Sequoiadendron giganteum, 3
Serbian Spruce, 27
Service-tree, 104
  Bastard, 105
  Wild, 105
Sessile Oak, 73
Shagbark Hickory, 92
She-oak, Drooping, 89
  Horsetail, 89
Shore Pine, 36
Siberian Crab-apple, 103
Siberian Fir, 21
Siberian Spruce, 26
Silver-berry, 151
Silver Birch, 64
Silver-fir, Common, 20
  Veitch's, 21
Silver-lime, 158
  Weeping, 158
Silver Maple, 145
Siris, Pink, 127
Sitka Spruce, 27
Small-flowered Tamarisk, 155
Small-leaved Elm, 79
Small-leaved Lime, 157
Smooth Alder, 63
Smooth Cypress, 44
Smooth Japanese-maple, 147
Snake-bark Maple, 146
Snow Gum, 165
Snowbell-tree, 169
Snowdrop-tree, 169
Snowy Mespil, 110

Index

phora japonica, 131
rbus aria, 106
  aucuparia, 104
  austriaca, 107
  domestica, 104
  graeca, 106
  hupehensis, 104
  hybrida, 105
  intermedia, 107
  latifolia, 105
  mougeotii, 107
  rupicola, 106
  torminalis, 105
  umbellata, 107
uthern Beech, 69
uthern Nettle-tree, 82
anish Bayonet, 180
anish Fir, 23
anish Juniper, 48
indle, 149
  Broad-leaved, 149
  Japanese, 149
ring Cherry, 123
ruce, Blue, 28
  Brewer's Weeping-, 29
  Colorado, 28
  Engelmann, 28
  Hondo, 27
  Morinda, 29
  Norway, 26
  Oriental, 26
  Serbian, 27
  Siberian, 26
  Sitka, 27
  Tiger-tail, 27
  White, 28
ag's-horn Sumach, 136
inking Juniper, 49
one Pine, 35
orax, 169
rawberry-tree, 174
  Eastern, 174
  Hybrid, 174
yrax japonica, 169
  officinale, 169
gar Maple, 145
mach, 136
  Stag's-horn, 136
vamp Cypress, 40
vamp Mahogany, 164
vamp Wattle, 129
edish Whitebeam, 107
veet Bay, 96
veet Chestnut, 76
veet-gum, 86
  Oriental, 86
veet Orange, 132
camore, 142
rian Juniper, 46

marisk, 154
  African, 154
  Canarian, 154
  Small-flowered, 155
marix africana, 154
  canariensis, 154
  dalmatica, 155

gallica, 154
  parviflora, 155
  tetrandra, 155
Tartar Maple, 143
Tasmanian Blue-gum, 163
Taxodium distichum, 40
Taxus baccata, 41
Tea-leaved Willow, 55
Thorn, Christ's, 152
  Hungarian, 113
Thuja occidentalis, 45
  orientalis, 45
  plicata, 45
Tibetan Cherry, 123
Tiger-tail Spruce, 27
Tilia cordata, 157
  × euchlora, 157
  petiolaris, 158
  platyphyllos, 156
  tomentosa, 158
  × vulgaris, 156
Torreya californica, 41
Trachycarpus fortunei, 183
Tree, Banyan, 85
  Coral, 126
Tree-cotoneaster, Himalayan, 111
Tree-of-Heaven, 134
  Downy, 134
Tsuga canadensis, 25
  heterophylla, 25
  mertensiana, 25
Tulip-tree, 95
Tulip-tree, Chinese, 95
Turkey Oak, 71
Turkish Hazel, 65
Turpentine Tree, 137

Ulmus canescens, 79
  glabra, 80
  × hollandica, 80
  var. hollandica, 80
  var. vegeta, 80
  laevis, 78
  minor, 79
  parvifolia, 79
  procera, 78

Valonia Oak, 71
Varnish-tree, 136
Veitch's Silver-fir, 21
Viburnum lantana, 179
  opulus, 179
  tinus, 179
Violet Willow, 53
Virginian Witch-hazel, 87
Voss's Laburnum, 130

Walnut, 91
  Black, 91
Washingtonia filifera, 183
Wattle, Green, 128
  Swamp, 129
Wayfaring-tree, 179
Weeping Silver-lime, 158
Weeping-spruce, Brewer's, 29
Weeping-willow, Chinese, 56

Golden, 56
Wellingtonia, 38
Western Balsam-poplar, 57
Western Hemlock-spruce, 25
Western Red-cedar, 45
Western Yellow-pine, 36
Weymouth Pine, 37
White Ash, 170
White-cedar, 45
  Chinese, 45
White-elm, European, 78
White-fir, Colorado, 22
White Holly, 93
White Mulberry, 83
White Poplar, 58
White Spruce, 28
White Willow, 50
Whitebeam, Broad-leaved, 105
  Common, 106
  Greek, 106
  Rock, 106
  Swedish, 107
Wild Cherry, 119
Wild Pear, 100
Wild Plum, 118
Wild Privet, 173
Wild Service-tree, 105
Willow, Almond, 54
  Bay, 51
  Chinese Weeping-, 56
  Crack, 51
  Cricket-bat, 50
  Dark-leaved, 55
  Goat, 52
  Golden, 50
  Golden Weeping-, 56
  Grey, 52
  Hoary, 54
  Purple, 53
  Rusty, 52
  Tea-leaved, 55
  Violet, 53
  White, 50
Willow-leaved Pear, 101
Windmill-palm, Chinese, 183
Wine-palm, Chilean, 184
Wing-nut, Caucasian, 90
  Chinese, 90
Witch-hazel, 87
  Virginian, 87
Wreath, Golden, 129
Wych Elm, 80

Yellow Buckeye, 141
Yellow Catalpa, 177
Yellow-pine, Western, 36
Yew, 41
  Plum-fruited, 41
Yoshina Cherry, 122
Yucca aloifolia, 180
  gloriosa, 180

Zelkova abelicea, 81
  carpinifolia, 81
  serrata, 81
Ziziphus jujuba, 152
  lotus, 152

Societies and Useful Addresses

Botanical Society of the British Isles
c/o British Museum (Natural History),
Cromwell Road,
London, SW7 5BD.

Men of the Trees
Crawley Down, Crawley
Sussex, RH10 4HL

English Nature
Headquarters for Great Britain and
for England
Northminster House,
Northminster Road,
Peterborough,
Cambridgeshire, PE1 1UA.

Scottish Heritage
12 Hope Terrace,
Edinburgh, EH9 2AS.

Countryside Council for Wales
Plas Penrhos, Penrhos Road,
Bangor, Gwynedd, LL57 2LQ.

Royal Society for Nature Conservation
The Green, Nettleham,
Lincolnshire, LN2 2NR.

Woodland Trust
Autumn Park, Dysart Road,
Grantham
Lincolnshire, NG31 6LL